GROWING
STRONG
DAUGHTERS

GROWING STRONG DAUGHTERS

Encouraging Girls to Become
All They're Meant to Be

LISA GRAHAM M^CMINN

Baker Books
A Division of Baker Book House Co
Grand Rapids, Michigan 49516

Published by Baker Books
a division of Baker Book House Company
P.O. Box 6287, Grand Rapids, MI 49516-6287

Printed in the United States of America

ISBN 0-8010-6324-8 (pbk.)

For current information from Baker Book House, visit our web site:

TO MARK,

*my good friend, husband,
and parenting partner*

CONTENTS

Acknowledgments

THE TELLING AND HEARING of personal stories allows us to connect our experiences with others' experiences. And from the composite picture of those stories we come to better understand the impact of social currents and trends on our personal lives. I am indebted to my students at Trinity International University and Wheaton College for their willingness to share their stories, first with me, and now with you. Their stories are true, though names have been changed to protect their privacy. I am also indebted to my daughters, Danielle, Sarah, and Megan, who have graciously given me liberty to discuss them in the following pages. From them I have learned much about God's love. They have shaped me as surely as I have shaped them.

This book is a composite of the wisdom of friends like Marcile Crandall, Donell Campbell, Jana Sundene, the "Wild Women," Zondra Lindblade, Ruth Bamford—there are so many. Their questions have been insightful, and their challenge to me profound. Publishing a first book requires a publisher willing to take a risk, and I appreciate Baker Book House for doing so. The editorial staff encouraged, supported, and taught me; *Growing Strong Daughters* is a better book because of their involvement. I am also thankful for Jana Sundene, Adrienne Buchanan, Patti Mangis, and Deborah Butman, who read and commented on all or pieces of this manuscript. Finally, this book is only possible because of Mark, my husband and parenting partner over the last twenty years. Together we have struggled with the questions, sometimes answering them in ways foreign to those around us. We have laughed, cried, prayed, and celebrated together in parenting, and pondered what we would have done differently if we were to begin raising daughters again. The message that we can raise strong daughters in the context of God's creative design for women needs to be celebrated and embraced.

INTRODUCTION

"WOMEN'S BATHROOMS are the confessionals of the '90s," a student wrote in her journal for my Gender Roles course. One bathroom in particular stood out to her. A small group of friends and coworkers were eating together at a restaurant. In the aftermath of an unsettling argument with some of the males about a woman's place, her roommate disappeared into the restaurant's bathroom. My student wrote:

> We ordered. Our food came. We waited. I excused myself and found the bathroom. "Are you in there?" I called underneath the stall. With tears glistening on her cheeks and fists clenched in rage she emerged and fiercely whispered, "Sometimes I hate that I'm a woman." In that bathroom I realized that I had given up the fight. Her statement set me on a journey to find my voice again and come to terms with what it means to be a gracious, non-bitter Christian woman who is empowered to interact intelligently, compassionately, and justly with the world around her.

Being gracious, empowered women is what I hope for my students and my daughters. To be a non-bitter Christian woman is to feel blessed, after all, to *be* a woman. And to be able to hold graciously the tension that, on the one hand, broadens opportunities for women while, at the same time, continues to perpetuate patterns limiting women from participating fully in society. Christian women who are empowered to interact in the world recognize the strength endowed them from being made in the image of God.

Thus they are able to respond confidently to God's call to be co-stewards over creation—seeking to bring peace, justice, and mercy to a broken world.

Ultimately, defining a gracious, empowered woman leads to questions about whether women should be encouraged or allowed to fight fires and wars alongside men. Or seek to initiate relationships with men. Or be corporate and political leaders. I wanted help determining which of the new opportunities available to my daughters fit within their co-steward calling, and which, if any, still seemed outside that calling.

Our culture is in transition, broadening opportunities for women. As parents we are uncertain and sometimes uncomfortable with these questions. Like many of my peers, I was raised by loving Christian parents to be a submissive wife and stay-at-home mom. But, as our youngest daughter joined her kindergarten cohorts for their trek through the educational system, I headed off for graduate school. My own need to figure out what I could do, and ought to do, piqued my initial interest in these questions. Could pursuing a full-time career be within God's call on my life as a co-steward over creation, or would it compromise my obligation to our children? Mark and I have three daughters, Danielle, Sarah, and Megan. As we contemplated how best to direct our adolescent daughters, my desire to adequately answer these questions intensified. Danielle entered high school about the same time I became a college professor. I continued to seek wisdom and clarity, desiring to offer college students wise counsel in their own struggles with these questions.

In the 1950s, roles were more clearly defined, and women and men pretty much understood and accepted their gender-defined tasks. In the 1960s, almost every taken-for-granted assumption about how society ought to function was challenged, shaking the values and traditions that had stabilized society. The problem with our current dilemma is not the questioning and debunking of traditional ways of arranging our lives (much of this has been good for society, particularly as it has allowed us to profit more from the contributions of women). Rather, the problem with our current dilemma, particularly as it relates to how we should raise our daughters, is the lack of a system, or set of criteria, replacing that which we cast off.[1] We no longer have a set of rules to help us decide what is good, less good, and bad for our daughters or our society.

Some of the confusion young women face is experienced profoundly from within Christianity, where many assume the gender-defined tasks of the 1950s come closest to the plan God ordained in the Garden of Eden. At school our daughters are encouraged to believe they are gifted in the same way boys are and can be assertive leaders, initiators in relationships. Yet on Wednesday nights at youth group they are taught to be submissive followers of the boys. Girls in the youth group may agree with youth leaders who talk about how girls and boys are created differently and yet leave unsatisfied, believing that being created "differently" somehow means being less than boys, since, after all, girls are the weaker vessel.

While girls may resent their assumed exclusion from the paintball outing or the hockey game trip because they are girls, the more confusing exclusion is when their preparation for adulthood leaves them ill-prepared to be co-stewards over creation—a task they are encouraged to take more seriously in secular spheres. Girls may be encouraged in one realm to discover their gifts and determine how God may be calling them to use those gifts in nontraditional ways. Yet in church they may be discouraged from pursuing or acknowledging certain gifts deemed inappropriate for women.

Our confusion as parents, a society, and a church is partly due to our not having a set criterion to use in directing the paths of our daughters. Postmodern society rejects putting too much stock in any one set of criteria, suggesting there is no one right path for our daughters. Rather, decisions should be based on what seems right to any given individual, according to the particular situation. If a woman can shoot and kill as easily as a man, and if the social context would benefit from her being allowed to shoot and kill, then she ought to be fighting wars alongside men. A postmodern answer to the confusion is: "If she can do it and wants to do it, she ought to be free to choose it."

Our Christian tradition rejects this postmodern approach to determining the paths of our daughters. As Christians we believe in absolute truth that does not shift with the changing tides of cultural change. God has made it clear that we are to love and serve God and others, to be merciful and just. Less clear is how our daughters are to go about loving and serving, showing mercy, and being just. Our understanding of how God calls us to live always takes place in the context of a cultural setting. Christian traditions that claim they can transcend culture, know God's absolute truth with certainty, and thus determine what God wants for girls, are unable to recognize that their ideas are inevitably rooted in the very culture they seek to transcend.[2]

Our understanding of what God calls women to be and do has become yet another battle line drawn in the sand. Changing social forces clash with tradition in a war to determine which side knows best how God wants our daughters to fulfill their responsibilities in the twenty-first century. Christian parents would do well to step away from the battle and try to understand where ideas about men and women's roles come from. In stepping away, we can explore the good pieces that both sides bring to the conversation and perhaps draw closer to an accurate understanding of how God has prepared our daughters for different kinds of stewardship responsibilities.

An insight we gain from a postmodern worldview is the recognition that there is more than one way to organize and run our societies. They are not all equally good, but there is more than one productive, right approach to the way our daughters live their lives. A grounding we gain from a Christian worldview comes from our belief in a God who created us and gave us some clear ideas regarding overseeing and organizing ourselves in that creation. Wrestling with how these two inform each other has the potential to free parents from the paralyzing fear of needing to find the one correct direction to point their daughters toward.

While the postmodern worldview and our traditional Christian worldview offer us valuable insight, they also hinder our ability to use that insight well. Both worldviews make a fundamental mistake that limits the ability for women to fulfill their obligation to be stewards over creation. Even though postmodernism encourages the swinging open of doors and invites participation of women in arenas traditionally shut off to them, female ways of knowing, being, and doing are not valued as much as male ways. The balance that could be brought to the task of stewardship is thus diminished. Our traditional Christian worldview makes the same error of valuing male ways of knowing, being, and doing as superior to female approaches. In this context what women are allowed to contribute is limited, so that female ways of knowing, being, and doing are largely absent in our churches.

This book begins by considering what it means for our daughters to be made in the image of God. An understanding of this concept gives parents a more solid footing to help their daughters respond to the challenges and opportunities confronting them as they enter the twenty-first century.

To explore how both postmodern ambiguity, traditional rigidity, and the low value placed on female ways of knowing, being, and doing have defined our daughters' choices, we will consider underlying assumptions (both theological and cultural) that have shaped our beliefs. God's truth *is* absolute, and some of it we can know absolutely. Yet pieces of it we see only through a glass darkly, giving us opportunity to draw nearer to God as we seek clarity about who God is, and how God would have us live. Ultimately, this is less a book about giving our daughters a revised set of roles to fill and much more about helping our daughters see who they have been created to be.

The first two chapters lay a foundation regarding what it means to raise strong daughters who have been made in the image of God. The next five chapters consider various aspects of being and becoming strong through the development of confidence, independence, and voice. As our daughters understand what they have been created to be, they will be able to make strong decisions about how to live. The final three chapters more closely examine our relationships with our daughters and their relationships with boys.

Jana Sundene, a good friend and colleague at Trinity International University, read a draft of this manuscript. In her response she wrote, "I have to tell you that I am a little sad that this book is marketed to parents with daughters because it really was a gift emotionally for me in that it ministered some healing to me. And as you know, I am not a mother."

While this book has been aimed at those who parent or work with girls and young women, it is my hope that it would be a gift that ministers healing to any woman who desires to read it. Certainly all women have *been* young daughters who made their way from childhood, through adolescence, and into adulthood. May we help our daughters, and perhaps even ourselves, toward a journey that will result in coming to terms with what it means to be gracious, non-bitter Christian women who are empowered to interact intelligently, compassionately, and justly with the world around us.

CHAPTER ONE

THE STRENGTH
OF AN IMAGE

GOD CREATED THE EARTH—with mountain streams, wooded forests, roaring oceans, open prairies, quiet jungles, and expansive deserts—and it was good, and it reflected God as creative maker of all. God created creatures of all sorts—giraffes and gerbils, cats and tigers, eagles and fireflies, rhinos and raccoons—which was also good and reflected God as creative maker of all. Then God created a special type of creature—these would carry his image within them, thus reflecting and mirroring his character and seeking after his heart as they went about ruling and taking care of the earth he had made. It was very good, and it reflected God as the most ingenious creative maker of all.

Then, of course, the image-bearing creatures sinned. Death and destruction came into the created world and began to destroy and pervert that which God had made. The ability of the special human creatures to accurately mirror and represent God as they went about their work of ruling and taking care of the earth also became distorted and perverted. But God set in motion a plan to restore creation, and part of that plan included sending Jesus into the world. Through the saving work of Jesus, God introduced the possibility of renewing and reclaiming the God-image in humanity. And this too was very good.

This book is about reclaiming that which is good in human nature and how we can nurture the image of God in our daughters, helping them recognize the strengths God gave them. Katy, a college student, was unaware of the strong and good traits she carried within her. Katy's image-of-God nature was buried under years of doubt and shame. Academically, she could compete with the best students, but socially she was insecure, awkward, and had no close friends. Physically, she was attractive, yet she curled herself in as though to hide in her body. She could think reflectively about social issues, but lacked confidence in her ability to do anything good for the sake of others. Katy knew intellectually that God loved her but felt distant and unable to respond to his love emotionally. She needed to be set free from a paralyzing image of herself as unable, unworthy, unattractive, and unlovable. She needed to embrace God's picture of her, the image of God within her, and celebrate who God had created her to be.

CELEBRATING OUR NATURES— WHAT WE NEVER LOST

> Then God said, "Let us make people in our image, to be like ourselves. They will be masters over all life—the fish in the sea, the birds in the sky, and all the livestock, wild animals, and small animals." So God created people in his own image; God patterned them after himself; male and female he created them (Gen. 1:26–27).

Being made in the image of God gave men and women the capacity to act as God's representatives on earth. However, the belief that men possess the image of God to a greater extent than women do emerged in part from Greek ideas, such as those suggested by Aristotle, who believed women were a mutilated or incomplete form of men.[1]

Augustine in the fifth century and Thomas Aquinas in the thirteenth century attempted to reconcile Greek ideas about women's defective state with Christian ideas that women were created by God. Women were inferior to men, but as creations of God they could not be *defective;* rather, they were created to be secondary, weaker, and subject to men as a natural and divine act of God.[2]

Our own ideas about how men and women reflect the image of God is perpetuated from within the context of fallen patriarchal cultures that, as a result of the fall, devalue women and women's contributions to the stewardship of creation. Subsequently our daughters' beliefs about themselves are also influenced by a ubiquitous and subtle acceptance of the belief that they are less than men and carry the image of God to a lesser extent than men do. The implications of believing women are not image-bearers to the same extent as men will be explored throughout this book, but it is fundamental to knowing how to raise strong daughters to challenge that belief and understand what it means that our daughters are image-bearers of God.

What the Image of God Means

Theologians such as Augustine, Aquinas, Martin Luther, and Calvin have worked to describe the unique aspects of being human that speak to the image of God embedded in us. They tell us that "image of God" as used in Scripture means a likeness, a mirroring of, a representation.[3] It is not so unlike my habit as a little girl of getting out my toy iron and ironing board and pressing doll clothes alongside my mother while she ironed our household linens. As I represented my mother, albeit imperfectly, so we represent God, also imperfectly. Woman as she was created was like God and able to mirror God's character. Furthermore, she was able to represent God, so that when one looked at a woman, one would see something of God in her.

Marcile Crandall is an example of a woman who well represents God. I met her over fifteen years ago at Newberg Friends Church. She was my first exposure to a female pastor. I held her at arm's length for a while, unsure if being a woman on the pastoral team was okay. Ultimately Marcile became a dear friend, one of the women I most respect. One can see something of God in her gentle ability to tell people what they needed to hear rather than what they wanted to hear when they went to her for counsel. She reflected her directedness toward God in the graceful way she walked with God through the pain of losing her husband in a plane crash. She mirrored Jesus in her ability to minister productively and live independently for a number of years before she remarried. And God's image was reflected in the humble and gracious way she persevered in her serving and loving others in full-time Christian ministry in spite of some resistance because of her sex.

While we lost some aspects of our image-of-God-likeness with the fall, other aspects we retained, though they are often expressed in distorted ways. In describing that which was lost and that which has been retained, Christian theologians often discuss the image of God as having two elements. The element we've retained relates to our essence—the core of our being that sets us apart as human creatures. The element we have lost relates to our ability to behave consistently in God-directed ways.[4]

Our God-image essence refers to all the abilities we have that allow us to interact with each other and oversee creation. That Martha could have a conversation with Mary is a result of being made in God's image. That Martha could now use an intercom, a telephone, e-mail, a fax machine, or the U.S. Post Office to interact with Mary is also a result of being made in God's image. That we seek community and are creative and inventive about how we build community reflects God's image.

The Essence Qualities of God We Have Retained

The essence of God that women and men retain as image-bearers in spite of the fall can be summarized in the following six statements.[5] Our parenting subtly encourages or discourages the development of each of these essence qualities in our daughters.

1. Our daughters are immortal and spiritual beings with souls that have the potential to respond to God. When our middle daughter

Sarah was about five years old she came up to me and said, "Last night I figured out how to hug God." I asked her to explain and she said, "Well, if God is everywhere, I figured if I wanted to hug him, I could just open my arms like this," she spread out her arms as far as she could stretch them, "and then hug the air and I would be hugging God." She brought her arms together, crossing them, and ultimately wrapping them in a hug around herself. Our daughters are created with a tender ability to respond to God, and in their childlike faith are able to remind us, to teach us, and to lead us into a greater understanding of who God is.

If our daughters (and sons) are spiritual beings with souls capable of responding to God, then the larger community would benefit from letting our daughters' simple faith draw us to God. And as our daughters grow, we would be wise to continue on as humble learners, eager to glean from the particular insights God gives them as women. We experience the fullness of God's nature as expressed through humanity when we allow other image-bearers, male and female, to teach and lead us. Our culture has led us to err and lose in two ways. First, we tend to be individualistic, and often assume we can achieve spiritual maturity in the absence of community. Thus we tend toward an arrogant self-taught spirituality rather than seek maturity as humble learners in community. And second, we have been influenced by a culture that disregards and silences women. Thus the unique spiritual wisdom women image-bearers could offer the community is underdeveloped, disregarded, or silenced.

2. Our daughters have a rational ability to reason, to take in information and draw conclusions, to be self-aware and self-reflective. Our daughters are as teachable as our sons, even though our educational systems have historically emphasized learning for sons over daughters. Before the 1800s, girls, if educated at all, were taught at home where they learned to play an instrument and were introduced to literature and foreign languages. It was not until 1832 that women were permitted to attend college with men, though it was still unusual for daughters to pursue a formal education. Following are a couple of explanations given then for why daughters should not attend college:

It was widely believed, for instance that women were naturally less intelligent than men, so that their admission would lower academic standards. A second popular argument was that women were physically more delicate than men and that the rigors of higher education might disturb their uterine development to such an extent that they would become sterile or bear unhealthy babies.[6]

Both of these myths have effectively been debunked. Educated women produce healthy babies, and the distribution of women with high IQs is comparable to that of men. God gave our daughters the capacity to be scientists, political leaders, and theologians who look at their social world and reflect on why it is the way it is. Marie Curie discovered radium and began the study of radioactivity. She won Nobel Prizes in chemistry and physics—the first person ever to win two Nobel Prizes. Sandra Day O'Connor was the first woman appointed to the Supreme Court—in 1981. Great Britain's Margaret Thatcher and United States Secretary of State, Madeleine Albright, brought a giftedness to their positions that reflected both their uniqueness as women and the image of God characteristic that enables us to be rational, reasoning reflectors of God to our social world.

Sally Ride became the first female astronaut in 1983. Theologian Ellen Charry was selected by *Christianity Today* in 1999 as one of the new theologians.[7] She writes about reclaiming spiritual nurture, connecting systematic theology (who God is) with practical theology (how we live).

Our daughters have powerful role models in all kinds of arenas. They need to be introduced so our daughters can believe that they too can do meaningful research and work to develop solutions aimed at restoring brokenness or exploring possibility, thus exercising their role as stewards over creation.

They can contemplate how social structures end up rewarding some groups of people with a huge slice of the pie while other groups get a sliver. They can develop theories to explain why those who receive so little don't rise up and revolt—and under what conditions they *will* rise up and revolt. Our daughters can do meaningful research on marginalized groups of people and work to develop solutions aimed at restoring their dignity and justice, thus exercising their role as stewards over creation.

Other strong women can contribute to our understanding of ourselves and our social world through the arts and literature. We learn something of our human condition in George Eliot's classic novel *Middlemarch* (Eliot chose a male pen name so that her work would be taken seriously). Alice Walker helps us understand the human condition through the eyes of black women who suffered much in her novel *The Color Purple*. Amy Tan teaches us about the brokenness Chinese women experienced in China and their struggle to relate to their Chinese-American daughters in *The Joy Luck Club*. Many women have used their reasoning capacity to be self-aware and self-reflective and have crafted stories that illuminate insights about ourselves and our social worlds.

God gave our daughters a capacity to reason and be self-reflective. And because God chose to embody that image in both females and males, our daughters' expressions of it will sometimes look different than our sons', bringing different emphases, raising different questions, offering alternative solutions. Creation has more balance when women are encouraged to use this ability alongside men.

3. Our daughters are intrinsically social (as God is, demonstrated by the Trinity) and are intended to be in community. This element is not difficult to see in our daughters. Women tend to be more focused on relationships than men, and are more naturally drawn to community. God made us to be social, to be interdependent in our need of each other. When this aspect of God's image is distorted for women it most often becomes an excessive dependence on others. When it is distorted in men it often becomes an excessive independence.

One of my friendship groups has been labeled "The Wild Women." Not that we deserve the title. We still haven't done anything really wild. We talk about skinny-dipping in the quiet, isolated lake we sometimes visit—but so far it's only talk. I prefer calling us simply "The Women," because it has a stronger ring to it. One cannot take "The Women" as lightly as one can take "The *Wild* Women." We go away for an overnight trip once or twice a year and meet together a few more times a year for someone's birthday, a Saturday morning breakfast, or coffee at Starbucks. We have shared our deepest pains and sorrows as well as our greatest joys and funniest moments. Every year we talk about how God has shaped and challenged us and revise last year's prayer requests to this year's shaping and challenging tasks. I know I am prayed for. I feel the power of God in these women. Together, hand in hand, we draw each other nearer to God and reflect the image of God as a relational God.

A number of theologians, Stanley Grenz among them, think we have gotten off track by talking about the image of God as something that is in individual people. Rather than the image of God being primarily an individual possession it is a corporate reality, present among humans in relationship with others.[8] God is too big to be captured in any one individual, so God created diversity—male and female, old and young, a multitude of different cultural and racial backgrounds—and *together* we more completely reflect who God is.

While God's image is reflected in our daughters individually, God's image *is* more completely reflected in the context of community. To bring to completion the corporate image of God, each of our daughters carries the capacity for relationship and community.

4. Our daughters are responsible moral agents who have a sense of "oughtness" about their lives and their world. Psychologist Robert Coles tells the story of Tessie, a little girl from the South, who was one of the first black children to experience desegregation in an all-white elementary school.[9] Parents lined up outside the school and yelled obscenities to her as she walked in the doors accompanied by the National Guard, who had been sent by President Kennedy to protect her from angry crowds. Robert Coles asked Tessie what kept her going, what made it possible for her to get up every day and face school. She said,

> If you just keep your eyes on what you're supposed to be doing, then you'll get there. . . . The marshals say, "Don't look at them; just walk with your head up high, and you're looking straight ahead." My granny says that there's God, He's looking too, and I should remember that it's a help to Him to do this, what I'm doing; and if you serve Him, then that's important. So I keep trying.[10]

Tessie had a strong sense of oughtness about her life and the world. She knew it was not the way it was supposed to be, and she was willing to work the front lines to make it better.

Billye could have been Tessie. She too is an African-American raised in the South during the late '50s and early '60s. For a time Billye directed the telecommunications department at a predominantly white, Christian college. During her time there, two male students wrote an editorial to the school paper expressing their displeasure at an outside donation that was to provide scholarship money to minority students. They said they didn't believe the school needed to be more diverse and were not supportive of efforts to recruit a more diverse faculty or staff. Billye asked to meet with them for lunch. She said, "I don't want to try to change you, I just want you to get to know me. And I want to understand where you are coming from." That is the action of a strong woman who refuses to let the devaluing of her race in our culture affect her. She built relationships with black students, helping them cope with the current culture and see beyond it to a bigger picture of God's kingdom. She built relationships with white students, opening their eyes to a world they have not understood, also helping them see beyond it to a bigger picture of God's kingdom.

God created our daughters with the capacity to serve as moral agents with a sense of "oughtness" about the world. They can do this within any context that bumps them up against the fallenness of the world. My daughter Danielle served as a moral agent when, in third grade, she refused to accept the special invitation to join the "cool girls" club because it meant she would have to snub all nonmembers. Refusing to join meant she suffered the snubbing of her best friend for two weeks. Danielle was acting as a strong woman—responding to the sense of oughtness God had placed within her. This story has a happy ending, because the club fell apart. Not all stories end that way. Billye did not perceive any change in the two students she met with for lunch. But her job was not to change them, only to respond to the sense of "oughtness" God placed within her by meeting them for lunch.

Our daughters can be moral agents in whatever circle of influence God places them. We can encourage them to become aware of public issues, of issues at school, to be informed women who write letters to school papers, or to members of Congress. We can encourage some to *become* members of Congress. Our daughters, with their sense of oughtness, can become judges, lawyers, or politicians who fight for a collective understanding of what is good and right that reflects God's character. Whether they are informed homemakers or lawyers, they can effectively minister wherever they are, like Tessie and Billye demonstrated, allowing God to bring their experiences, their voices, and their sense of "oughtness" to those who lack understanding.

5. *Our daughters are creative and able to create what is good and useful.* After Desert Storm, when our daughter Megan was seven years old, she wrote the following story as a gift to Stephen, a soldier in the war who visited our church.

> Once there was a soldier named Stephen who was the best soldier. He was a Christian. He hated to kill but he knew that he had to do it. Then the war started. Almost everyone died! But Stephen didn't die. And the next day other people died but Stephen didn't die. He was the only one left. Then he got really strong and killed Saddam Hussein and all the others. But he was sad. He wished he wasn't in the war. Then he sat down and cried. He buried all of them. Even Saddam Hussein. He cried and cried. He put a candle on Saddam Hussein's grave and the rest. But he still cried and cried. Then he heard nothing at all. Nothing at all.

Megan's story reflects her image-bearing ability to create something good and useful. She captured ambivalence regarding war in a story about the awfulness and sadness of war, even while recognizing the need to stop evil in a world that is broken.

What is good and useful includes beautiful gardens, welcoming homes, music, literature, programs to house the homeless or teach immigrants English, or a new surgical technique. When our daughters are young we can begin to affirm the image of God in their creations, especially those that reflect pieces of God's truth, goodness, and usefulness. George Eliot published under a man's name to find credibility in her culture, but she published nevertheless. A strong woman will create anyway and not let the devaluing of her giftedness keep her from creating. Strong daughters will seek to create using the gifts God has given them, which sometimes means crafting creations that have traditionally been created by men.

6. Our daughters possess an office of rulership and have been charged to be stewards over creation. Men and women were told to rule creation together. God did not spell out what this would look like but gave them the capacity to subdue and rule. Various cultures and times have fleshed that out differently. Cultures that saw themselves as set apart and above the rest of creation tended to define the stewardship relationship as conquering and subduing. Cultures that saw themselves as part of creation rather than separate from it defined their role more as stewards than subduers. Regardless of how it has been fleshed out, each culture and era has defined this rulership in ways that reflect the brokenness of the fall.

For instance, while we may say all humans are made in the image of God and given the stewardship/rulership authority over creation, the power to rule is only available to some. In our society we tend to assign value and grant power on the basis of economic worth. Michael Jordan was perhaps the most valuable basketball player ever—and we can see that because he earned over $300,000 per game from the Chicago Bulls. CEOs, who generally make at least twenty times what the janitors make, are more valuable than janitors, and we can see that because, in addition to their incredible salaries they have nice offices, great perks, and stock options, and wear $1,500 suits to work instead of blue uniforms. White Americans are more valuable than Mexican-Americans because they are seen as more motivated to get an education, and to pursue better paying jobs. Sons are more valuable than daughters because sons, with their larger paychecks, can contribute more meaningfully to society and maybe make a name for themselves that will bring honor to us as parents.

While we may say it is valuable that our daughters will grow up and become mothers that nurture and care for the next generation, we do not give any tangible evidence that we believe it. Indeed, we will pay the neighbor boy ten to fifteen dollars to mow our lawn (a job that takes an hour, maybe an hour and a half), but the neighbor girl gets four dollars an hour to baby-sit our children. What are we telling girls about the value of nurturing children? And what are we telling *boys* about the value of nurturing children?

Strong women will not let the culture's devaluing of women and femaleness inhibit their ability to be stewards of the earth. And whatever choice they make, it *will* be devalued by some group in the culture. A strong woman who decides to stay home full-time with her children may boldly decide to do so, even though the culture may accuse her of wasting her potential. Yet she will have opportunities to pursue other avenues of stewardship over the earth because she is not working. Another strong woman will pursue work out of sheer necessity, desiring to be a good steward of her children and provide for them, even though she may still be devalued and criticized for her poverty. Some strong women who could stay home with their children will engage in meaningful work and pursue stewardship in arenas associated with their work, even though the culture may accuse them of denying their children and trying to usurp power from men.

Brokenness in our world results in our daughters being discouraged from participating in their role as joint-rulers over creation. Yet God affirms the value of women as well as men. Both were given God's image to enable them to rule together and be stewards of the earth. To limit the ways our daughters can legitimately function as stewards/rulers further devalues the image of God in them and continues the imbalance and distortion of God's plan. The question that flows from this is whether or not men and women were given different tasks to perform in their joint-ruling, namely that women would be the nurturers and men the providers. A theological defense of women functioning beside men in the home, church, and society has been developed by theologians such as Stanley Grenz and Gilbert Bilezikian.

The above list of characteristics describing what it means for our daughters to bear the essence of God is empowering. Our daughters—image-bearers of God! We could not give them a higher compliment or responsibility than to assure them of their position as image-bearers of God. All men and women bear the essence of God planted within them, even though that image has been distorted. We will revisit some implications of these characteristics throughout the book.

CELEBRATING OUR NATURES— WHAT WAS LOST BUT IS BEING RESTORED

With the fall, people lost the second element of being made in God's image—the ability to act rightly. We've seen it in the child who fights for the toy in the store aisle, screaming and thrashing to get the parent, out of sheer embarrassment, to buy it. We see it in people who embezzle funds from companies that trust them. And we see it in parents who abuse the children they are supposed to care for. We see it in children who kill other children in our neighborhoods and on our playgrounds. We see it in our inability to resolve the race crisis, or to find politicians who are not bent in some way. If we look closely enough, we even see it in ourselves. We see it in our selfish desires to arrange the world so that it suits us, or in a passivity that refuses to do anything good for anyone, including ourselves.

The behavioral element of being made in the image of God refers to the ability to be perfectly aligned to God's will and perfectly in relationship with God, others, and creation.[11] This was utterly lost in the fall. Before sin, Adam and Eve walked spiritually, emotionally, and physically naked before each other and God with no embarrassment or shame. After sin, they blamed, they hid, and they died spiritually. We can no longer align ourselves appropriately to do the will of God, and we no longer have a perfect relationship with God. Instead we seek happiness by following our self-centered ambitions, then try to hide our shame and failure, running from honest intimacy with God and others.

The good news (and it is *very* good news) is that this behavioral element is continually renewed in Christians as God draws us closer into relationship with himself, restoring the distorted image of God within us. The goal of redemption is that God's people will be complete and flawless image-bearers of God.[12]

Having God come live among us as a human showed us what an undisturbed, unbroken, perfect image of God in humanity could look like. As Christians seek to follow God and experience a restoration of the behavioral element of God's image, we can look to Jesus as the perfect human representation of God. As commercialized as the "WWJD" (What Would Jesus Do) slogan has become, it speaks a simple truth about Jesus as our perfect model for how to live rightly. While Jesus lived among us he showed us three ways to better reflect God's image.[13]

1. Being Wholly Directed toward God

Our relationship with God is broken, and many have replaced worship of God with self-worship or thing-worship. Christians also struggle not to let other gods—materialism, power, or status—come before our worship and service to God.

As the perfect example of God's image in humanity, Jesus was wholly directed toward God. Mark and I have seen the renewing of our daughters' ability to be wholly directed toward God when they have talked to us of the ache they feel when they disappoint God through neglecting their relationship with him. A number of years ago, when Sarah celebrated her one-year anniversary for rededicating her life to Jesus, a friend gave her a cross to commemorate this event. She wore it around her neck as a daily reminder of her commitment to seek after God. Sarah and Megan have both had opportunities to lead groups at their high school in prayer and Bible study, increasing their confidence as image-bearers capable of directing themselves and others toward God. They are burdened and pray for those they know who are seeking but have not yet found God. I am profoundly challenged and encouraged by God's work of renewal in our daughters' lives and their obedient participation in that work. They are strong women who are seeking to direct their lives wholly toward God.

We were created to be totally dependent on God for our existence. We can experience renewal in the part of God's image that was lost only when we are properly related to God. Thus to be restored as the image-bearers God intended, we need to recognize our fallenness and need for redemption. The best gift we will ever offer our daughters is to invite them into a saving knowledge of Jesus. Augustine said in his *Confessions,* "You made us for yourself, and our hearts are restless until they rest in you."[14] The proper alignment of all other relationships will flow from this one. Once our daughters have come to God, we can begin to help them see what it means for them to be image-bearers of God.

2. Being Wholly Directed toward Others

As Christian women and men we struggle with our distorted relationships with each other. Instead of seeking each other's best interest we often use each other for our own selfish intent. We also distort our relationships with others by narrowly defining who our neighbor is and thus closing our eyes to the hurts of others. When Jesus was asked, "Who is my neighbor?" he told the story of the good Samaritan. Instead of answering the man's question directly, thus allowing his listeners to limit the extent of their responsibility, he ended the parable by asking them who acted neighborly. Upon hearing the answer, "the one who showed him mercy," he told them, "Yes, now go and do the same" (Luke 10:29, 37).

Jesus was wholly directed toward others. He loved them actively, whole-heartedly, and equally. Jesus served his disciples by washing their feet, and the multitudes with his teaching and healing ministries. Jesus boldly confronted sin and compassionately forgave the sinner. He drove money-changers from the temple. Jesus loved and served those outside the mainstream of society—children, women, the poor, lepers, the handicapped, prostitutes, tax collectors, and those possessed with demons. Jesus challenged the religious leaders who had lost sight of God's vision for a chosen people.

Mother Teresa beautifully mirrored God's image as a woman wholly committed to others. She spent her life quietly serving the poor, seeking no fame, yet gaining much credibility. When she boldly addressed world leaders on their responsibility to protect the lives of the unborn, her credible life gave power to her voice. When people chose not to heed her words, the integrity with which she lived made them respect her, and gave her a voice that could

31

not be easily hushed or ignored. We encourage our daughters to be directed toward others when we introduce them to models of women directed toward others and when we model Jesus' example of other-directedness in our own lives.

3. Ruling over Nature

God created a beautiful earth capable of sustaining many, so long as we share earth's bounty with each other and manage earth's resources wisely. Being created in God's image, we had the capacity to rule over nature as wise stewards. However, in our broken state we have exploited the earth's resources without regard for future generations. Wealthy, powerful countries have not only hoarded bounty, but they've also taken bounty from weaker, poorer countries. Our market-driven system is sustained by creating false needs and convincing consumers to buy the products designed to satisfy them. Sometimes this means taking resources from poorer countries. Do we *need* coffee? Plantations in South America grow coffee to satisfy our desires when the land could be used to produce food for the undernourished people of South America. In many cases, United States companies own these plantations. Do we *need* pineapple in our diet? Dole, a multinational corporation that worked with government leaders in the Philippines to displace local farmers growing rice for their livelihood, grows much of the pineapple consumed by wealthy countries. In these distortions we use the earth for our selfish gain rather than for God's glory.

Jesus often ruled over nature by performing miracles such as calming raging seas, walking on rolling seas, turning water into wine. While none of us will perform such miracles, we learn from Jesus' life that rulership over nature is an important part of functioning in God's image. We mirror God's rulership over creation when we bring usefulness, beauty, and healing to God's created earth in ways that bring God glory. This is accomplished by those working to stop or reverse the effects of disease, developing creative uses for recycled plastic, improving agricultural knowledge and technology that allows us to feed more people, or replanting trees in an area where the timber has been clear-cut.

As image-bearers of God it is good for our daughters to learn about the world over which they have been given dominion and stewardship. Yet they often grow up with messages that challenge whether or not they have the ability or even legitimacy to act as rulers or stewards over creation.[15]

For instance, Rosa was the first in her family to go to college. All her high school friends were getting married and having babies while she pursued a bachelor's degree. When she returned home she felt out of sync with their lives and awkward. Neither her family nor her friends understood why she wanted to go to college. Unfortunately, as a Latina student she was not particularly at home in her college environment either. Her values about family, life, and work were different from those of her peers. She had a hard time understanding her peers' apparent lack of family loyalty and their ardent focus on success. Yet Rosa was not derailed by her own neighborhood culture that neither understood nor embraced her desire for an education. Nor was she derailed by the college culture that neither understood nor embraced the diversity she brought as a Latina to the corporate picture of the image of God. She is a strong and persevering woman who prepared herself to be a steward and ruler over creation by pursuing a liberal arts education.

A liberal arts education encourages students to see the world more broadly (and as it is, rather than as we wish it to be) and to be critical analyzers of the social systems we organize ourselves around. However, college is only one avenue that prepares us to be good stewards and rulers over creation. Some of our daughters and sons will have interests that take them into different kinds of learning opportunities and various kinds of work. The challenge for us as Christian parents is to affirm the potential we see in our sons to find meaningful and significant work and see that potential also in our daughters. Our daughters ought to be encouraged to be salt and light in the world, not discouraged from representing the image of God through science, art, philosophy, architecture, forest preservation, urban development, or politics. In this way our daughters bring balance to God's mandate that males and females bring God's image to bear in the co-stewarding of the earth.

CONCLUSION

Our daughters have been created in the image of God. Embedded in their essence is an ability to be in relationship with God, to be rational, reflective, responsible moral agents, and to be creative and active stewards over the earth. Yet because of sin our ability to correctly align these characteristics to God's will has been perverted. Theologian Anthony Hoekema summarizes the travesty of fallen humanity by saying:

> The very greatness of man's sin consists in the fact that he is still an image-bearer of God. What makes sin so heinous is that man is prostituting such splendid gifts. *Corruptio optimi pessima:* the corruption of the best is the worst.[16]

Yet there is hope. We have the hope and promise of a renewed image of God through Jesus' redemptive work on the cross. Therefore, we are empowered by God to not only look to Jesus' example, but to follow the one who perfectly reflected God's will for humanity.

As image-bearers of God we can claim with confidence the lofty goals for our daughters to be wholly directed to God, committed to serving and loving others, and active participants in ruling over creation. Strong daughters won't let the devaluing of femaleness and women in our culture keep them from functioning as image-bearers of God. They know they have been made in the image of God and are empowered by God to reflect that image in a broken world.

CHAPTER TWO

MASCULINITY AND FEMININITY: ORIGINS AND IMPLICATIONS

> So God created people in his own image;
> God patterned them after himself;
> male and female he created them.
>
> —Genesis 1:27

GOD COULD HAVE MADE one sex, but he chose to create two distinct image-bearing creatures. Articulating conclusions about how women and men bear God's image differently is difficult, perhaps because we believe we must first figure out which differences to attribute to environment and which are knitted into our beings at conception.

That men and women see the world and behave differently is not so much the debate. Rather the controversy is over the extent to which our differences are biological, thus coming from nature, or learned, thus coming from how we are nurtured. This distinction has important implications. If our differences are embedded in our nature, we ought to accept them and let what is *natural* dictate our roles and behaviors. Women then would perform womanly work and men would perform manly work; women would act in feminine ways, men in masculine ways. However, if our differences are learned from society, then we can rightly challenge gender-based roles and behaviors and encourage both men and women to participate in what has traditionally been considered manly or womanly work, or masculine or feminine behaviors. Men can become compassionate nurturers; women can become protective providers.

Differences can be overemphasized ("boys are hardwired to be competitive and girls are hardwired to be compassionate") or ignored ("all differences are created by one's social environment"). In both cases we build boxes around our daughters and risk limiting or distorting God's image as expressed through maleness and femaleness. Our culture errs in both ways.

NATURE OR NURTURE?

In the 1960s, the penis of eight-month-old John was destroyed during an operation intended to repair some fused foreskin. John's parents were counseled to have additional surgery to reconstruct John's anatomy to that of a girl's and to raise him as one. John successfully became Joan for the five to eight years she was initially observed. Thus, the nurture side concluded: Gender behaviors are learned; they are *not* biological.

Yet, quip the nature folks, those who checked up on Joan later found that by early adolescence she was having extreme difficulty coping with life as a girl, even though she was receiving hormone treatment to help with details like breasts (desirable) and facial hair (undesirable). At fourteen, Joan learned the story behind her confusion and opted to have the surgery necessary to return to her previous male state. John is now happily married to a woman and has adopted children.

Furthermore, continue the nature folks, the fact that the courts accept premenstrual syndrome (PMS) as a defense for irrational criminal behavior in women shows that women are influenced by their hormones, causing them to become unpredictable, temperamental, and highly emotional. Likewise, higher testosterone levels show that men are more aggressive than women are. The proof is self-evident; gender differences between men and women are indeed biological!

The nurture folks, however, argue that PMS is not present in all cultures. In cultures that see menstruation as an honorable blessing PMS is *absent*, suggesting how much a culture values (or devalues) menstruation affects how women respond to it. Furthermore, male aggression studies have tended to overlook social factors for aggression and have misidentified aggression in women. For instance, in one study, observers were shown a baby startled by a jack-in-the-box; the baby becomes agitated and finally begins to cry. Observers who were told the baby was a boy described the baby's response as anger. Those told the baby was a girl described the baby as frightened. Thus, attributes such as anger can be identified according to what one *expects* to see. Thus, the nurture camp concludes, societal influence has much more to do with gender differences than biology.

And so the battle rages. Whenever we see a long-standing debate a couple of considerations are in order. First, long-standing arguments are long-standing because the issues are complex and cannot easily or definitively be resolved. Second, a good question to ask in long-standing debates is: What underlying values are at stake to create such a passionate debate? Rather than relive more of the battle,[1] let me summarize the noncontroversial pieces of the argument, move into a consideration of the values at stake, and then address the social implications of this debate for our daughters.

The Noncontroversial Pieces

Men and women have different distributions of body fat and hair. They also have different body shapes and different genitals. Females bear the children and are able to feed the newborns. Males are needed to impregnate the females. Males tend to be larger, stronger (especially for tasks requiring upper body strength), and thus more capable of performing physical tasks requiring strength. Females better resist disease, starvation, and have more long-term endurance. Males have more male hormones (e.g. testosterone) and women have more female hormones (e.g. estrogen), but both males and females have both testosterone and estrogen. These pieces are not controversial. The behaviors one associates with being male or female are what define the battle lines. Are men biologically more logical and less emotional than women? Are men biologically more aggressive than women and therefore better suited to be leaders, protectors, and warriors? Are women biologically more intuitive than men and better at noticing and responding to subtle nonverbal forms of communication? Are women biologically more social and therefore more suitable for nurturing children than men are?

Cross-cultural studies from anthropology,[2] as well as hormone and chromosome studies, suggest that the issues are complex and cannot be reduced to simple answers. There are enough exceptions to how men and women behave in other cultures as well as exceptions to the effects of hormones and chromosomes on behavior to merit one staying tentative about one's conclusions. In most cases it is very difficult to separate out behavioral differences from learning. Is Sam more aggressive because he has X and Y chromosomes and testosterone or because he was raised in an environment where he sees male aggression reinforced? Is Julie more nurturing because she has two X chromosomes and female hormones or because she was raised in an environment where she sees nurturing reinforced for girls? Whether nature or nurture has the strongest influence over Sam and Julie will not likely be answered to everyone's satisfaction.

What Is at Stake

What is at stake on the surface of this debate is the power to define legitimate roles or choices for women and men. What is at stake more fundamentally is the value a culture places on masculinity and femininity. In most cultures the failure to recognize or legitimize women's ways of being, knowing, and doing have resulted in women's contributions being devalued. For women to contribute in a way that "counts," they have had to prove that, given a chance, they can function just like men.

The surface argument suggests that if women are biologically more sensitive, less competitive, and more intuitive, then women are best suited for roles that don't require rational, competitive, or logical abilities. But if women are more sensitive and intuitive because they are *taught* to be that way, then girls can be socialized to be more like men and doors will open for them to enter spheres traditionally reserved for men. The unspoken subtext of this argument is that sensitive responses are worse than rational ones, cooperation doesn't get one ahead as much as competition, and intuition is much less reliable as a way of knowing than logic. Some will read that comparative list and think, "Well, yes, but those things are true, aren't they?" This question will be addressed in a minute. But asking the question shows that we have been socialized well to devalue, or at least question, the ability of things feminine to contribute meaningfully to stewardship responsibilities over the earth.

Where the Devaluing of Things Female Came From

Women historically occupied a sphere of life that revolved around reproducing babies for the next generation. A woman bore and nursed children, clothed, fed, and taught them the rules of society. In many cases she also gathered berries, worked in the rice fields, or sewed garments in a sweatshop, but, nevertheless, her life necessarily revolved more around children than her mate's did. Men had not needed to invest much in the reproductive process and so had more time to invest in the making of things. They crafted tools for hunting and war (from spears to atomic weapons), tools for communicating (telegraph systems to computers), and ideologies to help us organize our social lives (political and religious systems). These inventions of men came to be seen as more valuable than reproductive tasks—after all, it is these kinds of inventions that set humans apart from the rest of creation as thinking, creative beings. Thus, those who participated in these activities were demonstrating a natural superiority over those who did not. This was not a male conspiracy. Rather, male domination resulted from what was initially a convenient division of labor; women labored too but fashioned their labor around the producing and nurturing of offspring. Men's labor more directly resulted in the development of civilizations. Once the pattern of dominance was established it was easy to maintain through traditions and laws passed down through the generations.

Things masculine came to be seen as separate from and superior to things feminine. Indeed, a boy who is a sissy is a worse offender to his gender than a girl who is a tomboy. However much she is made fun of for being a tomboy, she at least can be applauded as one who recognizes the value of maleness and desires it for herself.

As discussed in the previous chapter, the devaluing of things feminine was embedded in early Greek ideas about women that then influenced early interpretations of New Testament passages about women. If those interpretations had been built on the values and beliefs about women in Sparta, who were renowned in the Greek world for their social and legal freedoms, instead of Athens or Rome, perhaps we wouldn't need to read books about growing strong daughters.[3] For instance, the Greek philosopher Socrates argued that being a woman was a divine punishment, since a woman was only halfway between a man and an animal.[4] His student, Aristotle, who believed women were actually a deformity, thought that equality between the two would be hurtful and was very critical of the situation in Sparta. In Rome, women were perceived either as objects for men's pleasure or sources of temptation.[5]

Church fathers like Tertullian, Augustine, and Aquinas were heavily influenced by these and other Greek philosophers, and brought their ideas into early interpretations of Scripture regarding the proper relationship between men and women. While these men established important theological groundwork for Christianity, they were not flawless, nor were they able to transcend the culture that influenced them. Our Christian ideas about women were built on an ideology that, at its core, held women and all things feminine in disdain. Tertullian saw women as the curse that led to God having to die, Augustine viewed marriage as the advent of death for men, and Thomas Aquinas's careful and good work also solidly tied Greek ideas about devaluing women into Christian theology.[6]

The erroneous and damning conceptions of females we inherited from our western tradition need to be corrected and given context. Even given the possibility that the value of female characteristics in our culture *could* be raised, to gain any voice or credibility, doubt needed to be cast on the argument that gender traits were primarily biological, and that to be female was to be misbegotten and thus inferior. Consider the following quotes that speak to our deeply ingrained ideas about women:

> There are a large number of women whose brains are closer in size to those of gorillas than to the most developed male brains. This inferiority is so obvious that no one can contest it for a moment. . . . All psychologists who have studied the intelligence of women . . . recognize today that they represent the most inferior forms of human evolution and that they are closer to children and savages than to an adult, civilized man.[7]

The next quote, from 1970, demonstrates that even one hundred years later women battled against biological arguments that constrained their involvement in the public sphere.

> Even a Congresswoman must defer to scientific truths. . . . There just are physical and psychological inhibitants that limit a female's potential. . . . I would still rather have a male John F. Kennedy make the Cuban missile crisis decisions than a female of the same age who could possibly be subject to the raging hormones and curious mental aberrations of that age group.[8]

Why don't we wonder whether or not we are safe with men's decision-making ability during a crisis—men who are subject to their raging testosterone level *every* day of the month?

The first step in reclaiming women's full participation as image-bearers of God commissioned to be co-stewards over creation involved challenging the assumptions upon which statements that devalue femaleness are based. Doubt has effectively been cast on the biology-as-only-explanation-for-gender-traits theory. The social sciences, as well as large segments of our society, recognize there is an interaction between nature and nurture that influences gender behavior and characteristics. Even so, we have had less success effectively casting doubt on the assumption that females are biologically inferior to males and that female characteristics are less desirable than male characteristics. Whether Jim's rational decision-making style is a result of his being born male or his exposure to an environment that fostered rational thinking for boys may be important. But it is less important than recognizing that rationality is considered a male trait and is more highly valued in our society than intuitive thinking, which is considered a female trait.

THE PREFERENCE FOR THINGS MALE

The Michigan Board of Education researched elementary-aged students' perceptions of what it was like to be female in our society. When asked how life would be different if they were the opposite sex, almost half of the girls talked about advantages of being a boy. Only 7 percent of the boys saw any advantage to being female. Almost 20 percent of the boys responded with extremely negative and debasing comments about being female. A number said they would commit suicide if they were girls. One boy wrote, "I would *kill* myself *right away* by starting myself on fire so no one knew."[9]

Since being female is worse than being male, attributes associated with being female become inferior or undesired for males, while attributes considered male have positive connotations and are valued. Rationality is more valued than emotion; logic is a better way to arrive at truth than intuition; competition yields more profit than cooperation. We have been exposed to this bias so much that most of us assume things male *are* better than things female. I saw this bias as a student in seminary classes. Several times authors of texts or professors called arguments *intuitive* or *emotional* to debunk them as foolish, though I never quite saw what was intuitive or emotional about them. Conversely, the *logic* or *rationale* of an argument was offered to show its strength.

But think about these characteristics. Do we respond to God primarily through logic or emotion? We may come to a logical understanding of God, yet ultimately our response to the amazing grace of God is an emotional one. Do we understand each other better on the basis of what is rational or what is intuitive? Those who try to understand others rationally often ignore, or don't trust, the clear, gut-level messages that are trying to inform them and so bungle up their relationships. Even if competition yields more profits, is "profit" always the best end product?

By valuing what we have labeled as male attributes more than female attributes, we have devalued the feminine characteristics of God as expressed in humanity. Furthermore, when this devaluing of certain traits is combined with an exaggeration of whatever real differences exist between males and females, our ability to effectively partner as co-stewards, fully reflecting the feminine and masculine traits of God, is also diminished. The losers? Women, men, our societies, and the created order.

Women have attempted to fulfill their stewardship role by showing men they could partner alongside them by functioning just like them. We have met such a woman, or heard of one. She plays the ruthless game by the men's rules and becomes a top executive. She can be as cutthroat and backstabbing as the best of them. In the process she alienates every friend she has. But that doesn't matter much, because she is self-reliant, and nonemotional—just like a man. She has her job (and happily works the eighty hours a week her job demands), her six-figure paycheck, and an apartment that overlooks the bay. This caricature is meant to be unattractive. Perhaps stories like this are intended to discourage women from trying to compete with men. On the other hand they speak a truth about a woman who rejects anything "feminine" in herself in order to gain access to the power, prestige, and wealth that men have. And they speak an equally powerful truth about a man who denies anything feminine in himself in his effort to gain power, prestige, and wealth.

If we encourage our daughters to try to be "just like men" (competitive, rational, nonfeeling), we are joining the ranks of those who value attributes ascribed to males over attributes ascribed to females. Instead, we need to balance two goals.

One goal is to encourage women and men to regain some of what they deny in themselves because they believe a particular human attribute (for instance, sensitivity) belongs primarily to one gender. This perspective has limited the ways men and women perceive themselves and play out their roles. Yet David's view of God in the Psalms shows much more flexibility in attributes we consider male or female. For instance, while the deliverer, provider, and refuge-making roles are often assigned to the father, David consistently uses mother images to depict God in these roles. David frequently refers to God as a large bird, an eagle perhaps, sheltering, protecting, delivering from harm, and providing for her young (see Pss. 17, 61, 91). David also presents God as the father who is merciful, gracious, slow to anger, abounding in love, and compassionate (see Ps. 103:8–13), attributes more often assigned to mothers.

In addition to encouraging each other to embrace characteristics perceived to belong to only one sex, the second goal is to step away from the trend that sees progress as eliminating differences between the sexes and, instead, find ways to embrace those differences. Our daughters can only become confident in who they have been created to be when the value of femaleness is recognized as equal to the value of maleness and when the representation of femaleness in society is seen as necessary to reflect the fullness of God's image. A fairly recent shift in feminine thought shows how some are beginning to think differently about women and success in a man's world. Cultural feminism seeks to overcome sexism and patriarchy by fundamentally shifting the way people think about female and male qualities. Cultural feminism celebrates women's unique characteristics—ways of thinking, being, and doing—as being equally useful as men's ways. This shift acknowledges that some fundamental differences between men and women exist but challenges the rules of the game. Must women become like men to be successful? Can we assign greater value to qualities seen as particular to women and so benefit from encouraging the expression of those qualities in public arenas? Not until the feminine aspects of God's image are valued as much as the masculine aspects of God's image are will women stop working to gain credibility by being "manly."

EMBRACING THE DIFFERENCES

The approach that says women have to become like men to gain equality is reactionary and ultimately devalues the uniqueness of femaleness. The alternative way to empower our daughters is to embrace the differences by recognizing their value. Following is a sampling of characteristics women appear to demonstrate more than men in our culture. I am not addressing whether these differences come primarily from nature or nurture. I want to move beyond that debate to examine the differences *as we see them* and what might be valuable about them. By focusing on raising the value of attributes ascribed to females, we ultimately free our daughters, our sons, and even ourselves, as fathers and mothers, to experience and benefit from feminine characteristics.

Intuition

Intuition at its best is an incorporation of a woman's own history and experience, a trust in the inner voice that speaks to her emotions and feelings, and an evaluation of the input of others' experiences and opinions. Women who trust their intuition bring all of their being to bear on how they evaluate and judge people, events, and ideas. Intuition is thus a voice of reason, though often cast off as utterly emotional and illogical. Women have intuitions about others' intentions, about a danger their child is entering, about the truth claims of some ideology, about the consequences of a potential decision. Neither intuition nor logic is always accurate. Intuition is a holistic way of feeling and thinking through and about issues, events, and people. While logic is given more credibility in our society, some situations are best determined on the basis of intuition as a way of knowing and evaluating, especially situations full of ambiguity.

Nonverbal Cues

Part of what gives women strong intuition is their ability to attend to nonverbal cues. Some anthropologists ascribe this ability to generations of caring for infants who could not describe their needs.[10] Women more often than men notice particulars at a social gathering—such as when someone is uncomfortable in a conversation, or bored, or offended, or who is coming on to whom, or how the hierarchy of power plays out.

Sustained Attention to Detail

It has long been assumed that women are better than men at staying on task for menial, repetitive, detail work because women have less need for change than men and can attend to detail for longer periods of time. Again, perhaps this comes from generations of attending to the needs of infants and small children. However, this ability to attend to detail means women are not only great assembly line workers, but they also make superb brain surgeons.

Value Given to Life

Historically, women have been seen as life-givers and sustainers. Many ancient cultures worshipped goddesses—a recognition of the esteem given women because of their godlike ability to create life. Women tend to be more opposed to war than men, more likely to favor gun control laws and, although many women support the death penalty, support the death penalty to a lesser degree than men do.[11]

Sensitivity to God

Women are more religious than men are.[12] Women attend religious services more, report religion as being more important, and have more confidence that God (or their religion) can answer the problems of the day than men do. Some church traditions have used women's greater sensitivity to God to support the belief that men need to be leaders in the church and home. To keep men active in religion, these traditions argue that men must be given the leadership of the church, otherwise men would drop out altogether. Other traditions approach the issue differently. If women are more receptive to God than men, perhaps women ought to be the ones leading and mentoring—not only other women but also men who recognize a need to emulate this greater receptivity and sensitivity to God.

These few examples recast into strengths characteristics typically ascribed to females that are sometimes perceived as weaknesses. If we can embrace female characteristics as necessary in our stewardship role over the earth, then we will move toward the restoration of balance that comes with reflecting all of God's character in our stewardship responsibilities. If it is our broken culture, rather than God, that has limited women's participation in stewardship roles, then we are partnering with God when we work to restore that which our culture has broken. As Christian parents we shouldn't wait for our culture or even our churches to begin to value these traits. We can do it by identifying and reinforcing these attributes when we see them emerging in our daughters.

EMBRACING DIFFERENCE WITH EQUALITY

An assumption in some of our churches is that men are to be image-bearers of God in the public sphere and women are to be image-bearers in the private sphere of home. Many would say they consider these roles to be equal, just different. And thus the conversation ends. Traditional roles are embraced, and we teach our daughters to be good wives and mothers and our sons to be good leaders and providers. We teach our sons to look for wives who are committed to staying home and our daughters to look for men who exhibit strong characteristics of leadership. Certainly women are image-bearers in private spheres, but difference with equality does not mean that women only or primarily serve God in private spheres, nor that men primarily serve God in public ones. Indeed, most Christians would argue that men should also be active leaders and participants in their homes. If God didn't limit men to participate only in one sphere, has God limited women to only participate in one, or is that a message from our broken culture?

Competition on the Job

Several male-dominated fields have come under scrutiny in recent years. Women who want to fight fires are challenging the right of men to dominate a field on the basis of superior physical strength, but the fear of dumbing down the standards for women has some of the public disconcerted. If one needs to be hauled out of a building, one generally wants to be sure the firefighter can do the hauling. If the job requires being able to handle a heavy ladder or fire hose then the public wants people capable of doing so—as do the women firefighters who can meet the male standards. They don't want standards reset for women either. If that means only a few women are capable of handling the job, then so be it.

Women who have the upper body strength to be firefighters can be just as effective at fighting fires as men. However, because upper body strength is more common to males, firefighting may be *generally* more suited for males. But what about police officers? Are women capable of carrying out patrol duty effectively? Some have argued that women are *better* patrol officers than men.

> The truth is that the vast majority of police situations call for tact, flexibility, and the ability to read a touchy situation. [Male police officers] are more likely to produce or to escalate violence. Women . . . may have greater success in cooling down violent situations. (This last statement has been supported by police studies).[13]

A partnership linking together male and female traits may yield the strongest team for police work. However, other male-dominated fields may be more suited for females. If women are better communicators, are better able to read nonverbal cues, are capable of making intuitive judgments of character and events, and are more committed to peaceful alternatives than men, then they may be better suited for high level jobs dealing with foreign affairs and national security. Again, a team that is blending the best of what men offer with the best of what women offer will yield the most balanced outcomes. A cabinet dominated by women will come to have its own set of weaknesses, as have our cabinets dominated by men.

Whether or not women should be fighting in the military is perhaps the most heated of the debates regarding differences in men and women and beliefs about what constitutes men's work versus women's work. War, in most cultures, has been a man's job, and resentment about women gaining entrance where they are not wanted has made headline news in ways the military would never desire. Perhaps the most infamous example was the Tailhook Scandal, where eighty-three women and seven men were assaulted at a naval aviators conference in 1991.

Yet if one believes men and women are to be ruling the earth together, then perhaps women ought to be engaged in the business of war (that is, assuming *any* of us should be engaged in war). Inasmuch as women tend toward life-giving and preserving characteristics, they ought to be involved in discussions of war. Yet female perspectives are rarely valued in this arena. Carol Cohn quotes a male physicist who tells this story:

> Several colleagues and I were working on modeling counterforce attacks, trying to get realistic estimates of the number of immediate fatalities that would result. . . . At one point, we remodeled a particular attack . . . and found that instead of there being thirty-six million immediate fatalities, there would only be thirty million. And everybody was sitting around nodding, saying, "Oh yeah, that's great, only thirty million," when all of a sudden, I *heard* what we were saying. And I blurted out, "Wait, I've just *heard* how we're talking—*only* thirty million! *Only* thirty million human beings killed instantly?" Silence fell upon the room. Nobody said a word. They didn't even look at me. It was awful. I felt like a woman.[14]

Part of what it means to be a man discussing war is that men less often contemplate the personal reality of the dead during calculations of war. While soldiers who are sons, brothers, husbands, and fathers, or civilians who are mothers, fathers, and children may be in the background of one's mind when one is discussing casualties of war, they are not brought to bear in professional discussions. This physicist violated that rule, and by emotionally "blurting" out his realization, he acted like a woman.

What gets left out of discussions about war is another perspective. Women might bring an uncomfortably passionate voice that insists on talking about the eighteen-year-old soldiers whose legs are blown off by land mines, and the children whose skin is burned off their bodies by chemical warfare. To bring this concrete and personal reality to the table would make it more difficult to contemplate only the abstract calculations of anticipated casualties. But perhaps making war more uncomfortable and difficult to pursue is a *good* thing. War is perceived to be a man's job, and women, and women's ways of knowing, are believed to have no place in it. Yet on this issue of women's participation in the military, John Arnold, a Vietnam veteran, had this to say:

> During my tour in Vietnam, I was astounded at my peers' capacity to do exactly what was most likely to make enemies of the people we were there to help. Malicious desecration of shrines, limitless sexual harassment, destruction of people's livelihoods and other forms of inappropriate behavior were routine. Ultimately, it didn't matter how many battles our macho forces won because off-battlefield macho behavior eroded away every gain. The lesson of Vietnam should be this: regardless of who is piloting that jet or firing that rifle, if their efforts are not to be in vain, whoever is in command of them should be a woman.[15]

Arnold's experience in war gives power to his perspective. Perhaps having an intelligent, capable woman (who acknowledges the emotional side of war, that is, the concrete reality of the dead and maimed) making decisions during a military crisis is a good thing. Perhaps she could bring balance to an intelligent, capable man who may be more concerned about honor than life or is driven by an aggressive and competitive nature that enters too quickly into battle.

At this point in our history, women who want to join the military are generally resented. Nowhere are charges of sexual harassment higher than in the armed forces. Piloting an aircraft may be one of the jobs that women are better suited for than men because of their smaller body size and ability to attend to detail for extended periods of time. When a man crashes a plane, all male pilots are not discredited. However, when a woman crashes a plane, all women pilots are discredited. Colonel Cadick, a retired Marine fighter pilot, wrote a *Newsweek* opinion piece that said women were genetically unsuited for lengthy combat. His piece drew many letters in response, one from Manny Kiesser, a fellow Marine that had served with Cadick. Kiesser first highlighted Cadick's own crash during an air show that lost the military a thirty-million-dollar F–18, and then identified Cadick's opinion piece as a second public embarrassment to the Marine Corps.

> To imply that chest-thumping barbarianism is the appropriate character for those involved in a dangerous undertaking insults the intelligence of marines. To further imply that as a male pilot I would not trust or fly with a female pilot adds to that insult. . . . Some of the finest marines I served with were women. Given the chance, they would have made excellent fighter pilots, and I would have proudly flown with them.[16]

This is a very heated debate, not to be solved here. Not all arenas are so fraught with disagreement. Women's intuitive nature, ability to read nonverbal cues, and communication skills make them well suited to be lawyers, judges, surgeons, administrators, professors, and counselors. Many occupations that were once dominated by men have come to benefit from the contributions of women.

Competition at School

Certainly our daughters will still feel devalued on the playground and in the classroom. The words *sissy* and *wimp* are used primarily to demean boys who act like girls—who cry, are not good athletes, are timid, or are not adventurous daredevils (a trait some refer to as intelligence!). By implication girls are all these things. One of our daughter's young and inexperienced physical education teachers tried bonding with the boys in the class by mimicking how one of the girls ran. The girls were not impressed. Neither were the parents who heard about it. Our daughters are taught subtly and not so subtly to devalue things feminine.

Our youngest daughter is a distance runner. Although the runners only competed with their own sex, during middle school track meets boys and girls of the same grade ran the mile at the same time. I felt sorry for the boys the girls beat—not because I believe the boys *should* be able to beat girls but because I know our culture *expects* boys to be able to beat the girls and mocks them if they cannot. Until we can eradicate this competition between boys and girls, and women and men, some men will continue to feel threatened and resent the accomplishments of women. These men will continue to devalue the feminine characteristics, seeing women not only as different but also as inferior. Our first challenge is to examine how we as parents, teachers, and youth leaders unknowingly participate in and communicate this devaluing of things feminine to those we parent, teach, and lead. Our second challenge is to seek to celebrate and value differences between men and women, remembering God chose to create two distinct image-bearers—males and females.

Where to Go from Here

Connecting abstract ideas to concrete action is often challenging. Following are several suggestions for how we can begin to challenge the messages girls receive that devalue traits considered feminine.

1. Celebrate Typically Female Attributes

At church when a woman stood up and shared during prayer time, I used to cringe if she started to cry. "One more peg in the coffin of female credibility," I would think. Yet to cringe is to deny the sensitivity to God and others that characterizes women. It is to accept the culture's value of emotionless rationality over expressive sensitivity. Similarly, it is good to celebrate typically female attributes when seen in men. If men are willing to be vulnerable, to cry, it is a sign of affirmation that things typically considered female are not anathema to things male. Parents affirm female characteristics in their daughters when they give legitimacy to expressions of them.

2. Encourage the Development of Intuition

As we encourage the development of logical and rational thinking in our sons and daughters, we should also encourage the development of intuitive ways of thinking. Intuition is undervalued, underrated and underdeveloped. Megan is very intuitive. In an almost uncanny manner she can read a situation for what it is. In fourth grade she picked up on and identified the subtle racial prejudice of a librarian attending to one of her classmates. She has often identified how someone is feeling in incredibly insightful ways. As we acknowledge the trustworthiness of our daughters' insight and intuition, they are encouraged to use and trust it.

3. Explore Atypical Applications of Gifts

Encourage daughters in fields for which they have aptitudes, whether or not these fields are dominated by males. Encourage the notion of partnerships between men and women rather than competition, where women and men bring balance to fields typically dominated by one sex or the other.

4. Do Not Neglect the Androgyny Principle Entirely

Androgyny focuses on how men and women are more similar than different. Thus an androgynous person is one who exhibits both male and female characteristics—emotional and logical, cooperative and competitive, nurturing and aggressive. While God created us with some differences, our culture and church have overemphasized these differences and put us into boxes based on our sex. We should not neglect the point of androgyny. Boys can be taught to be nurturing and cooperative, and girls can be encouraged to be strong and competitive. Our biology does not preclude us from making these choices.

When we release ourselves from the boxes that constrain choices on the basis of typically assigned female and male characteristics, we experience humanity more fully. By drawing such stark (and at times arbitrary) lines between that which is masculine and feminine, we close off half of the human experience to ourselves. Men who have allowed themselves to become nurturing fathers and to cry with friends should not feel "sissified" for doing so, because they are richer in their experience of what it means to be human. Women who can maintain a logical position on an emotional argument, who can compete effectively against competitors, should not feel like they are denying their womanhood by doing so, but feel richer in their experience of what it means to be human. Differences should be seen as general tendencies, not moral codes that define what we can and cannot do, feel, or be. A narrow focus erodes our ability to consider how God created us.

SOME CONCLUDING DISCLAIMERS

I conclude this chaper with two disclaimers. First, this book only focuses on daughters. Certainly a discussion of our sons' unique capabilities would also be appropriate. Its omission here is not intended as a devaluation but rather an attempt to focus on those characteristics attributed to our daughters, though not often valued.

Second, later in the book I will make a case for active parenting from both mothers and fathers. When I talk of careers and encourage us to encourage our daughters to think broadly about their capabilities, it is with recognition that life is much longer than the years we invest in our children. If the average family has two children and spreads them two to three years apart, this means, on average, parents spend seven or eight years in intense parenting of small children, plus another ten years parenting them through school until they leave home. Depending on when the process started, this leaves the average person twenty-five to forty years of life to fill with meaningful activity.

We need to attend to our children. As a society we are letting children fall through the cracks as both men and women pursue their own dreams. Both parents are equally responsible for parenting their children. Families will certainly play this out differently. In some cases, mothers will stay home with small children; in a few homes, fathers will stay home with small children. For the majority, both will be working, and the challenge is most pressing for them. Mothers and fathers bring different dimensions of maleness and femaleness into parenting. Children need to receive from each of them. Together, mothers and fathers are to steward in this realm as well. These issues will be discussed in later chapters. For now, suffice it to say this chapter's dialog is not meant to suggest that all women should go out and get careers. Rather, it is to open the horizons for how our daughters think about their femaleness and how God may intend to use them to reflect his image in the world.

CHAPTER THREE

DAUGHTERS
AND CONFIDENCE

The very little engine looked up and saw the tears in the doll's eyes. And she thought of the good little boys and girls on the other side of the mountain who would not have any toys or good food unless she helped. Then she said, "I think I can. I think I can. I think I can." And she hitched herself to the little train.

—Watty Piper

MEGAN WAS A GOOD DISTANCE RUNNER, the best on the Franklin Middle School cross-country team. But in seventh grade she had never come in first overall in a meet. Franklin hosts the Girl's Invitational each fall, which fell on a particularly cold, rainy day her seventh grade year. Some of the teams arrived late and did not have enough time to walk the course prior to the race. But they had maps, and the course at North Side Park was well marked. The race began, and several top runners pulled out ahead of Megan. The pack disappeared around the bend. We waited in the rain for them to reappear at the far side of the lake. . . .

Types of Confidence

In *Women's Ways of Knowing*,[1] Mary Field Belenky and others develop five perspectives on knowing, and confidence in the capacity to know, that they have observed among women. To a large extent, these perspectives were influenced by the homes these women grew up in. As we read *Women's Ways of Knowing*, many women recognize their own homes and come to better understand why they are as they are and perhaps why other women are the way they are. I've adapted the authors' five ways of knowing to corresponding *types of confidence* that underlie what a woman knows, how she knows it, and how much confidence she has in it.

The Absence of Confidence

Some women seem to experience the world as though they are deaf and dumb. They have no confidence in their ability to learn or comprehend and thus depend entirely on others to direct them. Obedience is important, because the one thing they learn well is that obedience will keep them out of trouble. These girls are often raised in isolated homes and have few friends while growing up. Not much talking occurred in their homes, and when it did, they more often heard hurtful words rather than nurturing ones. These daughters accept the extreme sex-role distinction they observe in their homes. Men are competent doers and women are incompetent and passive. The incompetence they see in their mothers they accept as true of themselves.

Daughters from these homes do not occupy any seats in my college classes—or anyone else's classes. They do not attempt college. Though many would be intellectually able to succeed, they have no confidence in their ability, nor do they see any value in their obtaining a college education.

Listening Confidence

These daughters have confidence that they can listen and learn from others. Authority figures hold the truth, and they willingly submit to the truth of authority figures. Yet, while they absorb what others have to say, these girls lack any confidence that they have something to contribute to the ongoing conversations around them.

More of these women come to my classes. They take great notes, comprehend the readings, and can retain and recall the facts and concepts. But they are quiet, preferring to listen to others rather than contribute their own ideas. When they have to evaluate, analyze, or apply the concepts to some real life problem, they lose confidence in their intellectual abilities. These women often come from homes where parent-daughter conversations were primarily one-way: from parent to daughter. Parents did not encourage their daughters to think about issues but instead told them *what* to think about issues. The homes are usually structured along a hierarchy where men have the most authority and do the most talking. Daughters observe that men talk more than listen and that women listen and encourage men to talk.

Much of our evangelical tradition encourages women to be listening learners. The pattern where men do most of the talking and women do most of the listening is witnessed in many of the evangelical churches these daughters attend, thus reinforcing a listening confidence.

Confidence in One's Self

Daughters who have confidence only in themselves are strong and independent. Yet they have lost (or never had) confidence in the authority of others. They have confidence only in what they know, feel, or experience. In Belenky's study, these girls seldom came from supportive, stable families. These parents frequently belittled their children and expected obedience without question. Fathers were often absent. These daughters have been hurt by the authorities that were supposed to protect and support them and learned instead to only trust themselves. Thus they are sometimes rebellious and have shut their parents out, respecting them only when the parents would listen to them.

I have had a few students in this place. It is a challenge to work with them, to bring them back to a point of enlarging their confidence circle to include others. Professors who can support these students' efforts to be self-directed are more often able to connect and reengage with them than those who try to rein them in. This is true of parents as well.[2] It is especially challenging to help these women reconcile trust in God with their disappointment in the church. Some have been disillusioned by the church and no longer have confidence in religious authority. Truth as they were taught it by various authority figures has not measured up to the real world or the critiques of other authorities. Thus their confidence about what they know to be true comes to reside in themselves. Our postmodern culture, which values the acceptance of multiple claims of truth, fosters the belief that one's best shot at discovering truth is to rely on one's own gut feelings.

Confidence in Reason

Some women come to believe truth is not easily accessible but needs to be studied, evaluated, critiqued. It takes work to know with confidence. These women may feel overwhelmed by what they do not know and anxious not to appear stupid, so they may be quiet reflectors and listeners. But unlike girls with listening confidence who do not believe they can think carefully, girls with reasoning confidence believe they can reach truth by reason but want to approach it carefully. Sometimes thinking rationally dominates their values: "It doesn't matter what you think about homosexuality, only that you have thought it through carefully." The content of the value sometimes becomes less important than how one thinks about it.

These women trust in authority, but they also have confidence in their ability to reason and think critically. The women in Belenky's study often described their families as caring, connected, and having good mutuality and reciprocity. Mothers could speak with confidence as well as listen, and fathers could listen carefully as well as speak.

Holistic Confidence

Women who have holistic confidence have confidence in their ability to integrate and evaluate what others (both friends and authorities) tell them, their subjective intuition, and the voice of reason. These women have confidence in their ability to think about, make, and follow through with decisions. They also come from caring, connected homes that have good mutuality and reciprocity. In addition, they did not see fathers as having primarily intellectual abilities and mothers as having primarily emotional ones; rather, they saw their mothers and fathers as having both. Mothers could speak and did so from the gut as well as from the mind.

Emotions and intuition come from God and were given as tools to help us fully experience and comprehend the world. Confidence that reflects God's character is an integration of discerning listening to others, to reason, and to one's inner voice. These daughters will be able to discern whose authority to trust and then trust it; they can trust their ability to evaluate with critical reasoning along with their intuition and emotion.

Few college freshmen come into my classes with holistic confidence. Some graduate with it. Others, I am certain, acquire it later. Many never will. I have grown, along with some of my friends, into a holistic confidence. These friends are wise and confident women who are able to listen to the voices of others and to reason, to trust their intuition, and to speak confidently. They are wonderful role models for their daughters and mine.

What do we want for our daughters? If we believe that being made in the image of God means that daughters have the ability to bring all of who they are into wise decision-making, then we want them to be confident in their ability to do so. How do we build a foundation for holistic confidence in our daughters? By being aware of currents that undermine confidence and by being intentional about strategies that help our daughters gain a strong sense of self in spite of cultural factors that erode the confidence of girls.

CURRENTS THAT UNDERMINE CONFIDENCE AND STRATEGIES TO OVERCOME THEM

Women today can be lawyers, astronauts, businesswomen, and movie producers, yet adolescent girls are more depressed and less optimistic than their mothers were a generation ago. In *Reviving*

Ophelia, Mary Pipher talks about something dramatic that happens to girls in early adolescence.

> Just as planes and ships disappear mysteriously into the Bermuda Triangle, so do the selves of girls go down in droves. . . . In early adolescence, studies show that girls' IQ scores drop and their math and science scores plummet. They lose their resiliency and optimism and become less curious and inclined to take risks. They lose their assertive, energetic and "tomboyish" personalities and become more deferential, self-critical and depressed.[3]

Maintaining or restoring our daughters' confidence is an important part of keeping them out of that Bermuda Triangle. This is particularly challenging given the obstacles in our present culture. A number of factors contribute to this downward spiral our daughters experience in adolescence, all of which erode their confidence.

Current 1: Cultural Expectations for Girls

I remember the summer each of my daughters transformed from a carefree little girl who loved the swimming pool to a self-conscious preadolescent who felt on trial before a crowd of gawking critics. In turn, they each went from being unaware of her scantily clad body, immersing herself in the pleasure of sun and water on skin, to a budding woman-child, painfully aware of every inch of her body—whether exposed or not. It was harder after that to glean much pleasure from the kisses of the sun and water. I grieved for them this loss of childhood pleasure and ease with their bodies. And it happens earlier now. What I began to experience in late junior high, girls today begin to experience by fourth grade. A study of nine- and ten-year-old girls in San Francisco showed that while only 15 percent were actually overweight, over half of them thought of themselves as fat. Eighty-one percent of the ten-year-old girls were dieters.[4] This obsession with beauty and obsessive critical analysis of their own flaws by the fourth grade demonstrates a strong cultural undercurrent.

Another type of cultural undercurrent that our daughters encounter comes from invisible social structures like the "glass ceiling." Cultural traditions allow females to advance only so far, and social structures reinforce those traditions in ways that hold our daughters back. A female student may be the most qualified in the class to be class president, but if tradition upholds only boys as class presidents, she will have a hard time winning the election. Even though girls now may have more opportunities than their mothers, they still run up against barriers that limit how far they can take their aspirations. The inconsistency between what they are told they can achieve and their achievement of it gives rise to doubt and self-criticism, as well as a loss of confidence in their abilities.

A third type of cultural undercurrent is ideological, like the individualism of our culture that carries an expectation that girls (and boys) separate or distance themselves from their parents by adolescence.[5] While people in the United States, who value individualism, tend to see babies as dependent and needing to be differentiated from parents, people in Japan, who value close bonds between people, see babies as too autonomous and needing to be coaxed to be more dependent on others to encourage bonding.[6] This results in different parenting styles and different cultural expectations for growing children. Thus, in our culture, by adolescence—a time daughters (and sons) need parents for support and encouragement—children are pulling away from parents.

Strategies to Combat Cultural Currents

How our daughters think about their bodies is partly learned from their mothers and fathers. Are mothers obsessed with weight control? Beauty? Is aging an enemy? Do fathers perpetuate this obsession by their own response to beautiful women portrayed in the media? If parents can resist the tendency to judge and critique others or themselves on the basis of beauty, they will begin to break a cycle that negatively impacts how their daughters think about their bodies. Another strategy is to monitor media influence. Some parents choose not to have televisions or go to movies. But pressure will come from peers whether or not our daughters watch television, so we need to become astute critics of the media: ask questions, point out unrealistic portrayals of beauty, wonder out loud about the cost of beauty. Are these models and actresses starving themselves? Have they undergone surgery to have various parts of their bodies enlarged, reduced, or reshaped? We need to question whether the images of beauty we are exposed to are natural and healthy.

One strategy to combat a social structural current like the glass ceiling is to remind ourselves and our daughters of ceiling breakers. Women do rise to the top, and they make great contributions when they do so. There have been female world leaders (Margaret Thatcher), significant scientists (Marie Curie), and at the close of the twentieth century, 12 percent of presidents for colleges in the northwest are women.[7]

A related strategy for young girls is to keep stories like the *Little Engine That Could* around. The little engine in Watty Piper's story decides she will try to pull the train over the mountain (clearly beyond what is expected of her), and as she tries, she succeeds. And so can our daughters. Parents can challenge the voices in a culture that undermine their daughters' confidence and thus instill in them a sense of confidence that they are capable of being stewards and caretakers over creation, even if it means butting up against glass ceilings.

A strategy for overcoming ideological cultural currents, like the expectation that our daughters pull away in adolescence, is to buck the culture while being sensitive to our daughters' need to live within their culture. Our daughters grew up in a community where, by adolescence, it was uncool to be seen in public doing things with one's family. Forcing our girls to go on a family bike ride would not help us stay connected. But it was okay to do activities with subunits of the family. The girls and I could go into Chicago to shop at resale stores. Mark and/or I and one daughter went to movies or Cubs games, or any two or three of us went on walks. Look for avenues that your daughters will accept that allow connection without forcing it. This is not to say parents should not insist on social family time. We occasionally have "Forced Family Fun Night," where we plan an evening around games or a movie. (And every so often it happens anyway, without having to be forced.) We still take family vacations, because it *is* okay to be seen as a family out of town. We insist on certain kinds of sisterly support and wish we had insisted on more—attending a sister's drama production, at least one track meet or basketball game. Families can work creatively to eat together; for example, some have breakfast together because schedules seldom work for dinner. Be intentional, creative, and persistent in staying connected with daughters through adolescence.

Current 2: Broken Family Patterns and Broken Daughters

The positive messages that parents give daughters from infancy onward will be significant motivators that can help enable girls to overcome negative messages they receive from culture. However, come adolescence, some daughters (especially those separating from their parents) reject those messages and succumb to the negative voices in culture that erode their confidence. Other daughters are never offered support from their family to begin with. Thus, the family is also sometimes a factor that undermines confidence.

Children first gain a sense of confidence (or lack thereof) from parents, siblings, grandparents, or other extended family. Whether Angela thinks she is cute or ugly, smart or dumb, fun to be around or obnoxious begins at home. The impressions of self-confidence formed in the family are strong ones, whether these are negative or positive. These early socialization patterns are so strong that when girls' self-confidence is eroded at home, it is difficult for teachers, friends, and youth pastors to build it back up.

My student Autumn's father eventually committed suicide after his wife took Autumn and left. After his suicide Autumn's mother went away for awhile, spending time in and out of mental institutions. Autumn described the brokenness in her family, prior to her father's suicide, in this way:

My mother was passive and my father was aggressive. My father yelled a lot. My mother took it a lot. My mother yelled back sometimes but was passive and let Dad walk all over her. My sister yelled back, but she was miserable. I never did. I was the youngest. My sister had the best of both genders. She was beautiful, she had attitude, she could fix cars and control the relationships she was in. I couldn't compete with her on any front. Because of my perception of her perfection, I didn't try to be feminine.

Couldn't try to be a tomboy either, cause she had that licked too. She would ridicule me a lot. I cried a lot too. Had lots of reasons too. My father would yell, I'd cry, and get yelled at for crying. I was a crybaby.

Broken families yield broken daughters. Autumn had never been given much reason to feel confident in anything—particularly her ability to be in relationships with others or to attempt what she was capable of achieving. But somehow she made it to college, and she was gaining confidence. More often than not the Autumns never get that far.

Some parents undermine confidence by overprotecting daughters so that they never come to see themselves as capable. Generally, we believe sons need to be confident and learn responsibility, so they are pushed harder to get good grades, become active in sports, or get a job. Girls are more often taken care of and seldom have to test their ability against hard challenges.

At least this is a general pattern among white families. This tendency is reversed in African-American families. Billye is raising a daughter, and she tells me that girls in African-American communities are often raised to take care of their brothers. They cook for and clean up after them, and are expected, as women, to take care of themselves financially. While the boys go off to shoot hoops after school, the girls flip hamburgers at the local hamburger joint before coming home to start the spaghetti and gather the household laundry. While this does not necessarily cause higher levels of confidence (certainly minorities in the United States have many cultural and structural challenges that undermine confidence and the ability to succeed), African-American girls grow up assuming they will have to take care of themselves and learn they can do so.

Strategies to Counteract Broken Family Patterns

The family plays a powerful role in the development of confidence. Broken families will likely need help to break the cycle that yields broken daughters. But many families unwittingly undermine their daughters' confidence by maintaining lower expectations for daughters than they do for sons. Meeting challenges and learning to persist, even when met with failure, instills confidence. Danielle, who almost always meets success rather than failure, had a particularly difficult sophomore year in high school. She had tried out for, and did not make, the fall musical. She tried out for, and did not make, the soccer team, even though she had played her freshman year. Come tryout time for the Treble Choir, she was fairly certain she did not want to face another rejection. But she tried out anyway and made the choir. Not all real-life stories end with persistence paying off, but many of them do. Parents need to prepare daughters for failure and keep encouraging them to find something at which they can succeed. The morning Danielle was to find out whether she made the soccer team, I picked her up for lunch. She dealt with her disappointment by deciding that after lunch she wanted to gather job applications. If she was not going to be on the soccer team, she wanted to get a part-time job. So we visited Starbucks, the grocery store, and the drugstore to pick up applications. Danielle was learning not to let failure in one area erode her sense of confidence that she was capable of success.

A second way families unwittingly undermine confidence is by raising their daughters to only have listening confidence. One-way conversations with daughters do not instill confidence in our daughters that they can think for themselves. Parents need to have dialogues with daughters, not monologues. We can ask our daughters what they think about NATO involvement in places like Kosovo, whether or not gun control would help decrease the numbers of kids killed by kids in the United States, or how the highly sexualized and violent entertainment culture affects adolescents. Encouraging them to speak what they are thinking and feeling about significant issues increases their confidence that they may have something to say that is worth listening to.

Current 3: School and the Attention Deficit

Even for parents who do an excellent job instilling confidence, the battle to maintain confidence is engaged as soon as our daughters walk out the door and into the world. Usually the first taste of that world is school or day care.

Some girls who begin school with very little confidence do gradually gain more. However, it is more common for girls who begin school with confidence, to gradually lose it by early adolescence.[8]

Boys tend to get more attention from teachers than girls.[9] Boys get more positive attention; they get called on more to answer questions and receive more help with correcting errors or thinking through answers. They also get more negative attention for things like throwing spit wads. While boys are praised for the intellectual quality of their work, girls are praised more often for the neatness of their work. One result is that girls sometimes sink into the "silence ghetto," where they get into the habit of not answering questions or participating in class and instead become passive bystanders.[10] Another result is that girls have a declining sense of their abilities. Findings from a study conducted by the American Association of University Women (AAUW) showed the following:

> Adolescent boys have a greater sense of confidence in their ability to do things in their lives than girls do. Twice as many boys as girls consider their unique talents to be what they like best about themselves. Sadly, twice as many girls as boys consider what they like best about themselves to be some aspect of their appearance. Further, adolescent boys dream bigger dreams than girls do—and they are more likely to believe that their dreams can become reality.[11]

One theory behind why girls doubt their success is based on research that revealed explanations for girls' and boys' failure or success. Both parents and teachers tended to attribute boys' successes to being smart and their failures to bad luck. Conversely, parents and teachers tended to attribute girls' successes to luck (or that the task was easy) and their failure to not being smart.[12] What parents believe their children are capable (or incapable) of doing will effect their children's level of confidence. What children attempt to achieve will be based, in part, on what they think parents and teachers believe they can do successfully.

While many studies in the social sciences continue to identify difficulties girls confront in school, a 1998 study reported in *USA Today* showed some reason for optimism in how girls are perceiving their abilities and opportunities. A survey of 1,200 students found that 60 percent of girls were trying to take the most difficult and challenging courses available, compared to 44 percent of boys, and that 75 percent of girls believe they will have many opportunities after they graduate. Eighty percent of girls said it was personally important to them that they do their best, compared to 65 percent of boys.[13]

This optimism and expectation for opportunity sometimes throws the arenas of school and church into conflict: In school girls are encouraged to do well and to think big dreams about their future contributions to society, while in church they are being prepared to become helpmates for their husbands.

Strategies to Combat Undermining of Confidence at School

Another piece of good news is that girls often bounce back from some of these confidence-eroding currents by late high school.[14] In fact, colleges tend to find it easier to locate women with good grades and high SAT scores. In spite of the lack of attention given to girls, many of them do well in school. This is partly due to expectation differences. Boys are supposed to be rowdy, daring, and distracted; girls are supposed to be quieter and attentive. The expectations in behavior differences seem to pay off for girls come college admission time.

Daughters can be encouraged at home to be active learners, confident in what they know and how they come to know it. Discussions at home about ideas raised in school, amongst peers, or at church can encourage daughters to participate and think reflexively, building a sense of confidence in their ability to be trusting of authority, yet critical analyzers of authority, rational, yet attuned to their intuitive responses. While they may not build holistic confidence at school, it can be developed and reinforced at home.

Current 4: Media and the Climate of Helplessness

The media reflects ambiguity about women's roles in the mixed messages found in contemporary films and on television. On the one hand we find a plethora of women who need saving, sometimes from bad men (or evil women), sometimes from their own stupidity. On the other hand we see strong women who are credible and sometimes even likable. Walt Disney gives us females that need saving *(Little Mermaid)* and females that do the saving *(Mulan)*. Movies intending to attract women viewers give us strong women, some more admirable than others, in films such as *Fried Green Tomatoes* and *Elizabeth;* women trying to be like men *(GI Jane);* and women who are out to get even *(The First Wives' Club)*. In movies intending to attract male viewers women tend to be either absent or present for the purpose of showing how strong and brave the men are. The Lethal Weapon series, Chuck Norris movies, Arnold Swarzenegger and Sylvester Stallone movies and perhaps most notably, the James Bond movies all illustrate this. Occasionally movies for men depict smart and strong women, but they still come in second to their male leads, and according to one of my colleagues, are largely present for their "yumminess quotient" (male viewing pleasure). Catherine Zeta-Jones in the movie *Entrapment* is one such example.

Television serves up the same ambiguity we get in the movies. Ally McBeal is supposed to be a smart lawyer, but she is dumb when it comes to her personal life. Girls are shown as ditsy *(Clueless),* or sexy and available for sex (Rachel, Phoebe, and Monica in *Friends). The X-Files* switches the stereotype by giving us an intuitive male (Fox Mulder) and a rational female (Scully). However, the male still wins. In one episode Fox Mulder asks Scully how many times his intuition has been what solved the puzzle over her rationality. The answer: every time.

One conclusion from this analysis is that the media merely reflects the ambiguity in culture rather than shapes it. However, our daughters are still susceptible to the shaping power of the media and assume the characters they see reflected on the screen are true representations of what women are supposed to be. The media both helps and hurts us, and most of us have some sort of love-hate relationship with it.[15] We are drawn to the very characters that repel us. Producers and writers that give us strong female characters who think well, love well, and do good offer our daughters positive alternatives as they sift through ambiguous messages. We are most hurt in the world of advertisement where the goal is to convince consumers that they need to buy a particular lifestyle or product to fix whatever is wrong with them—most notably for girls, their inability to get or keep a guy.

Flipping through a typical teen magazine girls can learn to "Get the hair guys worship" and "Get him to gush with love talk." They learn about the six signs that he's ready to fall in love and how to get rid of zits forever. They learn how to handle sex stress: "He wants it, you're not sure, now what?" Teen magazines sell our daughters unrealistic ideas about body image, boys, and sex. None of these add to their confidence level, though I imagine the magazine editors would claim that is their intent. Indeed, if girls were truly confident, they wouldn't need teen magazines to help them figure out how to live in a complex culture that says the essence of life is body image, boys, and sex.

The media culture perpetuates the belief that women will be evaluated purely on their physical appearance. On the one hand, society places unrealistically high pressures on our daughters to be successful (defined as beautiful, smart, sexy, and outgoing), yet, on the other hand, girls confront a culture that continues to devalue female attributes and abilities—except for perfection in beauty, which is unattainable.

Strategies to Combat Media Messages

Disney has created some strong female characters, and poked fun at "real men" types, most notably in *Beauty and the Beast* and *Mulan*. Other exceptions grace the screens as well. Dorothy, in *The Wizard of Oz*, is a smart, courageous girl who, although she still needs saving, at least helps the process along and ultimately kills not one but two wicked witches. The movie *Elizabeth* is another story about a strong young woman—a queen's fight to maintain and establish her reign over England.

Expose your daughters to movies that challenge or reverse stereotypes, such as *Elizabeth*, and *Courage Under Fire*, where a female helicopter pilot loses her life in an act of valor as she rescues some soldiers during the Gulf War. *Ever After* is a story where Cinderella saves Prince Charming and herself as well. In one scene she walks nonchalantly out of the castle of the Big Bad Man, having gained her freedom, just as Prince Charming arrives at the castle to save her. But a review of top ten movie lists will include many more damsels in distress than damsels who can think and act and save. *Ever After* didn't make the list. *Courage Under Fire* didn't either. We are uncomfortable with women heroes. Especially when they are saving men. But the film world received *Elizabeth* well, and it was nominated for best picture in 1999. These alternatives give girls something to think about besides being saved.

We parents can be intentional about what movies we watch with our young daughters, and teachers and youth leaders can pay particular attention to the portrayal of women in the movies we show in class and in church activities. We can read, watch, and listen with them to learn the nature of what they listen to, read, and watch. We can teach them how to critique movies for stereotypes about women, girls, boys, and men. We don't have to change our tastes in movies—maybe we enjoy the adventure of a James Bond type movie. Okay, so enjoy it. But be up front with your daughters about how women are usually used to further the plot or how they help the men look like really *manly* men. Do not let the subtleties go without exposing the underlying message. In this way, we can begin to combat destructive images and messages and help our daughters forge their adolescence with a stronger sense of confidence.

Current 5: Peers and the Contagious Nature of Depression

In addition to media troubles, our daughters sometimes confront peer troubles. Often peer groups are wonderful social arrangements that give our daughters a safe place to express themselves, to talk about outrageous ideas, and to try on different ways of being. Sometimes peer groups are less than wonderful and drag our daughters' confidence downward.

When Deborah, a student in our community, attempted suicide, she got a lot of attention from her friends. They brought her flowers, sent her cards, and showered love and attention on her for a few weeks. A small group of Deborah's friends became consumed with death and dying. They talked a lot about suicide, the awfulness of life, the tragedies of abusive homes, the pain of dealing with parents who had high expectations and low levels of understanding. The more they talked, the more depressed they *all* became. They became withdrawn, unhappy at home, and desired to be with this small group whenever their parents would allow it. They felt constrained by rules and suffocated by their parents' desire to know what was happening in their lives.

Depressed adolescents, especially those who talk about suicide, often end up trapped in a downward spiral that erodes confidence in their sense of self. Friends may seem concerned at first, but after a while they tire of providing support and withdraw emotionally from the friendship. As a result, the depressed person feels more isolated and alone. Parents have a harder time trusting depressed adolescents, because depressed adolescents are notorious for the bad choices they make. This adds to the problem, because the adolescent starts thinking, "I can't do anything right or please anyone." But this is not a true belief—it is the product of depression and other people's normal responses to depression. Those who want to get out of this trap must look somewhere other than to friends for help. Talking with friends about depression is often *not* a way out for adolescent girls but can instead be a pathway into deeper depression.[16]

Friends sometimes encourage our daughters and propel them forward, increasing their confidence. Other times, peers discourage them, erode their sense of confidence, and pull them down. Parents face choosing between what appear to all be bad options when they know their daughters are hanging out with a group that is sending them spiraling downward. Sometimes, forbidding involvement with a particular group may be just as bad an option as doing nothing. A friend of mine uses a canoe and river metaphor to explain her choice to let her daughter stay involved with a questionable peer group. As she and her husband watched their daughter maneuver through adolescence, they chose to follow along at the shore, allowing their daughter to forge the river, wanting to be there if she tipped out of the canoe, all the while praying for her ultimate safety.

If we have instilled a strong sense of self and confidence in our daughters, a ride through the river may better build their confidence and strength for challenges ahead. Sometimes, parents do best by pulling their daughters out of the river. If a daughter is in life-threatening danger, most parents will not hesitate to remove her from it. Yet the older the girls get, the harder it is to do so. Do we pull our daughter out of college to remove her from an abusive boyfriend?

Parenting is a balancing act. Sometimes we stay on the bank, carefully watching, praying for safety; sometimes we intervene and pull our daughters to safety. Ultimately, the goal is to help them gain confidence and the ability to learn from their mistakes as well as their successes.

Strategies to Combat Potential Peer Problems

A good first strategy is to know about your daughter's activities. Parents who monitor their adolescent's activities are sometimes perceived as busybodies who should mind their own business and grant their children some independence. I am disturbed at how frequently commercials aimed at preadolescents undermine the authority and relevance of parents. It is an unfortunate perception that follows from a culture that believes children should separate from parents in adolescence. This belief is further reinforced by teen magazine articles and columns advising teens how to deal with difficult parents. One such article addressing staying out all night after prom stated, "Name a time that's really later than you'd like to stay out (to give you some bargaining room), and throw in that you'll call them once to check in. Odds are they'll extend it—at least a little."[17] Parents who monitor their adolescent's activities are neither busybodies nor untrusting but recognize a need to stay informed and involved in their adolescent's life. To be a good watcher from the riverbank, we need to know the signs that our daughter is in trouble. Are her grades falling? Is she becoming deceptive? Are her eating or sleeping patterns changing? Is she withdrawn and apathetic? Is she self-mutilating? Certainly there is also a need to respect our daughter's privacy. Our daughters should not be expected to tell us everything. Again, parents must balance letting go with staying informed. But my perception is that our culture has tended to incline us the other way, so that we feel it is not our right or responsibility to know about and monitor our adolescent's activities.

Getting to know our children's friends is another strategy that combats negative peer influence. When our homes are places where kids like to hang out we have a great advantage. Encourage various gatherings, parties, and sleepovers at your home. Jess, one of Danielle's friends, often came to our house for lunch one semester in high school because her scheduled lunchtime did not coincide with any of her friends. Sometimes I was working at home when she came over. We began to talk and I received a delightful picture of what Danielle is like through her friend's eyes. "She's a free spirit; I'm more cautious, so we balance each other well," Jess said. Mostly though, we talked about her classes at school or a past or upcoming event. This was a rare opportunity. An easier way to get to know our daughter's friends is to participate in their activities. Volunteer at sporting events, host speech, athletic, or drama team parties or dinners, have pre-homecoming pictures at your house. The goal is to expose yourself to your daughter's friends. Let them know you; get to know them.

Current 6: Church and a Climate of Suspicion

One truth the evangelical church communicates very well to both men and women is their amazing value to God. That God loves women as much as men is not doubted in our churches. Neither do evangelical churches doubt that women, like men, are gifted and called to service. Yet a climate of suspicion begins with the church's skepticism or refusal to broaden that giftedness to service beyond traditionally defined roles for women. This climate of suspicion undermines the capabilities of women to perform in public spheres by eroding the confidence of women.

Our daughters are often getting mixed messages. When students write, "The beliefs of man were transformed by the enlightenment," some teachers will circle "man" and encourage them to be inclusive with their language. But some preachers and Sunday school teachers are either unaware that a discussion about inclusive language is occurring outside the church or are opposed to using it. Our daughters may have a woman principal at their high school but know that women are excluded from the deacon or elder boards at church. This chasm between what they see at church and at school will cause them to evaluate one or the other suspiciously. Either the church will seem irrelevant and out-of-touch, or women who transcend traditional roles will seem dangerous, or at least inferior to men and disillusioned for trying to "compete in a man's world."

Thus the church's own struggle over the role of women impacts how our daughters think about themselves. The inconsistency from one sphere to another raises questions that may not have been present before. When society agreed with the church on traditional roles for women, girls experienced less internal conflict figuring out what it meant for them to be female. The inconsistency they now experience heightens issues of confidence.

Once I started thinking about going to graduate school with the eventual hope of teaching college students, doubts crept in and eroded my confidence. I had to challenge a worldview that said God would never call a woman to a *career*. I also had to confront a perception (which I still believe is mostly accurate) that to have credibility as a woman professor, I would have to be better than the average male professor. The standards felt higher because expectations were already in place that women were not "natural professors" and thus could not be as good, or capable, as men.

For a semester research project, one of my students replicated a study by Sandler and Hall[18] where college students were asked to evaluate an author's article according to specific criteria (e.g., credibility, style, persuasiveness). Only one article was distributed, but half of the articles identified a female as the author; the other half identified a male. In 1986, Sandler and Hall found that articles thought to be authored by a woman were consistently ranked lower than articles thought to be authored by a man. The student replicating the study at our school expected similar findings. However, her findings showed an extra twist: Male students were more willing to grant credibility to a female author than female students. Women more fiercely criticized the writing of another woman than men did.

I draw two observations from this. The first is that female students from some Christian liberal arts colleges have less confidence in the abilities of women and thus may be less willing to allow women to expand their roles than male students are. Women have a lot at stake, especially Christian women raised in conservative homes. They have internalized the belief that women were not created to function, therefore not capable of functioning, in the same spheres as men. To challenge this assumption is to shake much of how they have come to think about themselves and their capabilities.

The second observation is based on a presumption that the women who ranked the female author lower are likely to be stay-at-home moms. I've observed a chasm among evangelical women between stay-at-home moms and working moms. Both feel disapproved of by the other. Both resent the disapproval and so stay on opposite sides of the debate to protect themselves from each other. Women become defensive about what they think is the best choice and create antagonism between themselves and those making different choices. This is acute for these women, because how they live their lives reflects their beliefs about how God intends them to live their lives. Yet we often lack confidence in our choices, uncertain whether or not those choices are best.

Working moms often feel inadequate in their mothering, and at-home moms often struggle with feelings of insignificance. Both have grievances and fears. However, to strengthen the confidence of our daughters, and ourselves as women, we need to reconcile these groups of women and work to build each other's confidence rather than erode it.

Strategies to Combat a Church Climate of Suspicion

Some churches are challenging assumptions regarding women's roles, recognizing how much our culture has always influenced how the church defined godly or ungodly gender roles. For instance, the idea that women should not contribute economically to the family is a relatively new one and only assumed by middle- and upper-class families. For women *not* to contribute economically has never been a reality for families below the middle class. Are these families outside of God's plan because they are poor and because the women work? The concept of men or women working "outside the home" was ushered in with the industrial revolution. Prior to that, the majority of families worked homesteads together or plots of land they were "renting" from the wealthy. The economic viability of the family depended on everyone's contributing. Did God prefer the expanding jobs and opportunities ushered in with the industrial revolution to only be available for middle-class men?

The woman described in Proverbs 31 is an industrious businesswoman. She considers a field and buys it. She manages a staff of people working under her. She takes responsibility for the well-being of her family and works to protect that well-being. She is a strong and confident steward even within the constraints of her culture. How unfortunate when those constraints come from the church itself. If our churches want to build up and prepare its daughters to be strong image-bearers of God, they need to be willing to ask questions about their assumptions. As long as the church uses culturally defined roles to answer the question of what women can do, it will confuse and inhibit our daughters' confidence in their ability to contribute as God has created and gifted them.

Some evangelical churches encourage women to have confidence in all areas of giftedness, including spiritual giftedness. These churches use women gifted in teaching to teach, those with spiritual discernment to counsel, or those who are spiritually mature and sensitive to God to lead. The controversy of women in ministry continues to be played out between evangelical theologians who believe the Bible supports an interdependency where women and men serve God together and those who believe the Bible teaches a hierarchy where women are to be followers and men are to be leaders.

Some parents may support a hierarchical position in the church while also supporting greater opportunity and voice for their daughters in society. While this position may feel incongruous at times, daughters can be encouraged to participate with confidence in arenas outside the church and still be encouraged to use gifts within the church in avenues open to women.

A second way the church can combat the eroding of women's confidence is to encourage bridge-building between stay-at-home moms and working moms. Women's retreats or for women only

Sunday school classes can foster discussions of women as women, as friends, and as mothers. They can discuss fears, frustrations, joys, and in the process they will likely find common ground. Both groups of mothers are Christian women striving to make choices that honor God. Some feel that obedience to God means sacrificing financial comfort and self-fulfillment opportunities by being wholeheartedly available to their children. Others feel that obedience to God means discovering and using the gifts he has given in whatever capacity he enables them to be used, whether in a career or a church ministry. Still others feel God calls them first to raise their children and then to a ministry or career. All three groups of women contribute to the body of Christ; the first two are hurting for the respect of the other. Both struggle, at times, with feelings of inadequacy, and both are moms, striving to parent in ways that bring God honor. A shared ground can be built on these similarities, diminishing the lines between them, especially if they seek ways to encourage each other.

WHERE TO GO FROM HERE

We have already discussed several strategies for developing a holistic confidence in our daughters. Following are other general suggestions.

1. Provide Good Models

One powerful way to increase our daughters' confidence is through models, and the Bible offers us many (an amazing feat given the patriarchal structure of Old and New Testament times). Consider Esther, a lovely virgin who was chosen to be part of King Xerxes' harem. Women were valued for their external beauty and chosen queen on the basis of their beauty and ability to "please" the king. Indeed, before Esther spent a night with the king, she spent twelve months under the guidance of eunuchs, receiving beauty treatments with perfumes and ointments. The queen was not supposed to think or act—that's what got Esther's predecessor in trouble. She was only supposed to be a passive and beautiful figurehead.

Yet when Esther's Uncle Mordecai pleaded with her to go before the king with an appeal for the lives of the Jews, she let his confidence become her own. She trusted in Mordecai's authority. She reasoned through the potentially life-threatening consequences of going before the king unsummoned. She trusted her gut-level intuition that led her to fast and pray, and she boldly asked all Jews to fast and pray with her. Esther designed a clever plan to aid her success.

By the end of the story, this young woman who had been taught her value resided in her beauty and passivity was exuding confidence. And God used her confidence to save the Jews. Stories like Esther's can provide strong models for our daughters. They are all the more powerful when they come from the Word of God that speaks with the authority of God.

2. Expose Your Daughters to Risk and Physical Challenges

Dad used to take us out to watch the brewing up of dust clouds in Kansas as tornadoes whipped across the ground in the distance. We'd watch thunderstorms from our living room in Arizona. Dad helped us climb up to the roof, one at a time, to look at the stars. I learned to identify Orion, the Big and Little Dippers, and the Milky Way, while perched with Dad on the rooftop. He climbed mountains with us in Colorado. I remember starting to cry on the long march down Mt. Princeton because my ankles and knees were hurting. I told Dad I couldn't breathe (understandable since these were the high Colorado mountains). He told me I would be able to breathe a lot easier if I'd stop crying—a rather atypical statement for a father to make to his daughter, a much more typical thing for a father to say to a son. Ultimately, I am thankful for that. I am less fearful than I could have been because Dad made me take risks. I am more confident in my abilities because I had to push and challenge my physical capabilities. So here are some suggestions:

- Climb rooftops, mountains, and trees with your daughter. Take her backpacking; teach her the skills necessary to take care of herself.

- Drive with your daughter on a snowy or rainy day in an empty parking lot so she can learn to handle a car with confidence in adverse conditions.
- Encourage your daughter to participate in prison ministry opportunities, the tutoring of inner-city kids, or mission trips to less developed countries. Churches and colleges would not plan these activities if they were not essentially safe.

3. Build Competency

We can nurture our daughters' confidence through puberty by helping them become competent at something. If their interest is playing the guitar, invest some time and money in someone who can give them lessons. If they like sports, encourage participation and go to their meets or games. If they like astronomy, check out the resources in your community. If they enjoy dance, enroll them in community-based programs. The goal is not to inundate them with busyness (indeed, pushing our children to be overinvolved is another problem altogether); the goal is to help them find an interest area that can be turned into a competency. If guitar lessons are not affordable, you may want to check out library books or instructional video or audiotapes. Be creative and active in encouraging your daughter to find and develop some area of competency.

4. Widen Your Own Friendship Base

The Women (a.k.a. The Wild Women) became a friendship group because of one woman (Deb) who initiated our first trip away from husbands and children. The rest unfolded in the success of that first venture. Someone has to initiate for friendship to develop. Too many people assume the initiator will be someone else. Our group includes six mothers who are making different choices about how they blend motherhood and careers. All six of us stayed home with our small children. Two women still have preschool or early school-age children and continue to stay home. Three others have entered careers. One woman has continued to stay home with her middle-schooler, high-schooler, and college student but is now going back to school part-time. We do not identify ourselves on the basis of whether or not we have careers. Our connection to each other is based on who we are as women, striving to be godly, good mothers, good wives, and good friends. In our diversity we enrich, support, and better understand each other's different choices. I have never felt condemned for working, nor do I suspect those who stay home feel condemned for staying home. Our relationship transcends this distinction. Developing relationships that represent a broad spectrum of experiences will enrich who we are as mothers and what we model for our daughters.

CONCLUSION

. . . A few minutes later the runners reemerged, and Megan was leading the pack! In fact, none of the initial top runners were in sight! We cheered, in the rain, wondering what had gone wrong. Megan sprinted toward the finish line and won the race (her team placed first, second, third, and fifth). We cheered, still wondering.

Megan won, not because she was the fastest but because at a critical point in the race she knew the right way to go and had confidence to break from the pack to go there. But Megan did not take full credit for that decision. Her running partner, Katie, had seen the other team heading the wrong way and had told Megan, "Don't go there, it's a dead end." Megan pretty much knew it was a dead end, but part of her thought maybe it was a shortcut, and she was tempted to follow them. Yet she had confidence in the voice of a friend to go the right way. If being made in the image of God means our daughters have the ability to bring all of who they are into what they know and do, then we want them to do so with confidence.

Even the best parenting will not always result in daughters who are confident. We battle against a broken culture that undermines what we are trying to do. Our daughters will struggle with confidence at times, feeling they have nothing to offer. They will likely be distant at times. It is a challenge to know how best to help our daughters. We need to learn when to go with the flow, praying and watching from the riverbank, and when to step into the river and intervene.

The parenting this book promotes is messy. It lets our daughters make choices we wouldn't make for them. But the outcomes for our three daughters have confirmed our choice to raise them as strong women. They are not perfect; they have not always made good choices. At the risk of discrediting myself, I share the following examples (with their permission) to illustrate the messiness of growing strong daughters and the importance of being watchful parents.

One of our daughters wasn't sure she wanted to go to college. That was absolutely her choice. She knew the value we placed on a college education, but we wouldn't insist she go. Another daughter was into facial piercing for a while. Since she was old enough not to need our signature on a permission form, we figured she was old enough to decide whether or not she wanted holes in her tongue and nose.

But we have pulled our daughters from the river. We pulled one out when we learned she had begun to cut herself as a way to deal with emotional pain and stress in her life. We gave her several options, and she chose and ultimately responded well in therapy. We pulled a daughter from the river when we said she could not go with her group of mixed friends to an After Prom unchaperoned sleepover at a cabin four hours away.

Sometimes our daughters will be pulled out of the river by others. During middle school, one daughter was pulled out by a store manager who caught her shoplifting, detained her, and called the police. Her ride to the police station with her hands cuffed behind her back, and all the thoughts and fears summoned up during that several-hour ordeal were part of a process that set her back on course. She graciously submitted to a rather harsh social contract that we established for her (severely limiting time with friends, time on the phone, and extracurricular activities). At her baptism a year and a half later, she talked about this before the congregation as the turning point in her life, a point that has drawn her powerfully to God.

Mark and I will intervene whenever we feel to *not* intervene might lead to a potentially life-threatening or life-changing event with such negative consequences that the impact will be severe. But we will use the power to intervene cautiously. We want our children to learn to make their own choices. Ultimately our goal is to be neither too quick nor too slow to respond. That requires us to be watchful.

We must always pray for our daughters. The same God who placed his image within us gave us the potential to be in relationship with him. We are invited to pray and to bring our daughters before God. They belong, after all, to God, not to us. And God has their best interests in mind, even as we do.

Our daughters have been made in God's image so that they can better be in relationship with God, reflect God's image in their relationships with others, and participate in being stewards over the earth. Confidence in how and for what they were created better enables them to do so.

CHAPTER FOUR

DAUGHTERS
AND INDEPENDENCE

I long to put the experience of fifty years at once into your young lives, to give you at once the key to that treasure chamber every gem of which has cost me tears and struggles and prayers. But you must work for these inward treasures yourselves.

—Harriet Beecher Stowe in a letter to twin daughters

MARK, DANIELLE, AND I were sitting together on our back porch one summer night. Our little house was in a newly developed rural area, forty-five minutes west of Nashville, Tennessee. Our back-yard wasn't fenced, none of the yards were, and it opened into uneven fields of wildflowers and prairie grass. The full moon looked particularly enticing to Danielle's three-year-old imagination, and she said, "I want to walk to the moon tonight." Mark looked at me, and we smiled that knowing-parent smile. Then unexpectedly he said, "Okay, Danielle, let's walk to the moon."

Together they left our yard, her little hand in his big one. They walked up and down the uneven field, becoming ever smaller figures as I watched from the porch. Mark later related to me that she soon asked, "Papa, will you carry me?"

He told her, "No, I think we should walk to the moon together."

After walking for some distance she said, "I think the moon is too far away to walk to tonight." So they came home over the uneven field and settled back into our porch chairs.

I have always loved this story because it encourages exploring the unknown realms of possibility. Helping our children experience the boundaries of imagination grows them as creative actors— able to work interdependently with others to explore the world of possibility.

INDEPENDENCE, DEPENDENCE, AND INTERDEPENDENCE

We encourage boys to be independent more than girls. If we surveyed one hundred parents and asked them whether they were more likely to let a sixteen-year-old son drive on first-day snow than a sixteen-year-old daughter, what do you imagine they would say? My bet would rest on the sons.

We encourage girls to be dependent more than boys. Even as infants we coddle and coo girl babies and bounce and toss boy babies. We teach our daughters to rely on others for help and our sons to rely on themselves.

Is this independence and dependence what God intended for men and women when we were created as social beings? Or did God have something else in mind that was distorted with the fall? God set apart humans as unique in creation, and one feature of that uniqueness is the privilege to be in relationship first with God and second with others.[1] Yet our relationship with God was broken in the fall and the relationship between women and men distorted. One result of the fall was that men tended to become overly independent and domineering and women overly dependent and passive.[2] Both excessive independence and excessive dependence distort God's intent for human relationships.

Excessive independence says, "I don't need help; I can make it on my own." Paul Simon expresses a strong independence in the lyrics, "I am a rock, I am an island. And a rock never cries, and an island feels no pain."[3] The strong man is the independent man who does not cry, does not need, does not feel. As we need to bring our daughters to a better recognition of their ability to function independently, we would serve our sons well to bring them to a better recognition of their need for dependence—in both cases seeking a balance of interdependence.

Excessive dependence says, "I can't make decisions or take care of myself. I must rely on someone else to do it for me." Existentialists say when humans remove themselves from the decision-making process or when they refuse to make decisions that they are trying to escape themselves.[4] To do so is to excise one of the characteristics of an image-bearer of God. While we recognize the waste of human potential in men who cannot take charge of their lives, we less often see this dependence as a waste of potential in women. Yet women too were created as reasoning, thoughtful, and reflective decision-makers. The value of instilling a sense of independence in our daughters is that it gives them the ability to act *inter*dependently in their social relationships rather than dependently.

God created us to be social, to be interdependent. There are two ways that community-building interdependence has been distorted in women. First, and more commonly, dependence becomes a distortion when it becomes a passivity that distances a woman from her ability to make decisions and act independently as a steward-ruler over creation. Second, independence becomes a distortion when it focuses on self and personal rights at the expense of others.

Numerous examples in Scripture show women acting independently in ways that reflect their interdependence with others. Abigail saved the men of her husband's household when she went to David and offered him the supplies her husband Nabal had refused—supplies David had asked for and deserved. Rahab saved her household when she recognized the spies of Israel as God's chosen and aligned with them rather than her own people. Mary acted obediently (and independently for the sake of all humanity) when she agreed to let God use her body to bring Jesus into the world. The Hebrew midwives acted independently to save baby boys born to Hebrew women during their enslavement in Egypt; Moses' mother and sister acted independently as they schemed and worked out the salvation of their son and brother Moses. Jael acted independently and brought peace to the Israelites when she welcomed Sisera, the general of the Canaanite army and enemy of the Israelites, into her tent for refreshment and then drove a tent peg through his temple while he slept.

These strong women are inspiring models for our daughters (though admittedly I hope mine never need to drive a tent peg through an enemy head). Recognizing their interdependence with others, and being secure in their ability to act for the sake of others, these women took great risks rather than wait passively for someone else to bring salvation. They allowed God to use them as tools to bring about God's mercy, justice, or salvation. These women are honored in various ways. David praises Abigail and she later becomes one of his queens. Rahab married into the Israelite community and was honored to be part of the lineage of Jesus (Matthew 1). Rahab and Moses' parents (though the Old Testament account lists only Moses' mother and sister as active in saving Moses) are listed in Hebrews 12 as great examples of those who acted in faith. Mary has been called blessed throughout the history of Christianity.

There are also women who acted independently for their own sakes and brought great pain and brokenness to those around them. Eve acted independently of Adam and made a decision that gave birth to sin in the world. Sarah acted independently and sent Hagar in to Abraham so Sarah could have the child God promised. Rebekah acted independently and helped Jacob, her favorite son, deceive her husband and steal Esau's birthright. The enmity between the offspring of Sarah and Hagar (as well as between Jacob and Esau) has had enormous implications for several thousand years. Though the hostility cannot be reduced to a single act of independence, nevertheless, these women's acts of independence contributed to devastating, unintended consequences.[5]

Extreme Independence

Most of us cringe at the stereotype of the independent woman. Evangelicals are among those who tend to label independent women "feminists" and, according to Susan Douglas, stereotype them very negatively.

> They (feminists) are shrill, overly aggressive, man-hating, . . . deliberately unattractive women with absolutely no sense of humor who see sexism at every turn. . . . Feminists are relentless, unforgiving, and unwilling to end or compromise; they are single-handedly responsible for the high divorce rate, the shortage of decent men, and the unfortunate proliferation of Birkenstocks in America.[6]

Most feminists are not man-hating, family-hating, deliberately unattractive types who are out to destroy America as we know it. But women who have acted independently in their own best interest (or in the interest only of other women who share their ideas) have given feminism a bad name.

We do not escape this error of extreme independence by casting it on a scapegoat we call feminism. Extreme independence emerges in many contexts. The woman who leaves her family to pursue a lover, the woman who knowingly overspends on the family credit card, or the woman who refuses to get a job to help make ends meet can all be acting from a self-seeking independence.

The absence of healthy interdependent relationships is one factor causing women to become extremely independent. A number of students in my classes report having mothers who were so controlled by their husbands that they lost any sense of who they were apart from their husbands. Many of these students have promised it will never happen to them. Some of them may become too independent in an effort to avoid becoming passive wives.

Another reason women may become too independent is because they will lose faith in the belief that men, who society says are supposed to care for them, will do so. By the age of eighteen, 27 percent of girls will have been sexually abused.[7]

A third factor that leads some women to extreme independence is that they accept the belief that the only way to make it in a man's world is to become like a man. The belief goes something like this: If you want to achieve the greatest economic success and rise to the highest echelons of power in America, you must become ruthlessly independent. While this trait of extreme independence is no more attractive for men than for women, it *is* more acceptable for men than for women. A man who is ruthless and crafty and circumvents normal paths to success with innovative shortcuts is not well-liked, but his behavior can be somewhat excused because he is, after all, acting out of a normal male sense of competitiveness. A woman who is ruthless and crafty and circumvents normal paths to success is also not well-liked, but her behavior is less excusable, because she is rejecting her normal female characteristics. However, neither sex here is acting out of an understanding of who God created us to be. Christians, whose lives are being renewed in God's image, mirror God's character when they act with interdependent concern for others.

Women are forfeiting who they have been uniquely created to be when they seek to become like men in order to succeed. As long as our society continues to value men's ways of doing and being more than women's, we will continue to see women who will try to copy men, even down to men's own broken distortions. However, in evangelical Christianity we have fewer women erring on the side of extreme independence than we do extreme dependence.

Passivity and Dependence

After God created Adam and Eve, God told them to fill and rule the earth together. In Genesis 1:28, God blesses them and says, "Multiply and fill the earth and subdue it. Be masters over the fish and birds and all the animals." God's intent in this matter did not change after the fall, but the fall brought distortion to it. Some might argue that God intended women to be passive and men to be dominant as part of the curse. However, a careful consideration of the intent of God's proclamations suggests otherwise.

First, God's declaration that women would produce children through great labor and that men would produce food from the earth through sweat and toil is more a statement about the current broken nature of God's creation than how roles should be divided (women at home, men at work). Because of the fall, what should have been produced with ease in a perfect world would now be produced through pain and suffering in a broken one.

Second, God tells Eve, "though your desire will be for your husband, he will be your master" (Gen. 3:16). According to some theologians, God is not setting forth a plan where men shall have dominion over women, but stating a consequence of brokenness.[8] Women will desire the intimacy of equals with their husbands, but they will not experience it. Instead men will rule as masters over the women they initially were intended to rule with together. Thus, after the fall, this shared sense of interdependence for the task given men and women by God was distorted and has led to a tradition of encouraging men to be dominant and independent and women to be passive and dependent.

Both our evangelical and cultural traditions have emerged out of an historical context centuries old, where women and children were considered the property of the men who owned them. As such, wives were perceived as dependents, in need of the same care and protection given to children. We see this not only in our traditions but also in our laws. It wasn't until 1891 that the Supreme Court prohibited the right of husbands to beat their wives.[9] And according to English Common Law, when a woman married it meant she could not vote, own property, administer estates, sign contracts, or keep her children in the event of divorce.[10] These were some of the reforms the early feminist movement of the late nineteenth and early twentieth centuries sought to change, with women finally winning a long battle for the right to vote in 1920.

Women in America are further along in regaining a sense of interdependency than women in other countries. In poor countries such as Malaysia and the Philippines, daughters are still sold as brides through various mail-order services. There are fifty such services in the United States. These firms reportedly help American men find the ideal, subservient wife they couldn't find at home.[11] Women from Muslim countries, Latin America, and many Asian countries have far fewer opportunities and many more constraints than women from the United States.[12]

Out of this cultural history of ownership and protectorship we came to believe a woman could not take care of herself and needed to be under the authority of a male. Bill Gothard, whose seminars were popular in the 1970s and 1980s, believed a girl should always be under the authority and care of a male. If she was unmarried, she was to be under the authority of her father. Once married, she should be under the authority of her husband. If a woman had neither a husband, nor a father, then she was to be under the authority of a brother.

However, this creates an extreme dependence in some women who are incapable of acting independently for their own sake or the sake of others. Sometimes this means that widowed or divorced women are left with no idea how to manage their finances, or do routine maintenance on the house or car. Many will not have skills they could use to earn a living if they needed to, and some cannot make any but the simplest of decisions without the input of their husbands.

Sometimes, though, the dependency is even more fundamentally damaging. Consider Kersten's family. Kersten was a quiet student in my Marriage and Family class. Classmates and other faculty assumed she was a typical student from a normal Christian home. But I learned her story as she evaluated her family in a case study assignment and later expanded on her story over lunch. Her family fell apart when her father died. She was ten years old, and her brothers were twelve and fifteen. There was no structure in her father's absence and no authority, because Kersten's mother had never been in charge before. Kersten said:

> My family lacks leadership, discipline, and the ability to get along. If I had to rate my family on the basis of a desirable family, I would give it a one with ten as the best. Since the death of my father eight years ago, my family has not done family activities as a whole family. We also have not sat down for a meal together for as long as I can remember. When I was in high school my brothers used to beat me for no reason. My mom would not do anything to them, so they decided they could do anything they wanted. There was no discipline in my family after the death of my father, since he had the discipline and authority.

Kersten was hospitalized five times due to her brothers' beatings. The oldest brother sexually molested her. Kersten's mother was also beaten by her sons but was unable to help either herself or her daughter. Kersten is trying to overcome the pain of her childhood and cope with the inability of her mother to protect either of them. Kersten hopes to marry someday and have the kind of family she has always dreamed of being in, but right now she's unable to let a male get close to her.

Passivity in women cripples their ability to act and results from an improper understanding of how God created us to be interdependent actors. Passive women have no confidence in their ability to understand social issues. One student told me she did not care that women had earned the right to vote. When I asked her why, she said, "My husband will decide who to vote for; I don't need to. And if you can't trust your husband, who can you trust?"

This could have been a cop-out for someone who did not want to bother herself about being informed, rather than a true claim about trust. But the position that says, "my husband will decide . . ." assumes that men care about politics more than women do, will be adequately concerned and informed about family and women-related issues, and that men can and will represent those issues adequately. That is an assumption many women voters are not willing to make. But instead of being a cop-out, more likely my student's statement was based on the assumption that women cannot understand politics and so should leave the responsibility to understand issues with men, who can presumably grasp the issues more clearly. Independence and confidence belong together. Assumed inability, or lack of confidence, leads to passivity and dependence.

Women's involvement in politics is reshaping society. Women tend to care more about the issues that relate to family concerns than men (e.g. health care, childcare, welfare), and candidates who care about the female vote know they need to attend to issues related to families to win them over.[13] Women fought for labor law reforms to prohibit the exploitation of child and women workers in sweatshops at the turn of the century. Women fought against slavery. To not be involved politically and to passively let the men do all the deciding is to forfeit the voice of women in society—a voice that God intended to be present to bring balance and wholeness over the stewardship of creation. God instructed both women and men to rule over the earth; they were to guard and subdue it together, each bringing to the task the unique abilities that God had created in them to ensure balance.

Passivity is modeled for our young daughters through the women often portrayed as a helpless kind of beautiful in our stories. It would seem that Buttercup (from *The Princess Bride*), Sleeping Beauty, and Maid Marian (from *Robin Hood*) exist in the prospective stories only to give the heroes someone to save. While some of these women attempt to be courageously independent, they all need to be saved by the man.

Most passive women are not married to heroes like Superman and Robin Hood, whose lives are fulfilling, adventurous, and go on happily ever after. In real life, extremely dependent women are unable to learn, unable to think for themselves, and thus unable to offer anything useful to others. The women we met in the last chapter who listen and learn from the voices of others but have no confidence in their own ability to speak, think, or act are further examples of extreme dependence.

Katherine was an ideal student. She was friendly, attentive, and did well in class. We met several times over lunch. Often the conversation about her plans for the future came back to her father's ideas. He wanted her to follow in his footsteps by attending law school and joining him as a partner in his firm. Her father cautioned her about getting too serious with her boyfriend—"it's not the right person if it's not the right time"—counseled her about which courses she should take, and instructed her about which politics and ideas she should embrace. Katherine admired her father and accepted and seemed to appreciate the guidance he gave her. His continued involvement in her life is admirable. Parental input is valuable for our daughters, even into college, but at some point along the way, we need to have instilled in them a sense of independence and confidence in their own ability to think, to reason, and to act. Daughters who are given a sense of independence and confidence will be the ones most capable of acting in ways that will improve the quality of life for others.

INDEPENDENCE, THE CHURCH, AND SINGLE WOMEN

We are dependent creatures, made to be wholly dependent on God. God also made us to be in interdependent relationships with other humans. The church sometimes responds to singleness as though the only way for dependent humans to have interdependent relationships is through marriage. While Paul put a high value on remaining single, contemporary churches do not. Neither does our society. Theoretically anyway, married people stabilize society, especially married people with children. They become more invested in the community as their children start preschool and later join T-ball programs or tumbling classes. Soon they're buying bigger homes, attending PTA meetings, and selling concessions at their children's athletic events. The more involved and invested members of society become, the less likely they are to throw it away by robbing the local convenience store, or deciding not to go to work. So the goal of society (on a collective level) is to encourage marriage and family life and discourage staying single.

Our churches value marriage for similar reasons. First, marriage gives an appropriate outlet for sexual drives. Thus, when people marry we worry less about the disruptive sins associated with sexual drives being met out of the context of marriage. Even though Paul affirmed that the ministry of women and men is less encumbered when they are single, we would often rather not take the risk, as evidenced by the difficulty single pastors have finding senior pastorate positions. Second, we believe families are a more stabilizing force in churches than single people. We believe they give more financially (married couples do tend to be better off financially, as a group, than singles).[14] We believe families are more committed to staying put and involving themselves by teaching Sunday school and serving as deacons. (While these beliefs may be well-founded for church-related involvements, it is single people who are most involved in community service, whether religious or secular.)[15]

Our society in general and evangelicals in particular tend to discourage singleness as a choice for our sons and daughters. However, single men do not confront the same negative stereotypes as single women. Single men become "available bachelors," single women become "old maids." Single men are encouraged to pursue avenues that will make them financially independent during these (assumed temporary) single years. Women, especially in evangelical circles, are encouraged to find a ministry and/or "some kind of work" until marriage, but they are not actively encouraged to pursue careers that may impede their desire for marriage and give them financial independence.

An example of the effectiveness of our "singleness is bad" socialization of women is illustrated in a student's class journal, where she articulates a concern frequently expressed by students.

> I went through a period of time when my greatest fear in life was imagining my life single—forever. At that time I saw having a boyfriend as an outward symbol of being lovable. So that meant being single had a stigma attached to it. If I were to be single for life people would look at me and wonder what was wrong with me. Maybe they'd think I didn't have the social skills to be in a relationship or that I was overly clingy or needy.

This student's image of herself became wrapped up in the stigma of being unwanted if she was not attached to a man. A social stigma against singleness distracts and limits the ways girls and women might otherwise develop certain gifts and contributions.

Our society and our churches do not foster a kind of independence that makes the life of a single woman acceptable. The years our daughters are single can be productively used to minister, but only if they have a healthy sense of independence that enables them to act. Many single women who are five or ten years out of college have unhappily put their lives on hold while waiting and wishing for husbands. Other single woman have joined the Peace Corps, become missionaries (the most acceptable activity for single women), gone to graduate school, started meaningful careers, traveled, and invested their lives significantly in others. The opportunities are broadest for our daughters while they are single. If we encourage independence in them, we free them to use their God-given gifts and allow their lives to be fulfilling and meaningful apart from marriage.

If we want to raise strong daughters, we will need to instill a healthy sense of independence so they can actively seek to live life, to love actively, and to use their gift of singleness. The opposite is to raise daughters who are passively waiting for someone to notice them and choose to take care of them, meanwhile grieving the lost hope of love.

SOCIETY AND DEPENDENCE FOR WOMEN

The inability for our daughters to look beyond marriage is not created in a vacuum. An underlying assumption in school is that the breadwinning responsibility of boys matters more than the success of girls.[16] Boys eventually need to be able to make a living and support a family; girls only need to be able to take care of a family. Thus, whether inadvertently or intentionally, teachers tend to focus more attention on educating boys than they do girls. Even when teachers were made aware of this imbalance in their teaching and tried to correct it, they still spent more time attending to boys than to girls. Granted, some of this may be the result of rowdier boys demanding more attention than the girls, but whatever the precipitating reasons, the result is that our daughters get less attention, encouragement, and praise than boys.

There has recently been renewed interest in all-girls and all-boys schools. The Julia Morgan School for Girls opened in California in September 1999. The independent school has engineering, science, computers, and math at the core of their curriculum. The school's goal is to get girls through school with their self-esteem intact and to challenge the idea that girls do not belong in technical fields.[17] Several Western High School students (an all-girls school in Baltimore) had this to say when comparing their all-girl education to their previous coed experience:[18]

> I knew that if I raised my hand a boy would at least be called on first. It's always expected that guys have the best opinions.

We need to be cultivated. It comes from growing up in a society that says women are supposed to take the backseat.

Now we go into a room with our heads high and shoulders back. When someone does that you know you have a leader.

You have to be a leader; you can't sit and wait for boys to make decisions— "Oh well, he can make the decision, he should know best." No, it's not like that.

These women are appreciative of their education and recognize the support they get in school to develop independent thinking and acting abilities.

I conducted a study at a Christian university on the west coast and looked at mentoring relationships between faculty and students.[19] The study considered the encouragement male and female students received to continue on to graduate school. While I found that some women were being specifically encouraged to pursue graduate education, this encouragement was more available to men. It seemed this was largely due to a gender factor: Male students tended to be mentored by male professors, and female students tended to be mentored by female professors. Because there are significantly fewer female professors, there are fewer women available to mentor and encourage women students.

Another social arena that fosters dependence for our daughters is the workplace. While career opportunities are opening up for women, there is still a pay gap between what men and women earn at all occupational levels. Overall, women earn approximately 75 percent of what men earn. This is a slight improvement over thirty years ago, when women were earning 60 to 70 percent of what men earned.[20] Some of this can be explained by women's more sporadic involvement in the workforce. They tend to be in and out of the labor force during their childbearing years, limiting their promotions and opportunities.

For example, proof of worthiness is often defined by one's résumé, rather than what one will bring to the position apart from a résumé. Imagine the following scenario: Company X has been experiencing low productivity in one of its sectors. The sector responsible has a high turnover rate due to employee dissatisfaction and low levels of morale. Mr. Davids, a man with a well-padded résumé representing years of solid management experience applies for the management position of this sector. Ms. Johnson, a woman with a much thinner résumé, also applies. The strengths Mr. Davids would bring are in project planning, development, and implementation. He has a very rational, businesslike approach to dealing with those who work under him. The strengths Ms. Johnson would bring are more relational. She is trained in systems management and brings a style of leadership that stimulates the development of shared vision, bottom-up project design, and personal mastery. Ms. Johnson is selected as the candidate who would best meet the needs of the sector. However, due to her limited work experience, she will not be offered the same salary Mr. Davids would have been offered. To offer her something less than Mr. Davids is not illegal and is justified according to a supply and demand economic system.

Men and women also still tend to hold different kinds of jobs. Women are more often in jobs where they answer to and are dependent on males. For instance, 99.8 percent of all dental hygienists, 99 percent of all secretaries, and 95 percent of all licensed practical nurses are women. Women are also more often in jobs that are considered extensions of what they do at home: 96.7 percent of all child-care workers are women, and 95.8 percent of all housekeepers are women.[21] These female-dominated jobs are less valued in society and thus bring in smaller salaries.

The underlying assumption of this economic structure is that men do the important work of society, and women, if they work, do the less important work of society. Women who choose male-oriented careers choose them for the same reasons men do, whether because of a calling, an interest, a dream, or simply to make money. However, they are often stereotyped as women who have something they need to prove, or who are ill at ease with what it means to be a woman. The ideal family in many Christian circles is still the one where the husband earns enough to allow the wife to stay home.

Yet, as we saw in the previous chapter, this idea of women staying home and being financially cared for is neither a universal nor a historical norm but emerged more recently, with the industrial revolution. Prior to that time, families were economic units and all family members were expected to contribute. Not until the industrial revolution did industry take the source for economic well-being away from home. And then only middle-class women could afford to stay home with children. A wife at home became a status symbol for those who could afford it. Many other families could not, of course, and those men, women, and, in some cases children, all worked in factories to meet the financial needs of the family.

Society, as well as the church, fosters dependency for our daughters, at least for our middle-class white daughters. Our daughters receive negative stereotyping for being single, are paid less than men (and thus have a more difficult time financially if they are not married), are less well-prepared for meaningful work, and are stereotyped as having something to prove if they choose independent career paths.

A healthy sense of interdependence involves recognizing that God has called women and men to be stewards and rule the earth together. Thus interdependence is speaking up against injustice and sin. It is actively seeking to bring God's mercy and healing to those who need it. It is the ability to make decisions independently for the sake of others.

Where to Go from Here

If we build on the premise that we are called to restore the image of God in our lives, thus mirroring God, then we have a foundation upon which to build criteria to guide our daughters. Image of God issues related to independence include recognizing our daughters' ability to be rational and reflective, helping them be in proper relationships to others,[22] and empowering them to be co-stewards of the earth (Gen. 1:28). From this premise the following recommendations emerge:

- We should encourage our daughters to act boldly when it is for the sake of others, including a concern for social justice, and a concern to preserve and wisely manage environmental resources.

- We should discourage our daughters from passive choices that limit their ability to act in interdependence with others as ruler/stewards over creation.
- We should discourage our daughters from choices that put the self above others and thus diminishes interdependent relationships.

Practical opportunities for parents to instill a sense of independence in their daughters can be readily found scattered throughout the opportunities of everyday life. Following are a few suggestions intended to stimulate how we think about raising strong daughters. The goal is to bring our daughters to a balance between too much dependence and too much independence, so they can function interdependently in their social relationships. Most of these suggestions assume the distortion for our daughters is on the side of too much dependence rather than too much independence.

1. Allow for a Future That Includes the Possibility of Singleness

I hope all my daughters marry and experience the fulfilling joy in marriage and family life that Mark and I have. But it may not happen. To encourage thinking about a future that includes the possibility of *not* marrying will stimulate our daughters to think of themselves as women who can function independently. It will open them up to hear God's call in their lives. If they assume they will marry and stay home (a wonderful call for those who are given it), then they will not be prepared for alternatives. Thus, they may become overly dependent, passive recipients, waiting for a man God may never provide to choose, marry, and take care of them. This passivity can stifle the sense in which God calls them to be active rulers and stewards over the earth in interdependent relationships with others.

2. Encourage Daughters to Problem Solve

Believing we need to solve our own problems can easily lead us to extreme independence. However, encouraging daughters who tend to be passive and dependent to solve their own problems will move them toward interdependence. Sometimes our daughters need us to intervene, and it is important that they know we will be there to help them. That is the essence of interdependency. However, other times (and more often than we think), it is important for us to resist the temptation to intervene, and allow them to learn they are capable of figuring out what needs to be done, and doing it. Following are some examples of opportunities for learning independence:

Financial obligations. Our daughters should be taught to budget and encouraged to figure out how they will save for or pay for expenses they encounter. Several of my women students say they were never taught how to manage money, although their brothers were. We may choose to help our daughters financially with car or college expenses, but we can let them work out the financing of it by initiating the loan process or contacting the insurance company.

Relationship quagmires. Daughters sometimes get caught in a messy relationship, and our tendency is to tell them what to do to get out of it. But to grow strong daughters we need to dialogue with them, help them ask the right questions, and lead them toward a solution that emerges from within them, rather than from us.

Scheduling. I used to be so tempted to control my daughters' schedules, especially when they overextended themselves. Yet the older our children get the more we must let go. They learn from their choices—how to say yes or no, how to prioritize obligations, how to think and act independently.

3. Create an Atmosphere of Interdependence at Home

We model interdependence by including our daughters in the circle of those on whom we need to depend. This has looked different through various seasons of our family's life. For one season, everyone was responsible for cooking one night a week; we depended on each other for sustenance. In other seasons we split up the household duties according to skill and interest. Sarah launders and folds clothes better than either Mark or I. Megan is a great detail person and does a terrific job cleaning the bathrooms. No one cleans floors as well as Mark. Recognition of each member's contribution brings us closer to interdependence. We relied on the drivers to help with transportation needs for the nondrivers. We negotiated the sharing of two vehicles among four drivers. For most years, that meant Mark and I shared one car (we drove to work together and one of us walked home), and the driving daughters (seldom more than two at once) shared the other car. Sometimes it meant driving a sister to school early, or picking her up from work or after-school activities, or walking or biking. This part wasn't easy, and Mark and I had to resist the urge to work out the details for them.

We encourage interdependence by asking for (and taking) our daughters' feedback and input on significant decisions. A few years ago I considered leaving teaching to pursue administration. I asked Danielle for input, explaining the benefits and liabilities of each choice. Her listening, questioning response was helpful to me. I still felt ambivalent up to the day of my interview. As we said our good-byes for the day she wished me well and said, "Let this be a clarifying day for you." Her statement reflected thoughtfulness with my dilemma and a gentle wisdom that blessed me.

4. Model Interdependence in Your Peer Relationships

We would all do well to evaluate our own balance between extreme independence and extreme dependence and seek to restore interdependence in relationships that lack them. Only then can we model interdependence for our daughters.

Interdependence is less about a particular set of roles than it is a way of relating to another. Interdependence in marriage means the wife says to her husband, "I am highly committed to your growth as a person," while the husband says to his wife, "I am highly committed to your growth as a person."

For some couples, interdependence may look like a traditional marriage with the wife working at home and the husband working outside the home. If they see themselves as partner stewards and rulers over that which God has entrusted to them, and if the husband is as committed to his wife's growth as a person as she is to his, then they can function interdependently. One does not need to change one's style of marriage to be interdependent, but they may need to consider how they view each other. Does he see her as a woman able to significantly function independently on behalf of others? Does she see him as dependent on her for growth as a child of God?

For other couples, interdependence may mean both the husband and wife have careers outside the home. They still need to be sacrificially committed to the other's growth. The challenge for these couples is how to rearrange the responsibilities that fell on the shoulders of women after the industrial revolution. Men left the home to work first, leaving the primary parenting tasks to women. If women independently leave home to work, children will suffer (and thus neglect this stewardship responsibility). The challenge for fathers and mothers is to work out, together, how best to meet the needs of their children. Thus they model an interdependence in parenting, where each spouse needs the other to holistically meet parenting obligations. If men or women pursue careers without giving thought to the consequences to their spouse and children, they distort interdependence. However, women and men who pursue career callings with a sense of interdependence are able to explore broader avenues to be stewards and rulers over creation.

5. Act Boldly on Behalf of Others

Since the focus of interdependence is not the specific roles we fill but our approach to others with whom we are in relationship, we also model interdependence when we, as parents, call a friend for help instead of attempting to take care of our problems by ourselves. This is especially powerful when modeled by fathers who tend to err on the side of independence. Mothers model interdependence more powerfully when they step forward to help someone who needs it rather than wait for someone else (particularly a male) to take care of it.

When Sarah and I heard a man belittling and harassing an older homeless woman we were quite disturbed. It would have been easiest to walk away and assume this was not our problem to address. But we went back to her and attended to the hurts of that encounter. We told her we were sorry for how she had been treated. It was a little thing really, but it meant a lot to her, or so she told us several times. Sarah and I went back that night with a sack supper for Sherry and returned about once a week throughout the summer to visit and feed this lonely, homeless woman. We found out that other people were taking care of Sherry too. We did our part, they did theirs, and Sherry's needs were met. The community effort demonstrated interdependence. If women are unable to respond independently, their ability to be stewards of creation is thwarted. Inasmuch as we can model interdependence as parents, especially as mothers, we encourage a healthy form of independence in our daughters.

CONCLUSION

We are dependent creatures, made to be wholly dependent on God. God also made us to be in interdependent relationships with other humans. Our construction of social and human arrangements reflects this interdependence. We need physicians to take care of our sicknesses, farmers to grow food, spiritual leaders to encourage our walk with God. Likewise, women need others, male and female, to be strong where they are weak, to affirm them, to listen to them, to minister to them. And men need others, female and male, to be strong where they are weak, to affirm them, to listen to them, to minister to them. In this interdependent fashion we bring wholeness and balance to our fallen tendencies to be too independent (an easy error in our individualistic society) and too dependent (an easy error for our daughters).

The point is less how we define this interdependence and more that we recognize that God created men and women to manage and rule the earth together. God did not specifically define what that would look like nearly as much as human societies have throughout history.

We need each other. God created us this way. To teach interdependence to our daughters we need to live it before them.

CHAPTER FIVE

DAUGHTERS AND VOICE

"But you will have to pay me, too," grinned the witch. "And I want no small payment. You have the most beautiful voice of all those who live in the ocean. I suppose you have thought of using that to charm your prince; but that voice you will have to give to me. I want the most precious thing you have to pay for my potion . . ."

"But if you take my voice," said the little mermaid, "what will I have left?"

"Your beautiful body," said the witch. "Your graceful walk and your lovely eyes. Speak with them and you will be able to capture a human heart . . ."

—Hans Christian Andersen

WHEN MEGAN WAS AROUND TWO YEARS OLD she used to try out her voice. She would screech quite loudly and Mark or I would say, "No, Megan, that is far too loud." Then she would screech just a little bit softer and Mark or I would say, "Megan, that is still too loud." She would screech one or two more times until we finally said, "Okay, Megan, that's okay." Then she would stop screeching altogether. All she really wanted to know was how loud we would let her screech.

Megan, like all of our daughters, will try out her voice. Our daughters will explore what their voices can do and learn accepted and expected uses of them. They will ask questions about their voices, such as: Will I have useful words to contribute? Is my voice credible? Will anyone listen to me? How they answer these questions and come to view their voices will shape many of their life experiences.

In *Mother Daughter Revolution,* voice is defined as the courage to speak one's mind. It is not to be confused with loudness or amount of talking, rather it is courage "to speak one's mind by telling all one's heart."[1]

A woman who has a strong voice will have confidence in her ability to think for herself and confidence in what she has to say. She will not be overly dependent, but she will have a good sense of interdependence and an ability to act independently. For our daughters to illuminate the image of God within them they will need the use of their voices.

The passive dependency women acquired after the fall meant that they gave up their voices and became silent. The little mermaid in Hans Christian Andersen's story offers a powerful example of one who literally gives up her voice so she can pursue love. In the Disney film version she wins her prince *and* gets her voice back. In the original story she gets neither: The witch cuts out her tongue, signifying a permanent loss of voice. Thus the little mermaid gambles on the seductive power of a beautiful body, gives up her voice and with it the power that could have enabled her to win a human soul.

However, the idea of women losing their voices contradicts the stereotype of women as talkers. In many jokes, proverbs, and cartoons, women are portrayed as gabbers while men are silent, suggesting women have plenty of voice—too much according to these proverbs. Do women really talk more than men? Deborah Tannen says it depends on the social context.[2] Women talk more in the privacy of their homes, and men talk more in public contexts. Tannen says men and women feel comfortable with different kinds of speaking in different situations. Men tend to feel most comfortable speaking in public spheres. Husbands can be the life of the party, dominate the conversation at a formal dinner, or contribute easily to a public forum, yet have wives with valid complaints that these men never talk to them at home. In contrast, women tend to feel most comfortable speaking in private spheres. They talk easily with husbands, friends, and neighbors about their lives—the events, feelings, and dreams that fill their days. But many of these same women have nothing to say in public forums, feel too self-conscious to make jokes at a party, or fear they may appear uninformed or dumb if they join a dinner conversation.

The different contexts in which men and women feel comfortable using their voices corresponds to what they grow up learning about the purpose of voice. Girls tend to cooperate in their play and boys tend to be competitive; so also in their use of language. Early on, girls see and model the use of language to build relationships, usually with other girls. Meanwhile, boys see and model the use of language to compete, to show others they are tough, funny, or smart. Tannen says that talk for women is primarily for interaction. It is a language of rapport, a way to establish and develop relationships with others. For men, language is primarily used to give information and to negotiate social position. Boys and men do this by showing knowledge and skill, or by telling jokes that draw attention to themselves. The male that can attract and keep the most attention wins by gaining the highest social position.

Thus boys and girls grow up learning different purposes for their voices. Boys talk more in school and volunteer more answers to questions, while girls become accustomed to being quiet, preferring to talk amongst themselves rather than speaking out in class.

In one study, the gender dynamics in the classroom of an evangelical Christian college were explored through observations and interviews with male and female students.[3] A male student had the following to say about women who speak up in class:

> It's not a good impression and I'm sorry I have it, but my impression is that the women who do speak out are abrasive. Sometimes it's true, but part of it is an awful stereotype and the other part of it is that it's probably difficult enough for women to speak out that the ones that do might have a bit of an edge. . . . Anytime there's a woman who consistently speaks up she's any number of things, but . . . it's never positive.

On the same topic a female student said:

> When the women are confident it's seen as something on the negative side. When you know a little bit too much or you take on the professor, you think "you're so smart," and it's kind of a smarty-pants attitude. Whereas men will never be seen as smarty-pants.

Our daughters get reinforced for being talkative in private spheres and silent in public spheres. Not only do a lack of good models and the silence ghetto in schools reinforce this lost public voice, but girls will criticize other girls who try to use their voice to stand out or appear better than others in public spheres.[4]

If both our sons and daughters could learn to speak in the realms where they have lost their voices, communication and use of voice would improve dramatically. Women would contribute more (and with greater confidence) to the public spheres, and men would engage in more cooperative, relationship-building communication with their wives, children, other relatives, and friends.

God has watched over the voice of women throughout history, not allowing it to be completely silenced. God ensured that some of their profound insights, ability to recognize God, and words of praise would be recorded in Scripture for public use. The Magnificat, a song of praise written by Mary, the mother of Jesus, is recorded in Luke 1. The song of deliverance sung by Moses, Miriam, and the people of Israel after God delivered them from the Egyptians, is believed by many scholars to have been written by Miriam.[5] God used the voice of the prophetess Anna, who recognized the baby Jesus, to reinforce and strengthen the faith of Mary and Joseph. God chose women to be the first witnesses of Jesus' resurrection in a time when the testimony of a woman was regarded as so worthless that women were not allowed to testify in court.[6] Yet God used women's voices to bring the news of Jesus' resurrection to the disciples (Matthew 28).

A number of New Testament scholars believe women served side by side with men in the early church, in various leadership roles that required the use of voice. As Christianity became institutionalized, the church began to conform to the secular culture surrounding it which excluded women from leadership roles in public spheres.[7]

One challenge facing those who seek to rebuild the lost parts of the image of God is to rebuild the ability for women to use their voices in public spheres. Our daughters have the capacity to be in relationship with God, have an innate sense of "oughtness" about how the world should be, and are particularly gifted at being in community with others. Yet without voice, these aspects of the image of God cannot be fully utilized. So far we have seen that parents begin to restore their daughters' voices by reaffirming that God gave women voices to be used to help bring balance to the stewardship role humans have over the earth. The absence of female voices results in an incomplete effort for humans to rule over creation. Another challenge is teaching our daughters how to use their voices in spite of traditions that encourage them to keep silent.

BREAKING THROUGH THE SILENCE

Imagine observing a panel of experts on the advantages and disadvantages of affirmative action. The experts have been called together to discuss the issues surrounding affirmative action and make a recommendation to the president for action. Each expert has been invited because of her or his specific perspective or slant on the issue. Now imagine the outcome if half of the experts do not speak. While a recommendation would still be reached (indeed, perhaps more efficiently), it may not (likely not) be the best recommendation the group could have developed.

Half the bearers of God's image largely move in public spheres of silence. They do not have the courage to speak their minds about what is on their hearts. If that which is on the hearts of women and men is in any way different (and assuming that what is on women's hearts is equally valid and important), then the effectiveness of conversations and policies developed in the public sphere is hindered since not all represented perspectives are heard.

We saw the significance of the contribution of women's voice when we looked at women voters in the last chapter. Women's involvement in politics is reshaping society because women tend to care more, or at least differently, than men do about issues that relate to family concerns.

Various spheres of silence affect our daughters. Yet parents and those who work with girls can help break open these spheres in ways that will encourage girls to find and use their voices.

Breaking the Silence Sphere at Home

Even though women are supposedly the talkers at home, there are spheres of silence at home that need to be broken. At the most extreme end are homes where abuse occurs, but a code of silence keeps children and spouses from using their voices to get help from the outside. Sometimes these are chaotic homes, where alcohol or drugs are abused and/or parents are unemployed. Teachers, pastors, and youth leaders sometimes identify such homes as abusive and intervene. But, other times, abusive families have normal-appearing homes, where family members attend church and are productive members of the community. Abuse is less often identified in these homes. The code of silence works well to insulate these girls from outside help.

Girls who have learned that words cause pain experience another serious form of silence. These daughters learn that the best way to keep from getting hurt by words is to obey and stay silent. The childhood of my friend Rachel included divorced parents, an abusive stepfather, and a mother who did not know how to love her children. Rachel talked about how her mother would distance herself from Rachel if she tried to talk to her and draw close. As Rachel learned the cost of using her voice, she chose silence so she could stay in some sort of distant relationship with her mother and mitigate her sense of outright rejection.

Other silence spheres experienced at home are not life-threatening and cost less emotionally and physically than silence found in abusive homes, but these still erode girls' ability to use their voices. More common than abusive homes are homes where mothers, sisters, and daughters are supposed to talk about other people, events, fashions, and fads, but not ideas. The world of philosophical debate surrounding news and views represents a silence sphere for many women. Breaking the silence sphere at home means entering into dialogues with our daughters about ideas that matter. Breaking the silence sphere means encouraging them to develop skills in thinking through and expressing their conclusions about issues. One student described family dinner conversations this way.

> I can remember many talks that led to arguments and others that have been very engaging. If a controversial topic comes up it is usually my father who will debate it with someone who may not agree with his view. My mother does, of course, contribute to the conversation, but in a limited way. Also, any talks we have are very organized. To disagree with someone like my father you must have a very clear, concise argument about what you want to say or your view can and will be easily disputed. This is not to say that we have not had some great discussions though. There have been times (especially when we agree on a subject) when we have been able to explore an issue or discuss a topic—usually initiated by my father.

While some might read this description as a positive example of a father encouraging his children to discuss and debate issues (and there are some positive elements here), there are also negative elements. This scenario is about a family that thinks it is encouraging daughters and sons to explore the realm of ideas, but it does so in a very controlled way. Was this daughter's use of voice encouraged? Under what conditions? Her father clearly had the voice with which others had to contend. The father debated with those who disagreed and could fairly easily defeat his opponent. The mother contributed but in a limited way. Topics generally seemed to be initiated by the father, at least the ones she described most positively. On the upside the daughter was encouraged to use her voice, particularly when it agreed with the father's voice. Disagreement would be challenged and it would be uncomfortable, but it was allowed.

For daughters in homes like this to be encouraged to develop their own voices parents need to encourage them to build on their fledgling or unformed opinions, figuring out the strengths and weaknesses of positions as the discussion unfolds. The tendency is often to squelch dissenting ideas rather than develop the ability to think through them well.

A true dialogue implies receptivity on both sides to the other's position. A dialogue will challenge and probe, and although it emerges out of conviction, it is committed to understanding, not simply persuading. If getting a daughter (or anyone else) to agree with our position is the goal, the conversation isn't dialogue anymore, it is persuasion. Persuasive conversations may raise daughters who can use their voices to recite someone else's position, but these daughters are not speaking their minds from their own hearts.

Parenting certainly includes persuasion. We want to persuade our daughters to stay away from premarital sex, drugs, and alcohol. We want to persuade them to do well in school, to become godly women, to obey the rules we live by. We hope to pass our values on to them and give them a foundation rooted in God. But to send them off we must eventually let go. To send them off prepared to use their voices in public spheres, we need to eventually stop using persuasive conversations and begin having dialogues. The older our daughters get, the more our conversations should consist of dialogue rather than persuasion. A time comes when *dialogues* about abstinence, abortion, causes of poverty, or problems of various political parties become more appropriate than persuasion. Yet honest dialogue is difficult, because honest dialogue allows differences to remain unsettled. Our daughters may choose positions and views that we disagree with. Honest dialogue attempts to understand why they hold them, and continues to accept our daughters in spite of differences. Dishonest dialogue makes a pretense at listening and allowing for difference but exerts pressure for conformity by withholding acceptance as long as difference remains.

If we believe our daughters belong to God and that he will shape, mold, and craft them into useful vessels, then we can let go of our desire to recreate ourselves in our daughters. Each new generation brings new challenges and problems. Growing strong daughters means giving them a sense of confidence in their giftedness and voice, and allowing them to shift and change so they can be part of God's plan to address shifting and changing problems.

Sometimes breaking the silence sphere at home means having monologues with our daughters where they talk and we listen. We must listen without offering advice or interpretation unless they ask us. We listen to affirm their experiences and how they feel about them. When they say, "I feel fat and ugly, and my friends are all boring," we may be tempted to say, "You are neither fat nor ugly, and you should be more loyal to your friends." To affirm their experience and their feelings we need to listen. Often what is said in what appears to be off-handed triteness is a representation of some more deeply felt need.

It is especially hard to listen to our daughters when they have hard things to say to us about us. Just because they think we are unfair or too rigid does not mean that we need to change, but we do need to listen and affirm their experience. Okay, so none of their friends have a curfew, none of their friends have to call and say where they are when they don't come right home after school, and none of their friends have limited phone or TV time. What does this mean to them? That they are not trusted? That they are being treated like young children? That privileges have not matched their expectation for increasing responsibility and maturity? Only after we have heard what they are really saying can we respond in a way that validates development and use of their voices. Responding to their questions with the pat answer "Because I am the parent and you are the child" stops the discussion and squelches their voices. We may be able to find some places of compromise reflecting our belief that privileges should match increasing responsibility and maturity. We may be able to explain that calling home has nothing to do with trust but is a courtesy we extend to those who may wonder where we are, a courtesy we, as parents, extend to them and each other as well.

Learning to listen encourages our daughters' development of voice. Breaking the silence sphere at home gives our daughters the boldness to disagree with us, a confidence that what they have to say will be listened to, and an ability to express what is on their hearts without fear of rejection.

Breaking the Silence Sphere at School

I have already introduced you to Autumn, whose father committed suicide. Autumn was a good student, deeply reflective, and able to express herself well in writing, though she rarely spoke up in class. About her silence she said, "To make myself less noticeable, I remained silent. That worked because I was a girl and girls could be quiet at grade school and not get beat up as much as boys who were quiet. I couldn't express myself at all."

Daughters who are taught to be silent at home will often stay silent at school. Even daughters from homes that encouraged their use of voice will learn that girls are supposed to be quiet at school. The silence ghetto girls experience at school reinforces what some girls experience at home—boys and men talk, girls and women are silent. Before the silence sphere at school can be broken, girls need to exercise and develop their voices at home.

A cultural difference emerges when one considers African-American adolescent girls. They are better able to hold onto their voices through adolescence then either white, Latina, or Asian girls. African-American daughters are raised to be strong at home. To protect their sense of self they often distance themselves from institutions in our culture (such as schools) that devalue them because of their skin color and gender.[8] Unfortunately this distancing, while preserving their sense of voice and self, often means they avoid the paths that could potentially lead to better paying jobs and thus to lives with more economic stability.

Daughters can be encouraged to break the silence sphere at school by becoming active in ways that require them to use their voices. Drama, choirs, and the speech team are all voice-building activities. Parents who go to open houses, who volunteer in classrooms or on school committees come to be known by school teachers and administrators. Teachers notice and respond to cues signifying parents who are invested in the education their daughters receive. It is harder to overlook a girl whose parents are known in the school.

Breaking the Silence Sphere in Relationships

One study considered the effects of home environment on college women's experiences with unwanted sexual experiences.[9] The researchers found that women who came from homes where fathers were perceived as authority-holding initiators and mothers as submissive receivers had more unwanted sexual experiences than daughters who saw their parents in less rigid gender roles. All of these unwanted incidents were related to voice in some way. In some cases a "no" voice was ignored: date rape, incest, sexual assaults by strangers.

However, in 55 percent of the cases the women had "lost voices." In these incidents there was no force or coercion but a sense that, as women, they were to follow and could not say no, even when they wanted to. When girls are taught to be submissive followers in their relationships with boys and men, it increases their vulnerability to unwanted sexual experiences. Boys are taught to be masculine by taking charge, and girls are taught to be feminine by submitting.

Several studies have looked for the source of social status for girls and boys in high school. For boys, prestige and popularity were rooted in their athletic achievement. Girls were validated as being worthwhile, and thus gaining prestige and popularity, by having a boyfriend.[10] Like the little mermaid, adolescent girls and young women who care about having a relationship with a boy or man will often sacrifice their voices to save those relationships. For many this includes going further sexually than they want to.

Breaking the silence ghetto in relationships is more of a challenge for parents who endorse traditional gender roles for men and women. However, if we raise our daughters with confidence in who they are, independent of an attachment to a boy, and encourage them to exercise their voice by allowing them to disagree, think, and believe differently than fathers and brothers, then we better enable them to keep their voices in relationships with other males.

Breaking the silence ghetto in relationships is easier for parents who endorse flexible gender roles for men and women. Yet all girls are still confronted with messages that say girls who love their guys will help them assuage the tyranny of their sexual drive by saying yes when they want to say no. Boys and girls also pick up messages that imply girls secretly want to be overpowered by strong, sensual men—they are just *supposed* to put up a fight. One classic example is the scene in *Gone With the Wind*, where Rhett carries a mad, fighting Scarlett (seemingly against her will) up to bed for passionate lovemaking. In the morning the mad, fighting Scarlett has been transformed into a giddy, satisfied woman. Parents need to find ways to challenge these cultural myths and give daughters the boldness to say and mean no, especially to boys or men who really think they mean yes.

A challenge for daughters who have a strong voice may be finding men who will not be intimidated or put off by that voice. But as some girls are growing into strong women who desire to find a man who will partner with them, some boys are growing up into men who desire to find a woman with whom he can partner mutually. Men and women who thus come together can use their voices, sometimes in harmony, sometimes in unison, to partner together in serving God.

Breaking the Silence Sphere in Church

The controversy rages. Did the early Christian church really have women preachers and teachers? If so, what did Paul mean when he wrote to Timothy that women should be silent in the church? Church historians and theologians come to different conclusions, depending on what secondary sources they consider authentic and legitimate, how they do their historical research, and perhaps most importantly, what biases they bring with them to the discussion. I want to lay aside the controversy of women in ministry as teachers and preachers and focus instead on what it has meant more generally for women to enter a silence ghetto in the church.

Whether or not women are to be preaching and teaching, the silence ghetto in the church has meant a loss of God's essence as expressed through women's intuitive, sensing ways of being. If women generally are more intuitive, emotional, and sensitive than men are, it follows that women would also be more attuned to the inner workings of the spiritual life. Yet women's expressions of faith are sometimes devalued, as though women do the fluff stuff of faith—attend to their "spiritual journeys," go on spiritual retreats, journal, attend women's prayer meetings, or even fulfill various serving responsibilities. Meanwhile men do the tough stuff of faith—debate doctrine, prepare persuasive apologetics for the faith, and preach, teach, and lead Bible studies.

I assign *Space for God* by Don Postema as one of several books for a Capstone Integration of Sociology and Christianity course. The book invites readers to create space for God in their lives through reflections, poetry, Scripture, artwork, quotes from the Desert Fathers, written prayers, and hymns. One year, as a student was purchasing her copy, someone working in the bookstore said with a snicker, "The prof who assigned *that* book must be a woman." How good it would be if, instead, he had made his comment positively, affirming the importance of incorporating matters of the centered soul into class, thus introducing balance into our Christian academics.

I have had a few students complain about what they thought were required devotions as part of that course. The use of a book that brings one into an experiential place with God is sometimes viewed as inappropriate for an academic course. My defense is that true integration of our faith with any discipline must include the experiential with the intellectual. By far the majority of my students have welcomed this integrative approach. But when questions about the appropriateness of this kind of integration arise, they reflect a schism in our faith between what we perceive to be the experientially based "fluff" of Christianity (engendered as female) versus the intellectually based "stuff" of Christianity (engendered as male).

A colleague who taught in the Christian Ministries department had male students regularly come to her for mentoring. They saw her centeredness, her discerning and sensitive spirit. A hungry stirring in their souls drew them to her. Because of the voice she had in the context of her classes, she was able to minister to men and women who desired a deeper, more centered spiritual life than they had often been able to access in their churches. Not all female professors minister to students in this way, and certainly male professors have also been a magnet for students seeking a way to integrate their intellectual and spiritual selves. But this kind of integration is still often perceived as secondary to the more academically rigorous integration of thinking Christianly and sociologically (or philosophically, psychologically, theologically).

If men are taught to be tough and to do most of the talking, it may well be that women are best gifted to teach us how to listen, to be vulnerable and tender to the moving of God within us. Perhaps women who have learned to be listeners are best able to teach men to listen to the still, small voice of God.

Women have much to offer both women and men from the depth of their spiritual lives. While many women are granted an audience of women, few are given an audience of men. Thus men miss the opportunity to learn from wise women who have spent years growing in Christ. Women have much they can learn from the experiences and training of men. Likewise, men have much they can learn from women.

Unfortunately, since women are not encouraged to speak in public spheres in general, most women are uncomfortable with the thought of speaking publicly, and few women seek opportunities to speak from their hearts. Some women do so anyway, but with much fear and trepidation. As our sons are trained in the skills of public speaking—both formally and informally through the natural discourse of the day—so we need to train our daughters.

Breaking the Silence Sphere in the General Public

Being made in the image of God means we have within us a sense of "oughtness" about the world. Our sons and daughters see evidence of sin and a world broken from God's plan every day. We have a responsibility as image-bearers of God to speak out against what is wrong. Daughters can only speak out against wrongdoing if they have developed confident voices that speak from their hearts.

We begin judging and criticizing others by the time we march off to kindergarten. By high school we have learned these skills fairly well. We criticize those who do not fit in to better assure our place in the circle of those who do. Both boys and girls are fairly comfortable using their voices to criticize. However, to take a verbal stand against such criticism is to risk being ostracized. Fred was a marginalized kid in my daughters' high school. He showed up for class wearing strange makeup. One day he drew fangs on his face with lipstick, and another day he wore purple eye shadow in big circles around his eyes. Occasionally he showed up in a dress. Those he went to high school with either feared him, ignored him, or made fun of him. Few befriended him. Sarah did, largely because he tried to pick her up and so started a conversation. Sarah rejected his pickup attempts but added him as a friend. She thought he was just a guy who needed attention and told people they shouldn't judge him. It takes a fair amount of courage to take a stand against the crowd and risk your own spot in the circle for someone else's sake.

Some strong women have always been willing to challenge the inner circle to speak out for what they believed. Women like Sojourner Truth and Susan B. Anthony were the moving force behind the abolition of slavery. Emma Goldman fought for sweatshop reforms, and Rosa Parks helped get the civil rights movement underway by refusing to acknowledge the discriminatory Jim Crow laws of the South. Because those women had a strong sense of oughtness and a corresponding confidence in their voices, they impacted history. Likewise, we can encourage our daughters' sense of oughtness and boldness to respond when they see wrongdoing.

WHERE TO GO FROM HERE

Throughout this chapter I have offered a number of ideas for parents to encourage the voice development of their daughters. The following suggestions summarize various arenas where voice can be developed.

1. Awaken a Sense of God-Awareness

Those who attend to God's gifts of intuition and emotion have an enhanced ability for spirit to touch Spirit. If our daughters are intuitive and spiritually sensitive, we should recognize this as a strength and celebrate it with them. God's image in us means we have been created to be in relationship with him. Intuition, emotion, and spiritual sensitivity enable men and women to know they are deeply loved and known by God. Inasmuch as women have been encouraged to foster these traits more than men have, it is a strength that means they are capable of centering down and listening to the voice of God.

Awaken a sense of God-awareness in your daughters by identifying this gift from God within them. Look for and note moments of spiritual discernment and sensitivity when they express them. Affirm opportunities they take to use their voice to express the sense of oughtness God has placed within them.

2. Nurture Voice Development at Home

Parents can nurture voice development in many ways. Following are just a few ideas. A modified democratic decision-making model functions as a training ground for our daughters' voice development. Parents decide the basic rules and expectations by which the family will be run but allow many decisions to be made democratically. Planning a vacation, modifying rules, assigning responsibilities, and financial budgeting can all be accomplished in a way that incorporates the whole family. This allows the voices of our daughters to be heard and counted as significant.

Parents can also hold honest discussions about issues that come up for an adolescent daughter at school or church. In these conversations parents can dialogue with their daughter rather than attempt to persuade her of their own perspective. Parents can learn about their daughter's world when they try to understand why she thinks contraceptives for sexually active teens ought to be available at school. If parents respond with a rebuke and try to persuade her that contraceptives should not be available, then parents learn nothing, as well as squelch their daughter's attempt to use her voice. To truly listen to her and dialogue with her affirms her voice, whether or not you agree with her.

During some seasons in our family's life, dinnertime was an opportunity to bring a trivia question to challenge the rest of us. Sometimes the trivia would be a piece of news one of us heard or read about, such as "In which states is TV watched the most hours per day?" Other times the trivia concerned something one of us learned in school, such as "Which generals fought for the South in the Civil War?" That anyone can ask or answer such a question legitimates all of us as learners, teachers, listeners, and speakers.

Parents who seek input on things that matter from their daughters validate them. I've known parents who value the input of sons but not daughters. To ask our daughters for their opinions, perspectives, and ideas tells them we believe they have opinions worth listening to and encourages them to trust their voices in sharing them.

3. Encourage Activities That Nurture Voice Development

In every silent sphere lies a potential sphere of influence. In each sphere we can find ways that encourage and nurture the development of our daughters' voices. At home we can enter dialogues that encourage thinking, analyzing, and presenting skills. At school, daughters can be encouraged to join speech teams, debate teams, or drama. If they are writers, they can express their voice through the school newspaper. In their relationships, we can legitimate the right for them to be assertive in expressing their preferences and ideas. At church, they can be encouraged to take advantage of leadership and service opportunities available to them. These opportunities will give them a springboard for using their voices in the general public to share gained insight and experience with others and to boldly confront injustice and sin.

Mothers who model voice will reinforce the use of voice for their daughters. Daughters who see mothers who use their voices to teach or proclaim, to participate in intellectual discussions, or to speak out for the sake of others will learn that silence in public spheres is not a necessary part of being female.

4. Develop a Community of Women

Although women may generally be more cooperative and relational than men are, women are also in competition with each other. The effectiveness of advertisements that say the most beautiful woman will get the best man supports the notion that women compete with each other. Since women have largely been convinced that their worth is based on being attached to a desired male, they may put relationships with other women aside to compete for the affections of men. Each year, we empty our pockets of $20 billion on cosmetics, $300 million on cosmetic surgery, and $33 billion on diets,[11] and then rush into the competition to win the best man. Somewhere along the way we traded our voices and our community with other women for the seduction of beauty.

Cooperation and community with other women is also lost when we criticize them for making different choices regarding how they will use their voices. Women in the public sphere criticize those in the private for wasting their potential and not being all they could be. Women in the private sphere criticize those in the public for neglecting their families and denying who they are as women.

We do not have to continue along this trajectory. At any point we can leave it, stop competing and criticizing, and begin to validate each other's voices. Other women will be our daughters' best supporters, their best listeners. We need to encourage them to build community with other women, and in that community to find safety and encouragement to learn to use their voices.

Daughters who observe a community of women supporting each other in their attempts to use and develop their voices will be encouraged to do likewise. My daughters know my women friends do that for me.

We encourage our daughters by reinforcing them when they build friendships with girls and women who will go beyond discussions of boys, body image, and clothes to discuss ideas, fears, and goals. Jeannine is a friend of mine who also became a friend of Sarah's. They became friends over a connection with clothes—both Jeannine and Sarah have created a style that is uniquely their own. Jeannine walks between Sarah's and my generation, offering a bridge from one to the other. I value the time she spent with Sarah, cruising through the resale stores in Chicago and meandering through the Blues Festival. Although they don't see each other often, Jeannine can still affirm and build Sarah in ways that I, as her mother, cannot. Our daughters will grow stronger if they have relationships with other women who build and encourage their use of voice.

5. Give Voice to Women and Girls Whose Voices Have Been Silenced

Giving voice is not just something we do for our own daughters but also for daughters whose voices have been silenced in emotionally and physically abusive homes. We need to keep our eyes and ears open for those who come from abusive homes where a code of silence keeps them insulated from outsiders. This is easier for those of us who work with girls and young women in classrooms, in youth groups, or in other extracurricular activities. For instance, in classes when we discuss abuse issues I remind students that some sitting among us have been physically or sexually abused. I encourage abused students to find someone to talk with and have heard some of their stories over the years.

When our daughters come home with stories of friends in bad situations, we can figure out with them ways to support and give voice to their friends' needs. In one instance for our family, this involved opening our home to a high school student who lived with us for six months. We need to give voice to girls whose voices have been silenced, drawing out their stories, supporting them, and, in some cases, getting them the intervention they need.

CONCLUSION

The use of voice is one of the ways humans are set apart from other created beings. Certainly animals communicate effectively with each other—likely in more complex ways than we know. But for humans, the voice is our primary way of expressing the reasoning, thinking, feeling, and knowing that comes from our soul. If our daughters cannot speak honestly from their minds and hearts, the capacity for God to use them as co-stewards over creation is diminished. If they do not use their voices, their ability to reason, think, and feel from their minds and hearts will atrophy, like the muscles around a broken bone. Building voice requires intentionality, because we, like our daughters, become used to moving quietly in spheres of silence.

CHAPTER SIX

PHYSICAL ESSENCE

I have never worked with a beautiful young woman who thought she was
beautiful or thin enough.

—Joel Schumacher, movie director who has worked with
Demi Moore, Julia Roberts, and Sandra Bullock[1]

WOMEN HAVE BEEN MADE in the image of God. While our
focus is usually on the character traits we have that reflect God's
image, God chose to encase that image in physical human bodies.
We are knit together in our mothers' wombs by the hand of God,
and we are fearfully and wonderfully made. However much Scripture affirms our physical selves, few women (even few who read the
Bible) feel that they have been wonderfully made—even the Julia
Robertses and Sandra Bullocks of the movie industry. Rather than
celebrate the diversity God created in our differences, we accept some
standard we call beautiful and compare ourselves mercilessly to that
standard. We try to hide our thick thighs and mask our pronounced
chins or close-set eyes, because we know the value standard for female
bodies in our culture is based primarily on external beauty.

However, the real value of a body is to be a vessel for the soul.
Our body is the window through which our soul experiences such

pleasures as the taste of chocolate, the scent of lilacs, the sound of a bird's song, the spectacle of a sunset, the intimacy of sexual ecstasy. A body that functions well can climb mountains, swim, run, even carry a backpack eight or nine miles a day while exploring the wonders of the wilderness.

Jana, my friend and backpacking partner, and I lead a group of women on a trip to Isle Royale, a small island in Lake Superior, every summer. For a week we help women experience their bodies as windows to their souls. All of us are moved by the mysterious and eerie cry of loons, which are only found in pristine, secluded areas. We see moose, all kinds of birds, ducks, and yellow lady slippers, and walk along trails where the ferns come up to our waists. And for the few willing to be dragged from their sleeping bags at night out onto a dock or into a clearing, we see more stars than we ever imagined. We grow to appreciate the strength in our legs that carry us (and our packs) mile after mile along ridge and coastal trails. Our expeditions are called "Glorious Endurance," and they are. At some points, the trip feels only like an endurance, but by the end of the week, all say it was indeed a *glorious* endurance. Our bodies enable our souls to experience God at Isle Royale.

Our bodies also enable us to serve God. With our voices we praise God and bring the good news of Jesus to those without hope. We feed the hungry, welcome the stranger, dress the naked, care for the sick, and visit the prisoner (Matthew 25). Mother Teresa epitomizes a woman who used her body to serve others, earning the nickname, "The saint of the gutters."[2] At age thirty-six, she left her cloister in Calcutta where she taught rich girls to work among the most reviled of India's poor: lepers. She spent the remainder of her life blessing, working, and raising the awareness of the world to the plight of the poor. God gave us human hands and feet to bring Jesus' healing comfort to those who are suffering.

But we forget this goodness of our bodies and succumb to the pressure to allow the particular size, shape, skin tone, and features of our body parts to become a symbol of value, a measuring stick of our worth. And not without reason. Attractive people *are* more successful than unattractive people. This is especially true for women. Attractive people are perceived by strangers as more intelligent, kind, happy, interesting, confident, sexy, assertive, strong, outgoing, poised, and successful than unattractive people. Attractive babies get coddled and kissed more, attractive children get more attention from teachers, attractive women are sought out more in social situations, and attractive people get more lenient punishment for social transgressions.[3]

It is no surprise, then, that our daughters easily forget that their bodies are intrinsically valuable simply because they house and serve their souls. Most women, along with their daughters, have a distorted view of their physical selves. We focus more on the worth of our body as a thing and less on what our bodies allow us to experience and accomplish. To turn our daughters away from a damaging obsession that critiques their worth according to their physical beauty, we need to recognize the distortions in culture that shape women's perspectives about worth and then offer our daughters an alternative perspective. Three types of vessels are offered here as a metaphor for three different emphases one can have regarding the bodies of women.

THE BODY AS A BEAUTIFUL VASE

God created human bodies to be beautiful and gave humans the capacity to respond in appreciation to that beauty. To desire to be attractive and to appreciate a person who is physically beautiful are in keeping with the way God created us. However, like much in the fall, the value of beauty became distorted. Female beauty became the criteria wherein a woman found her value. Leah had delicate, dull, or weak eyes, we read in Genesis 29 (the Hebrew meaning is uncertain). But Rachel "was beautiful in every way, with a lovely face and shapely figure." Beauty is the only reason we are given for why Jacob preferred Rachel to Leah. When a vase is valued only for its beauty it is set carefully in a cabinet or on a shelf to be seen and appreciated, but it becomes useless as a vessel.

Cultural Notions of Beauty

In the 1950s Marilyn Monroe epitomized the beautiful woman. She wore a size twelve. Today the beautiful women wear a size two,

126

like actress Teri Hatcher. Every culture and era defines beauty and creates norms and expectations surrounding that beauty. The distortion of beauty has led to beauty norms that are seldom natural and never reflect what the "average" woman actually looks like. For instance, the average height and weight of a woman in the United States is 5'4" and 142 pounds. The average height and weight of a model is 5'9" and 110 pounds. The average measurements of that model are 33-23-33.[4] Some of the most beautiful actresses choose, or are required to use, body doubles for nude or seminude scenes. And at least 85 percent of those body doubles have breast implants.[5]

Our daughters are surrounded by images of artificial beauty in magazines, on television, and in the movies. *People Magazine* publishes an annual report of the fifty most beautiful people. A consistent feature for women is that they must be young to be beautiful. For instance, in the 1997 edition, twenty-two of the twenty-five women were thirty-six or under, and most of those were in their twenties.[6] Girls come to think that the beauty of these successful women is, or should be, the standard they need to try to achieve. Beautiful and thin women win. The not so beautiful and not so thin (that is, average) women do not. Thus, the *functioning* of one's body is forgotten with an overemphasis on the appearance of one's body. Girls and young women forfeit health and emotional satisfaction with what their bodies enable them to do as they try to achieve the culture's unrealistic beauty standard.

One year I had students in an Introduction to Sociology class fill out a survey about perceptions of beauty. One question asked how satisfied they were with their bodies. None of the women reported being Very Satisfied, although 33 percent of the men did. Forty-five percent of the women were Somewhat Satisfied with their bodies, and another 41 percent were Somewhat Unsatisfied. Fourteen percent of the women were Very Unsatisfied, though none of the men reported being Very Unsatisfied. Some of this is a result of socialization. Women are not supposed to feel great about their bodies, much less *say* they do. If a woman says she is very satisfied with her body she will likely be considered arrogant. Given these social facts, it should not come as too big a surprise to read reports that suggest somewhere between 4 and 20 percent of all college-age women are bulimic—they force themselves to vomit after meals.[7]

Eating Disorders

On the one hand, we are socialized to eat, drink, and be merry. We connect good times and good friends with good food. A missionary who was home on furlough told Mark and me how strange it seemed to her that whenever Christians gather together, they gather with food—unheard of in the poor country she serves. Many of our churches offer donuts and coffee during a fellowship time between or after services. It would seem that where two or three are gathered in God's name, there in the midst of them is food.

On the other hand, women are socialized to be feminine, and today feminine means thin. Bulimic daughters have usually accepted the feminine role society expects them to fulfill. They tend to be good students and eager to please others. Yet in their eagerness to accommodate to demands of femininity that offer a narrow definition of beauty, they forfeit acceptance of their bodies. Girls with bulimia alternate binging on food with purges—either by fasting, through the use of laxatives, excessive exercise, or most commonly through induced vomiting.

Anorexia is less common than bulimia but more dangerous. According to the National Eating Disorders Screening Program, one thousand women in the United States die from anorexia every year. Girls who have anorexia have a compulsive fear of being fat. They literally starve themselves to lose weight. It is difficult to get accurate estimates on eating disorders because they are relatively easy to hide. Some estimates suggest 5 to 10 percent of all girls and women in the United States are anorexic, though possibly as many as one in five college women.[8] As much as college women desire the thin bodies of models and movie stars, being thin is not natural for most models—even their thinness is artificially achieved. Model Aimee Liu claims that many models are anorexic.[9]

Similar to girls with bulimia, those who are anorexic tend to be good students, nice people who are eager to please others. For girls with anorexia, their eating pattern becomes a way of regaining control when they feel they have none. While anorexia often begins in adolescence with ordinary teenage dieting, these girls get thinner than anyone demands or wants and relish a sense of control in knowing that no one can force them to eat. Ironically, long after they are emaciated, most still feel fat.

Jean Antonello's book *Breaking Out of Food Jail* offers a list of warning signs that parents and friends can look for in those they suspect might be suffering from an eating disorder. Her list includes the following: anxiety, especially about food and eating; a need for control over eating and/or an exaggerated sense of power to control or limit eating; secrecy and sneakiness regarding food; mood swings, depression, guilt, and shame; preoccupation, irrational thinking or obsessiveness about food, weight, or body shape; evidence of symptoms associated with hunger, such as irritability, weakness, poor motivation, or trouble concentrating; bingeing or self-starvation; perfectionism.[10]

Antonello recommends intervention whenever a person's life or safety is in danger—definitely if physical or mental impairment is apparent. This would include emaciation, fainting, or threats of suicide. Eating disorders are supposed to be a secret, and often parents are confronted with anger or denial when the disorder is discovered and identified. Professionals who deal with eating disorders are well trained to help girls recognize and work through the causes of their disorder, though girls will often resist treatment. Seldom are parents or friends alone able to effectively help girls struggling with eating disorders to overcome them.

Obesity is considered by some to be an eating disorder as well. Whether or not the obesity is a result of heredity, metabolism, or nutrition, the social effects of obesity on women are powerful. Obese people are usually blamed for their obesity, and considered lazy or poorly motivated to change. The general public often considers obese people to be sloppy, stupid, and ugly.[11] Obese people are the brunt of jokes, and, especially for women, have a more difficult time finding jobs and spouses. Knowing this, some parents work hard to keep their daughters from becoming overweight or encourage overweight daughters to lose weight. However, if this effort is not handled carefully, it reinforces the idea that worth is based on external appearance.

Perhaps the most common eating problem for women is what Judith Rodin called "normative obsession." Cultures that overemphasize weight create an environment where obsession with weight, food, and scales seems normal. Many girls and women monitor their food intake vigilantly, and their self-esteem day by day is determined by whether they are at the bottom or top of the weight range they allow themselves.[12]

Many parents feel guilt over the eating disorders of their daughters. Parents are told they have been too demanding or too controlling. Yet if the estimates are accurate, which suggest 20 percent of college women are anorexic and at least another 4 to 20 percent are bulimic, we need to reconsider the problem by taking the focus off parents and putting it in a larger social context. Girls are bombarded with images that say, "To have value you must change yourself. You must be skinny and wear makeup and maybe have an operation." During preschool and elementary school, girls play with Barbies (whose real-life measurements would be 36-18-33) and Li'l Miss Makeup dolls. As junior high girls, they consume the adolescent magazines about boys, sex, and body image that promise them happiness and popularity if they buy the right clothes, cosmetics, and weight control products. Many women keep reading these magazines, simply replacing *Seventeen* with *Cosmopolitan*.

Eating disorders are one indication that women have internalized shame about their bodies. Some women give up and escape into food and obesity. Some will only see value in their bodies if they can make them thin through purging or starvation. Daughters are not born feeling shame because of their bodies, they learn it. Our consumer-driven culture ensures it. Dieting programs rake in over $30 billion per year, cosmetic sales are over $20 billion, the sales of women's clothes averaged $103 billion *per month* back in 1990, the year women spent over $1.5 billion on cosmetic surgery.[13]

Cosmetic Surgery

Women feel compelled to improve on the body God gave them in order to obtain beauty as it is defined by culture. However, this is not a new phenomenon. The Chinese practice of female foot binding began in the tenth century and continued until 1911. Foot binding is an early example of culture's tendency to alter natural beauty for women in a way that damages their physical health and well-being. The feet of five-year-old girls were bound so that their toes became twisted under their arches. The more tightly bound, the smaller the foot, and the more attractive they were considered to be.[14] Yet this painful procedure crippled them. These women could not run or even walk normally. They shuffled painfully through life so they could be beautiful.

In the sixteenth century European women began to bind their waists and busts with corsets of whalebone and hardened canvas. Bending at the waist and breathing were difficult, thus causing the common fainting spells of women. Contrary to popular thought, women did not faint because they were a more fragile sex but because conforming to the culture's beauty standards required them to compromise their ability to breathe. Iron bands were later introduced, which allowed the waist to be squeezed down to the ideal thirteen inches. These corsets, as well as the later version which showed up in the mid-nineteenth century, not only caused fainting but could also lead to pulmonary disease and internal organ damage. By the mid-nineteenth century full busts and hips were in vogue, but they were still accompanied by a tiny waist.

In the twentieth century the ideal changed from decade to decade. In the 1920s the young, boyish look was in, which included slender legs and hips, small breasts, and bobbed hair. In the 1940s and 1950s the full-figured Marilyn Monroe image became the ideal. In the 1960s the shift returned to the thin, lean, long, straight hair look, which was captured by the model Twiggy. The 1980s ideal remained slender, but with large breasts.[15]

Today's beautiful woman is still thin with large breasts, which is a combination that rarely occurs naturally. Thus, the most common type of cosmetic surgery is liposuction to get rid of the fat, and the second most common cosmetic surgery is breast implants. In 1998, over 120,000 women had cosmetic surgery to enlarge their breasts.[16] Naomi Wolf, author of *The Beauty Myth*, says,

> Looking at breasts in culture, one would have little idea that real breasts come in as many shapes and variations as there are women. Since most women rarely if ever see or touch other women's breasts, they have no idea what they feel like, or of the way they move and shift with the body. . . . Women of all ages have a fixation—sad in the light of how varied women's breasts really are in texture—on "pertness" and "firmness."[17]

Our fixation with the perfect breast seems to be growing. In 1972, *Psychology Today* found 26 percent of American women surveyed were unhappy with the size or shape of their breasts. By 1985, the percentage of unhappy women had risen to 32 percent. The 1997 study showed another two percent increase: Thirty-four percent of women surveyed were dissatisfied with their breasts.[18] We are in an upward trend of dissatisfaction. Following some new information about health issues and risks identified with breast enhancement surgery, the numbers of women undergoing cosmetic breast surgery declined after 1992. However, due to increasingly safer methods, interest in breast enlargement surgery increased between 1996 and 1998 by 40 percent.[19] Ironically, women are more satisfied with their breasts than most other body parts. Sixty-six percent are dissatisfied with their weight (up from 48 percent in 1972); 71 percent are dissatisfied with their abdomens (up from 50 percent); 61 percent are dissatisfied with their hips or upper thighs (up from 49 percent). Overall, 56 percent of women are dissatisfied with their general appearance, up from 25 percent in 1972. And we now have numerous surgeries available to fix all our unsightly body parts. We have not made significant progress in accepting the female body as God created it in all its diversity in the last several thousand years. Indeed, we have gone further backwards in the last three decades.

Surgery to fix unsatisfactory body parts is now beginning to take place in adolescence. Girls in late adolescence are beginning to have the fat sucked out of them with liposuction and are enlarging their breasts. One female junior at a high school in California said, "A lot of seniors at my school get breast augmentation as a graduation present. I know at least four girls who had it done last year."[20]

Other women return to the cosmetic surgeon for breast implants after having babies, so they can once again have firm breasts that look just like the ones bought by the body doubles in the movies. Later, women return to have their faces lifted and their tummies tucked.

An added expectation in recent years is that women's muscles are toned and the body is physically fit. So women are joining sports clubs and hiring personal trainers to help them accomplish this.

We share the desire to conform to cultural beauty standards with the women who came before us. We have exchanged the binding of feet and waists with an assortment of cosmetic surgeries. Although we read the numbers that tell us how common cosmetic surgery is becoming among those who can afford it, we still want to believe that a beautiful woman is naturally beautiful. However, even many Miss America contestants are surgically reconstructed before they compete. In 1989, five of the contestants were surgically "improved" by the same plastic surgeon. What cultures define as beautiful is often not naturally achieved.

Judging the Joneses—Criticizing Other Females

When our daughters are preoccupied with what their bodies look like, they are less able to appreciate what their bodies enable them to do. The energy that could be used productively *with* their bodies gets funneled into activity that is supposed to make their bodies somehow more appealing and attractive. The irony is that all girls will eventually lose this battle, because all of us age, and the advertisements tell us aging is the most ugly thing of all.

Another question on my class survey asked students to rate when women's beauty peaked and then to rate when they thought the other sex would say women's beauty peaked. Fifty-nine percent of the women said women's beauty peaked between the mid-thirties and mid-forties. Another 27 percent said between the mid-twenties and mid-thirties. Yet women thought men would say female beauty peaks between late adolescence and early twenties. However, 50 percent of the men said women's beauty peaked between the mid-twenties and mid-thirties and another 39 percent said from the mid-thirties to mid-forties. Sixty-nine percent of the men thought women would say beauty peaked between late adolescence and the early twenties. Yet no men, and only 4 percent of the women, really believed this to be true.

Advertisers do a pretty good job convincing us that everyone else agrees with what they say we value. We ought to challenge those assumptions more. But until we do, girls are entering a competition advertisers suggest they will have lost by the time they reach their twenty-fifth birthday. Thus they enter a pattern of evaluation—how do I measure up against other women's beauty?

As an adolescent I felt overweight and unattractive. I remember scanning the room, evaluating the other girls in a class or at youth group, hoping to find someone heavier and more unattractive than I was. I longed for the ease and comfort the thin and pretty girls seemed to have with their bodies. The attractive girls were winning; I was losing. Or so I thought. In reality, most of them probably did the same scanning routine and found others to have the beauty they seemed to lack. While we may not believe we ascribe any more value to a beautiful woman than an unattractive one, beauty is what we are conditioned to notice, and beauty becomes the basis upon which we evaluate our own value as we compare ourselves to others.

Even when our daughters leave adolescence behind, they will continue to be evaluated on their external appearance. For instance, the clothes or mannerisms of women who are politicians or business leaders are often discussed by news writers, minimizing their role as a leader by drawing attention to their gender. Consider this *Newsweek* piece about Hong Kong's Chief Secretary Anson Chan.

> To her many admirers, Anson Chan is the conscience of Hong Kong. The city's future prosperity, they say, depends on the dimpled bureaucrat with the Shanghai pedigree, the Westminster manner and the Jackie O style. . . . Beneath the baby blue tailored jacket, the peach nail polish and the mesmerizing grace is a distinctly Hong Kong version of the iron lady. . . . Without ruffling her formal manner or mussing her perfectly coifed hair, the chief secretary has spoken out loudly and often for the kinds of political and civil rights that Tung has played down.[21]

This evaluation of Chan's physical appearance and manner seems out of place in an article about her economic and political maneuvering in Hong Kong. Yet it serves to remind us that women are judged by their appearance, not merely by what they accomplish.

To resist the temptation to judge each other and ourselves according to external appearance is to fight a tendency that is a result of the fall. Rachel was more beautiful than Leah and thus the more loved and desired wife. Esther was in competition to become queen with all the other beautiful virgins in Xerxes's kingdom. David "noticed a woman of unusual beauty taking a bath" (2 Sam. 11:2). He sent for Bathsheba, a married woman, committed adultery and then murder to cover up his sin. But, in the end, we learn that beautiful Bathsheba also becomes queen. The beautiful woman still wins.

As women exchanged their interdependent relationship with men for a dependent one, they also entered a competitive relationship, based on beauty, with other women. If a woman was to be dependent on a man, to ensure her survival she (or her father for her) needed to catch a man who would take care of her. Beauty seemed to be the number one variable in catching a man. (Also fertility, though few cultures have required a woman to prove her fertility before marriage.) Women with beauty were secure and also most likely to receive the most prominent places society offered women. Success for women historically has been based primarily not on ability but on external beauty. The pressure our daughters face to be beautiful is an old one, with the weight of history and tradition that stretches as far back as Rachel and Leah. Thus history pushes forward, ushering in revised versions, but the same value on beautiful women who can be set on a shelf and admired.

Beauty is good. God created us for beauty—both to desire it and to appreciate it. Yet a distorted focus on narrowly defined beauty undermines the body's ability to function as a vessel for the soul. Most girls will inevitably feel the pain of not measuring up to the beauty standard. However, parents can offer their daughters alternative images of their bodies, which can help them resist the pressure to focus too much on their external appearance.

THE BODY AS A SPORTS BOTTLE

When our girls were in elementary school, we would sometimes go to Champoeg Park and bike, throw softballs or Frisbees, or have "contests." The contest I most remember is when all five of us would lie down on the ground and see who could keep their legs lifted six inches off the ground the longest. The contest always came down to Mark and Megan. Megan always won. Mark asked her how she did it and why she always screamed, "Help me! Help me!" while holding her legs in the air. She said screaming kept her mind off how much her stomach was hurting. "Once I decided it was okay to hurt, I could keep my legs up as long as I needed to win," she explained.

Daughters and Sports

"Once I decided it was okay to hurt" sounds like something a football coach would tell his players. Yet women in sports are deciding it is okay to hurt too. The women on the 1996 Summer Olympic U.S.A. gymnastics team brought home gold and introduced new questions about women and sports. When Keri Strug was encouraged by her coach to attempt the second vault after severely spraining her ankle on the first vault just moments before, some wondered if the coach had gone too far. However, when a sick Michael Jordan (he had been vomiting all the previous night and day) played for the Chicago Bulls in one of the final 1997 National Basketball Association championship games against the Utah Jazz, he was regarded as heroic. Some want to suggest that we have lost sight of the purpose of sport when we endanger health for the sake of winning. Regardless of one's perspective about that, women who participate in sports are being taken more seriously and are given more legitimacy than in previous eras. Women are coming off the sidelines and exchanging cheerleading skirts and pom-poms for shorts and track or basketball shoes. God created bodies to *do* things—not just to be admired for their beauty. This focus on what a body can do physically through sports is a healthy alternative to obsession about what one's body looks like.

Historically, sports belonged to the masculine world of competition and aggression and were not considered suitable for the fragile composition of women. Women who did compete participated in feminine sports such as swimming, diving, figure skating, and gymnastics. Women who participated in soccer, basketball, track, and softball ran the risk (and still do) of being labeled lesbian because they were regarded as women who denied their female traits.[22]

Girls who play sports do better academically, are three times more likely to graduate from high school, 92 percent less likely to get involved in drugs, and 80 percent less likely to get pregnant.[23] Yet, in spite of these advantages, some myths parents grew up with about females and sports have sometimes kept parents from encouraging their daughters to participate in them.

Debunking Myths about Sports and Girls

One myth about exercise and girls was that vigorous exercise would harm girls' reproductive organs. This myth kept women inactive for years. It has been soundly refuted by the medical profession. On the contrary, girls and women who exercise typically experience less menstrual discomfort and have an easier time giving birth. Consider cultures where women are accustomed to hard physical labor. Stories are told of women working in the fields who stop briefly to give birth and then return to work that same morning or afternoon.

A second myth was that too much exercise would make a girl's body look muscled like a boy's body. As a young adolescent I was discouraged from biking too much, because biking would build up muscle in my thighs, which would then become boylike and unattractive. This myth is losing power as a deterrent for exercise as the new beauty standard for women includes being strong and well-toned. Society at large may not be ready to call women bodybuilders beautiful (when I show my classes a picture of a woman bodybuilder they are always repelled by it), but well-defined arm and leg muscles on women are now considered attractive.

A third myth perpetuated the belief that men are naturally better athletes because of biological differences, so women do not really belong in vigorous athletic programs. Women do have a harder time jamming a basketball than men, but mostly because women tend to be shorter. In some sports, women are behind men in performance because of lack of involvement over the years. Consider track. Men's running times have been improving since the beginning of the twentieth century. However, women's running times have been improving at more than twice the rate of men's running times. If this trend continues, some speculate that men's and women's track times will be comparable in the not-too-distant future.[24] But, returning to the image of God question—if God created our daughters and sons to be different, are there some differences when it comes to sports?

Feminization of Sports

One issue regarding the impact of typically feminine characteristics on sports addresses women's capacity for aggressiveness and competition. Can women be as competitive as men? If not, will they water down the competitive nature of sports? One assumption behind this question is that winning, and winning decisively, is the most important goal of sports. This assumption reflects an ideology of sports in keeping with values such as Manifest Destiny, strong independence, and individualism. Not all cultures agree with that assumption. In Japan, for instance, the perfect game of baseball ends in a tie. Everyone goes home happy, no one loses face. A team will win the series, but not by a landslide victory. Harmony is valued in Japanese culture and is reflected in their sports.[25]

The goal of sports does not have to be winning at all costs. Indeed, in elementary school, children learn the important goal is to play well and have fun, not whether or not they win or lose. Usually by high school this is replaced with winning as the important goal. Some of the potential benefits of teamwork become lost when the focus is only on winning.

While women and girls tend to approach sports with less of a "win-at-all-costs" mentality, more flexibility, cooperation, and concern with fair play,[26] female athletes *are* highly competitive and seek to find space on the sports pages and time in the broadcasting spots. The success of women's soccer in 1999 leads women's sports editors like Mary Ulmer to hope soccer might be the competitive breakthrough sport that legitimizes media coverage of women's sports in the United States.[27]

Another issue regarding the impact of girls on sports is whether or not girls should be allowed on high school boys' teams, such as wrestling. Since there is rarely enough interest in wrestling to create a whole team of girls, let alone a division, is it reasonable to allow Jane to wrestle on the boys' team?

This issue was addressed in a 1999 segment on the television news magazine *20/20* about girls and wrestling.[28] One high school athletic director believed girls ought to have a chance to wrestle— but on separate teams. He mustered up enough support in his district for separate girls' teams. He believed putting a girl on the boys' team introduced variables unrelated to wrestling. To ignore or minimize these variables, he believed, was irresponsible. The holds used in wrestling boldly invade personal space. The physical nature of wrestling adds stress to adolescent boys and girls already struggling to make peace with their changing bodies and redefine their relationships with each other. Coaches said boys would sometimes forfeit a match rather than wrestle a girl for a win. Partly, boys fear losing. When the most uncontested of differences between the sexes is at stake (that men are physically stronger than women) then losing to a girl becomes failure at being a boy. Partly, boys have been taught to treat girls gently and might be inhibited wrestling a girl as they would another boy.

Those who support girls in sports are not trying to take over and feminize male sports. Let boys and girls compete separately when physiological differences suggest this as appropriate. Opportunities are available for the sexes to play together. Little League baseball and community and church softball leagues provide coeducational experiences where males and females benefit from playing with each other in team sports. But meanwhile, celebrate women's involvement in sports and begin to challenge assumptions about sports that suggest winning and proving toughness are the most important outcomes for involvement in sports.

A focus on athletics does not mean girls will not care about their external appearance. In fact, since healthy bodies are often beautiful bodies, involvement in athletics is one way to value and attain beauty as it occurs in a healthy body. One benefit for girls who play sports is that they are learning to appreciate what their body enables them to do. They focus on how their body functions and what they can do to make it function better. They are learning that their body is valuable because of what it can do, not merely because of what it looks like.

The sports bottle body image also works for daughters who may not be active in sports but who are physically active and healthy. These daughters are also able to shift the focus away from pampering a body so that it looks good toward keeping one's body healthy so that it works well.

Daughters and Health

In the mid-1980s, we experienced the beginnings of the movement away from superthin and toward superfit. While the movement was supposed to relieve women of the pressure to conform to an unrealistically thin standard of beauty, many felt one unreal expectation was merely replaced with another. Hopefully, the pendulum will someday come to rest in a middle ground that encourages health without insisting on the Amazon look of the superfit.

As always, the consumer industry was not far behind shifting trends. Jazzercise and other aerobics classes became popular in the 1980s, as did memberships at sports clubs. Our churches also joined the fitness and weight loss movement and began offering aerobics classes using Christian music. Churches began to sponsor weight control programs, and numerous books emerged on the market to help convict and cure the overweight and underexercised. Two of the best-selling Christian books in 1999 were *Eat and Stay Thin* by Joyce Meyer and *The Weigh Down Diet* by Gwen Samblin. This is not a bad thing. Christianity is holistic and demands that heart, soul, mind, and body be directed toward God. Evangelicals have tended to compartmentalize body and soul. We worship with our soul on Sunday morning, while worrying about our body. "Does this dress fit too tight? Is my hair okay?"

Some evangelical subcultures are more holistic in their view of soul and body. African-Americans are more comfortable with their bodies than many European-Americans, and African-American churches show much more comfort with the use of their bodies in worship. Even King David danced before God. When we have fit bodies and sound minds we can better worship and serve the God who placed us as stewards over creation. For the body to serve the soul to the maximum of its potential it needs to be healthy. In recent years, the myth that slender equals fit has been exposed. It is healthier, medical researchers are saying, to be overweight and well-exercised than underweight and poorly exercised.

I saw my dad consistently exercise three days a week. And whether or not my siblings and I wanted to go, Dad would take us out to an empty field where he taught us to pass and catch a football and catch, throw, and hit a baseball. Granted, if Dad had had three sons and one daughter, things may have been different. As it was, God gave him three daughters and one son, and Dad couldn't play football or baseball without us. He modeled an active lifestyle and an appreciation for a body that enabled him to do much. Others encouraged and modeled an active lifestyle for me as well. In eighth grade, a father and his two sons invited my brother and me to run with them in the mornings, beginning a habit of jogging that I still enjoy.

Parents (as well as others) set the tone for healthy habits. Parents who take bike rides, play ball, and hike or walk with their children, model personal exercise habits, and cook and serve healthy foods will strongly influence their daughters' views toward the importance of health.

THE BODY AS SOOTHING BALM

A third vessel image is one that recognizes our bodies as the human hands God uses to infuse comfort and healing in others. With our bodies we bring comfort. I remember how powerful touch was to my friend Robin during her fight against cancer. I walked with her through her diagnostic testing and some of her treatments. One night, during the diagnostic work-up, I held her while we both cried and then prayed together. She said later, "You were Jesus to me. You were his hands and arms." We held hands in the hospital and sometimes at a café, wondering, sometimes what people thought, but deciding not to worry about it.

A loss for our daughters' generation is one already experienced by our sons some time ago. While it is still okay for girls to hug, they are held in suspicion if they hold hands or hug too much or for too long. Yet the pleasure of touch is a gift—God gave us skin that likes to touch and be touched. Fortunately, we can still celebrate friendship with hugs and handshakes. We are somewhat less comfortable using touch for one in emotional pain. Yet touch is often a soothing balm of comfort. When I worked as a home health nurse and visited the elderly, I would sit and hold their hands while I talked with them. This meant much to people who lived alone and received so little touch.

Our bodies function as the hands and feet of God when we use them to carry someone else's burden—relieving them of their backpack for a stint of hiking, helping them with yard work, working in a soup kitchen, or delivering food boxes. God uses our bodies as a tool to bless others through us.

In summary, God gave us bodies, beautiful bodies, that function best and look best when they are healthy. We are to use these bodies to bring God's healing and comfort to those in the world—to be his hands and feet of mercy and justice. Using our bodies as vessels of the soul is part of our role as stewards.

WHERE TO GO FROM HERE

Many of the following ideas focus on what we model for our daughters. Others involve mothers or fathers encouraging their daughters along a specific path.

1. Take an Interest in Women's Sports

Mothers, take an interest in women's sports! Men are still more likely to watch women's basketball than women are. Fathers are the ones who start coaching their daughters in softball and basketball. Fathers were the ones who pushed for Title IX to pass so that schools would be required to invest money in girls' sports. As a general rule, women in the United States are not fans of most women's sports. Women seem to prefer watching figure skating, "where the women don't look like athletes, and gymnastics, where the athletes don't look like women."[29] Daughters will take sports more seriously if they see it as something their mothers value.

2. Value the Body as a Tool

Mary Pipher said:

> It makes me angry, the needless suffering by women who are putting energy into losing weight when they could be focusing on making themselves better people, making the world a better place. We need a revolution in our values.[30]

142

Strong daughters will value their bodies for what their bodies enable them to do. If they can look at their thighs and say, "I appreciate the strength you give me to run, to play, to work," rather than, "I hate my fat thighs," they are beginning to reclaim what it meant for them to be given bodies to serve their souls. When daughters are young, help them see and appreciate what their bodies enable them to do. "Isn't it great that God gave you a nose so that you can smell that fresh bread baking?"

3. Give Daughters an Active and Healthy Childhood

When the girls were young, and Mark was out of town at a conference, I would sometimes take them to the beach house Mark's parents owned. Every trip, we spent one day walking along the beach or hiking the Cascade Head Trail. When we walked along the beach we'd leave the house mid-morning and walk the four miles to Neskowin. We'd stop along the way and eat trail mix (one of the highlights of the trip). We always ate lunch in a little café and then walked the four miles back home, again stopping along the way to rest and eat trail mix. Once home, the girls would take turns playing in the bathtub or take naps. The first time we hiked the Cascade Head Trail, Megan had just turned three and wanted me to carry her part of the way. But then Danielle said, "Mama, Megan is doing such a good job! We'll have to tell Papa!" Megan didn't want to be carried after that and never asked for a ride again. Without knowing it then, I was instilling the value of an active physical life in my daughters—passing on to them a value that had been instilled in me by my father.

There are at least two ways parents can encourage an active life for their daughters. The first is to be active with them, another is to enroll them in community park programs. Either way challenges the messages they receive that their bodies are only for looking at. However, being active with our daughters also models a value of activity outside of organized sports or programs. Even now, Sarah or Danielle and I will head out for a four-mile walk from time to time because we like walking, not because we have to stay trim.

Parents should focus on helping their daughters value healthy, fit bodies rather than beautiful, skinny ones.

4. Attend to Looks Enough but Not Too Much

The goal is not to ignore or teach our daughters to ignore their external appearance, but to keep appearance balanced so it does not become an obsession. Parents may not have much to contribute at the point of adolescence when peers become the powerful voice that affirms or tears down confidence. Up until adolescence parents can build confidence based on personhood while attending to style issues enough so that confidence is not undermined by critical preadolescent peers. In adolescence parents can support their daughters' efforts to fit in by encouraging them to find a style that gives them confidence. Parents shouldn't be too quick to cast off social norms of cosmetic and clothing attire for their daughters. The daughters who are least obsessed with looks will likely be those who fit in with their peers without being overly concerned about being most attractive and stylish. Mark and I desire that our daughters be neither too attractive nor too unattractive so as to draw attention to themselves on the basis of their looks.

5. Focus on Characteristics Daughters Have Control Over

Our daughters will get enough reinforcement for the characteristics over which they have no control; they will get far less for those over which they have control. Compliment your daughter for some character trait or behavior and then watch her response. Compliment her knack at poetry, or her recent responsible choices, or how she greets the clerk in the store. She will be encouraged and blessed by your words. Her face will show it. To reinforce our daughters' kindness, confidence, and competence gives value to the essence of who they are, not what they look like.

6. Examine Your Own Critical Tendencies

Unfortunately, I modeled a self-critical attitude for my daughters. They all learned that what I weighed on a given day was immensely important in gauging whether or not I was going to feel good about myself that day. I would change that if I could. My daughters learned that much of my perceived value came from how I felt about my external appearance, a trait some of them have ascribed to themselves.

Some daughters learn the critical habit of judging others by their looks. I've seen families where yearly get-togethers include an analysis of some members' weight gain or loss—"Doesn't it look like Jennifer has gained weight?" This critical analysis reinforces our daughters' fears that what they look like will be the most important variable used to evaluate them.

7. Celebrate What Is, Not What Should Be

Some of our daughters, and some of us, have broken bodies. Some are born with deformities or bear the consequences of diseases or accidents that have taken away the ability to use their bodies as God intended. Some cannot run or walk or feed themselves. Some cannot see or hear. But even the most disabled have a window that opens their soul to experience the world. My niece, Faith, cannot walk, feed herself, read, or carry on a conversation with another. Yet she can experience the pleasures of sun and wind on her face, see the beauty of creation, relish the sound of music, and feel the joy of human touch. She is a content child who feels loved and expresses love.

Our challenge is to bear the pain of those with broken bodies, to mourn with them, to work with them to enhance their ability to function, to help them experience the joys of life through avenues their bodies leave open to them. Helen Keller, who was both blind and deaf said, "Life is either a daring adventure or nothing. To keep our faces toward change and behave like free spirits in the presence of fate is strength undefeatable."[31] We are not only in a position to help people with disabilities, we are also in a position to learn from them. Those with broken bodies who are reconciling themselves to their limitations yet who "behave like free spirits in the presence of fate" have much to teach those of us with more whole bodies who yet struggle with contentment. To live life fully within our limitations is to accept, work with, and celebrate what is.

CONCLUSION

God created us with limitations. These bodies that house our souls cannot fly or swim underwater indefinitely; we cannot keep them from aging or dying. We cannot grow back a spinal cord that has been broken or an arm that has been severed. We cannot see as well at night as we can during the day; we cannot hear or smell as well as many animals. However, God gave us phenomenal bodies that enable us to do much with our souls. We can worship God by raising our hands and voices in singing or by raking leaves for someone unable to rake his or her own. We can read and study, carry burdens, hold infants, hug. We can build and teach, plant and harvest, mend broken bodies and be God's tools to mend broken souls.

Our bodies are a great gift. How wonderful that God encased us in such bodies as these! We can choose to look at our still-too-thick-thighs and be thankful that they are strong and have carried us many miles and through many years.

While God created us to appreciate beautiful bodies, cultural norms of beauty make it far too easy for women to set their hopes on attaining a particular standard of beauty, so that they forfeit health and contentment to achieve it. By encouraging our daughters to be athletic and healthy, reminding them that their body is valuable just because God gave it to them to inhabit, we begin to offer an alternative perspective of their body. By showing them there is much a body enables them to experience and do, we can perhaps draw them away from the temptation to condemn and obsess about the external packaging of their body and draw them toward a thankfulness for it and a celebration of what it can do.

CHAPTER SEVEN

SEXUAL ESSENCE

August after Sixth Grade

I woke to the
red rose of womanhood
My sister helped me
don the paraphernalia

Thorns
tore my thighs
and searing confusion
conceive me a woman
now

Awakening,
I closed my eyes and inhaled the
rosebud's fragrance.

I STARTED MY PERIOD the summer after sixth grade. Kathy, a sister who is a year older than I, helped me figure out how to attach myself to the pad and belt gizmo menstruating girls used in 1969. The red rose of womanhood. I was a woman now. Even with the bloody yuckiness, the awkwardness of the elastic belt, the embarrassment of having to cancel out of the Junior Lifesaving Swim Class—even with the cramps—I relished the thought that I was a woman now. I could make a baby now.

Our daughters' sexual essence is much broader than attitudes and behavior regarding sexual activity. At the core, sexual essence is about being female. Girls' souls come attached to bodies that menstruate and have the capacity to bear and nurse children. Our daughters' sexual essence is also about culture—primarily what culture says regarding the value of being female. Developing a healthy sense of sexuality comes from understanding how a broken culture and broken people yield brokenness in our daughters' images of themselves as sexual beings. Part of the task of growing strong daughters is becoming partners with God to redeem our daughters' sense of who they are as sexual beings.

THE CORE OF FEMALE SEXUALITY

On the simplest level, our daughters experience pleasure through their sexuality as they work and play alongside boys who may approach play and problem-solving differently (which may either delight or frustrate them!). They experience pleasure as they notice and enjoy the differences between their bodies and boys' bodies, appreciating the fine features God gave the male gender. Many of our daughters will grow to experience pleasure through intimate lovemaking, which brings not only physical satisfaction but also children. Sexuality is good—a wonderful gift that drives us toward intimacy with another and reflects the intimate communion we long to have with God. However, like all good things, the fall led to distortions of our sexuality. Growing our daughters to be strong includes helping them understand and resist fallen, broken views of sexuality while embracing a positive view of sexuality that reflects the image of God within them.

Female Sexuality as a Curse

One way our culture has distorted sexuality is by associating bad things with being female. For centuries Jewish men said, as part of their daily prayers, "Thank you, God, that I was not born a woman." As discussed in an earlier chapter, when boys were asked what they would think of being girls, their responses were overwhelmingly negative—some even said they would commit suicide.

When boys' bodies change into men's bodies, the changes are usually accompanied with positive connotations about what manhood means for them. However, girls become women with much more anxiety. Developing breasts are an embarrassment, and menstruation is the curse that "lasts until you are too old to enjoy life anymore anyway." Some women resent that they are the ones who have to get pregnant and birth children. A few go so far as to welcome technology that would allow fetuses to develop fully from embryos to newborns outside a woman's body so women would not have to be encumbered with reproductive tasks.

The message our daughters receive is that being born a female is unfortunate. This belief is held not only by many boys and men but also by many girls and women. A subtext of this belief is the idea that the only (or at least most) valuable thing females do is reproduce. Some women fear embracing motherhood because they do not want to be defined or valued wholly by reproductive abilities. They want to be allowed to contribute beyond their ability to bear children, and they fear motherhood will strip away whatever credibility they may have in some other realm.

Our daughters' sexuality needs to be restored. To believe it is worse to be female than male undermines the uniqueness of how they represent an important part of God's image. In addition, the cultural belief that the most valuable thing females can do is reproduce reduces their worth to that of a reproductive machine. This may cause them to resist or resent motherhood, mistaking the honor of being able to create life as a curse that limits what they can do with their abilities and gifts.

Female Sexuality as a Blessing

Sarah came home from kindergarten one day and told me she was *never, never* going to have babies. I asked her why not. She said her teacher said that it hurt really really bad, because Eve sinned and God made it so it would hurt. I wondered if this was the teacher's sex education curriculum for kindergarten: "Scare the kid in kindergarten, and she'll never let a man near her." I tried to recast this story in a more redemptive light, but Sarah's teacher was the final authority for the remainder of that year. I grieved the fear Sarah had been given for having babies.

Some women continue to fear and feel threatened by the approach of motherhood even as they are pregnant. Some say they fear they will lose themselves when they become charged with the care of an utterly dependent infant. Others say that they are not "themselves" while they are pregnant and describe pregnancy as an alien process taking over their bodies. This alienation or inability to identify with themselves as pregnant women may reflect a discomfort with that part of one's sexual identity. Some women are not sure how to embrace the life-giving aspect of being female, or what it means that God has given them a body that has the power to grow, birth, and nurse babies. They do not know how motherhood fits with the rest of who they are.

Other women love being pregnant. For nine months they feel a special ability to create and participate with God in the bringing of life. They love the growing of their abdomen, and the stretching, stirring movements of the child in their womb. Some women even love giving birth. The process of bringing forth a child into the world is so magnificent and powerful that the pain is lost in the wonder of the birth. Women who love pregnancy and the anticipation of motherhood do not feel overly threatened by this life-changing, identity-altering experience. I suspect that women who do not feel threatened by motherhood already have a strong sense of identity. Some, perhaps most, of these women see motherhood *as* their primary identity and are glad to experience its fulfillment. Other women have a strong sense of identity aside from being mothers and thus embrace motherhood without fearing that they will lose other aspects of who they are by doing so.

How a daughter feels about being female and her potential to embrace motherhood will be shaped by multiple factors. On the list will be her perceptions of her own mother's feelings about motherhood and being female. A daughter's view of pregnancy and childbirth will also be shaped by the stories she hears—from aunts, grand-mothers, friends, and neighbors. The media culture's values and ideas about menstruation, pregnancy, birth, and motherhood will shape girls' perceptions too. Few of our culture's depictions of pregnancy and birthing mothers are positive. Most show an uncomfortably bloated and bitchy woman who eventually gives birth while hys-terically screaming insults to those around her—especially her hus-band. One exception to this image is that portrayed by women like Demi Moore, Lisa Rinna, and Cindy Crawford, who have posed nude while pregnant. We are challenged to recast our image of preg-nant women as fat and unattractive to instead being sexy and beau-tiful. Of course the flip side is that now women feel added pressure to be sexy, thin, and beautiful while pregnant. Depictions of moth-erhood in the media offer a mixed assortment of views that reflect the ambiguity and ambivalence our culture has about motherhood.

In contrast to the predominantly negative view of femaleness present in the dominant culture, there is a positive view of female-ness found in a countercultural religious movement—the goddess worshippers. While this small movement is far outside Christian-ity, goddess-worship at its core redeems female sexuality by valu-ing the intrinsic worth of the life-giving process. Different honors are bestowed women depending on what stage of fertility they are in. For instance, menstruating women are celebrated and honored as they wear red ribbons during their period.[1]

A concept in systems theory suggests that whenever a vital part is excised from the whole, it will eventually find a way to reinsert itself. So it is with the value of female sexuality. When distortions of a broken culture affected our ability to value and honor how women were created as life-givers and co-stewards, groups formu-lated their own religious structures to affirm that which was being denied elsewhere. Some of this denial has been related directly to women's sexuality. For instance, besides the daily Jewish prayer thanking God for being born a man, following every menstrual cycle, a Hebrew woman was required to present an offering—a whole burnt offering as well as a sin offering—as atonement before God for her menstrual discharge (Lev. 15:19–30). Although the cycle was a normal part of life, a God-given part of her sexuality,

Jewish tradition required her to make atonement for it every month. Although some biblical scholars see the woman's obligation to offer these sacrifices as a symbol of her right to come before God on her own behalf to make atonement for her sins, to the casual reader it appears as though she is required to make atonement for menstruating. Thus, as Jewish tradition and law are combined with examples of females in the Old Testament being poorly treated and devalued, we can begin to understand why some women reject Christianity and create religious structures that overtly celebrate the life-giving ability of female sexuality.

The effect of a culture's views of female sexuality may also influence biological processes. For instance, premenstrual syndrome is more common in cultures where menstruation is perceived as a nuisance than in cultures where menstruation is celebrated as a reminder of the life-giving potential in women. The skeptic may wonder if, in these cultures, symptoms of PMS are still present but are not identified with menstruation. Perhaps. But maybe they are *not* experienced at all because of a social climate that regards this aspect of female sexuality as positive rather than negative. Regardless, parents can help craft in their daughters a positive view of their sexuality by affirming menstruation as representing the life-giving status God has granted them.

Having children is, to some extent, a social responsibility. Couples have to be about the business of making babies for the society to continue. A religious sect called the Shakers abstained from sex altogether, and, predictably, the sect did not survive very long. If a group fails to reproduce itself either biologically or through in-group migration (e.g. adoption, conversion, or immigration), it will fail to survive. Thus, to reproduce our culture, we need women to bear children and parents to socialize them according to culture's values. The value of reproducing is so strong that couples who choose not to have children are often perceived as selfish and irresponsible.

Perhaps because the continuing birth of babies is a social necessity, the management of pregnancy and birth by outside experts became desirable and expected. The medical community decided birth outcomes could be improved by providing standardized care. Providing standardized care did, for the most part, enhance the physical well-being for infants and mothers. However, an unintended by-product of sending women to clinics for care during their pregnancy and to hospitals to have babies is that many women feel alienated from and uncomfortable with pregnancy and birth—and, to some extent, motherhood. Since pregnancy and birth became "conditions" needing medical supervision and intervention, motherhood, to some degree, also became a condition needing supervision and intervention to "get it right."

A culture that treats menstruation, pregnancy, and birth as unnatural conditions to be endured results in women who have a diminished sense of their sexuality and a distrust in their ability to do the job of reproducing well. I can't help but believe that God intended women to experience honor as the ones gifted with the privilege of bearing and nursing babies.

Motherhood is given high honor in the Scriptures when God is described as a mother giving birth, nursing, or nurturing her children. When Moses speaks to the people of Israel, he says, "You were unmindful of the Rock that bore you; you forgot the God who gave you birth" (Deut. 32:18 NRSV). Earlier in the same chapter, God is described as nursing Israel with honey from the crags and oil from flinty rock.[2] In Isaiah 66:12–13, God says of Israel, "Her children will be nursed at her breasts, carried in her arms, and treated with love. I will comfort you there as a child is comforted by its mother." God is also described as a mother eagle hovering over her young (Deut. 32:11) and a hen gathering her chicks under the protection of her wings (Matt. 23:37). Images like these restore a sense of blessing and uniqueness that women are image-bearers of God who birth, nurse, and comfort children even as God births, nurses, and comforts nations. Even the birth process itself is given significance as Jesus uses the metaphor of new birth in John 3 to describe to a seeking Pharisee named Nicodemus the process of coming to God.

With the capacity to give birth came the capacity to do motherhood right. Again, that capacity has been distorted by brokenness. Mothers who were never nurtured have to learn to nurture. Women who feel alienated and uncomfortable with their reproductive abilities do not know how to listen to the cues of their bodies. Women need to learn to trust the intuitive messages and listen to what their bodies are trying to say. Sometimes, listening to the cues of your body means it is time to lay down and rest, because the making of a baby is demanding. Some women feel thirsty as they sit down to nurse, a cue that it is time to drink, because the nursing of a baby demands extra fluids. To give birth to children and have the capacity to mother them well is a powerful and wonderful affirmation of female sexuality.

Reclaiming a positive sense of our sexuality and instilling in our daughters a positive sense of their sexuality does not have to lead to home births attended by midwives (though a number of women do reclaim childbirth this way). However, parents, especially mothers, need to reflect on their own feelings about menstruation, pregnancy, and birth and redeem these for themselves before they can recast the negative vision of female sexuality the culture offers their daughters. Being female is a wonderful gift of God. It is not a curse to be borne by women.

Notions of Broken Sexuality

Because human cultures have distorted God's sense of female and male sexuality, our daughters are at risk for being wounded in two significant ways. First, they are wounded as they learn about and internalize a distorted view of their sexual essence. Second, and far more severe, is the wounding that occurs when they are victims of sexual violence.

Internalizing the Distortions

When girls and women are not being defined according to their beauty, they are often being defined according to their sexuality. Our western culture approaches female sexuality by disembodying the whole person and assigning pieces of the body as sexual objects. Thus, "Did you see those hooters that just walked by?" reduces a woman walking down Main Street to one identifying feature—her breasts.

Our daughters will blush or cringe. Perhaps they feel flattered; perhaps they feel devalued for being evaluated on the basis of their breasts or legs or buttocks. Or maybe they feel confused because they experience both flattery and devaluation. Feeling both is a natural outcome of a fallen, broken society. What was designed for beauty and pleasure has become sullied. Our daughters feel good when they get attention, because God created women with an intrinsic appreciation for the beauty and pleasure of healthy, well-proportioned bodies. So of course our daughters feel good when those body parts are evaluated positively. However, the good is sullied as our daughters sense that it is only, or primarily, their sexual body parts that make them desirable or give them value as a person.

Breasts, buttocks, and legs become the focal point on billboards, in magazine ads, and on television commercials selling products that may or may not have anything to do with breasts, buttocks, or legs. Often, sexy women are shown as available and eager to please men who drive certain cars, wear a certain brand of shoes, or use the right deodorant. In cases where the product is related to a woman's body, the ads become more blatant in their devaluing of women. An ad by Wonderbody Fanny Shapers shows a woman in Wonderbody underwear and nothing else, though she modestly covers her naked bosom with her arms. The copy reads simply, "Learn to manage your assets." The message: A woman's primary asset is her sexuality. This ad attempts humor with a play on words which suggest a woman's buttocks are her assets. Whatever other gifts and abilities she has are secondary to her asset as a sexual female.

One ad by itself is silly. But, as Jean Kilbourne discusses in her film documentary, "Still Killing Us Softly," the effect of being exposed to these subtle ads over and over again distorts the way women think about themselves, as well as the way men think about women.[3] Consider the posture of women in ads. They are often lying on a bed or on the ground, bending over at the waist, or kneeling in a sexually provocative way. In the early 1990s, Calvin Klein was accused of using underage models and soft porn to sell products. At least some of the public assumed he would respond to the negative press by changing his advertisement techniques. But Klein knows sex sells, and he likely believes those who don't like his ads are too small a minority to hurt his business. This was evidenced by a 1997 ad in *Teen* magazine that showed a girl who appeared to be fourteen or fifteen wearing Calvin Klein panties and a cropped tank top. She sat on the ground, leaning back on her arms, with her long, bare legs bent slightly at the knee and spread apart. The sexual imagery was not very subtle.

Our daughters pick up cues and values about sexuality from a culture that has broken and distorted God's intention for sexuality. These values need to be countered so our daughters can emerge from adolescence with a healthy view of their sexuality. Following are several values strong daughters learn to challenge.

"I Need to Be Beautiful to Be Sexual"

Beauty has come to equal sexuality in our culture. According to media representations, those who are beautiful are the only ones who are truly sexy, as well as the only ones who can have good sex. The movies rarely depict a woman over thirty-five going to bed with a man and having rapturous sex, though we often see men in their sixties having rapturous sex with women in their twenties. When women over thirty-five have sex, it is usually to ordinary husbands or losers, and their sex is made to look silly. Their desire to have sex is an embarrassment to their children (or whoever else is part of the scene). Viewers are supposed to be embarrassed, perhaps disgusted, as well. It is not surprising that girls often find it disgusting to think that people who are overweight or over forty have sex. I asked a middle-schooler why it bothers her to think of older people having sex and she said, "It's gross because they are *old*." The message is that sex is for the beautiful and young—and you better take it while you still can.

Parents can help daughters confront this myth by challenging media stereotypes when they see them and limiting their daughters' exposure to negative ads and articles in teen magazines. Parents who have experienced the deep intimacy and sexual satisfaction that comes with knowing and loving a partner over a period of many years relay this to their daughters by living out an example of intimacy in marriage and through conversations that span the child-rearing years.

"I Need to Be Sexy to Be Liked by Boys"

Early on in the brokenness of our human history, girls got the idea that they needed boys to like them. Anthropologists say this is part of our human nature. To propagate and ensure the survival of the human race, a female needed to catch the attention of a strong male who would be able to help protect and provide for her off-spring. One way females accomplished this was by wearing certain kinds of clothes and acting in certain flirtatious ways. If our daughters follow typical cultural norms, they will act and dress in ways that show off their sexuality.

Our youth culture teaches preteens to dress to be sexy. Before their breasts are much more than buds, they are learning how to dress provocatively. But of course it's not called provocative. Rather the style is sold as: Fun! In style! Cute! All the rage!

As a mother of daughters, I was not too distraught when the baggy look came back. Whether or not one liked the look, baggi-ness offered one way out for girls who wanted to dress "in style" without having to dress provocatively. Certainly our daughters can dress in ways that are fun, cute, comfortable, and stylish without dressing seductively. There have always been alternatives to the pressure to conform.

Moreover, our daughters can be encouraged to ask themselves whom they want to dress for and how they want to be perceived. Fitting in is as important for our daughters as it was for us. God created us to be social creatures and with a desire to fit in with our peers. Fortunately, our diverse culture accepts much in the way of fashion these days. Being "different" is a key stylistic value (and hard to manage when everyone is so quick to conform to some-one's latest attempt at being unique). But since different is in, our daughters can find many ways to dress uniquely that do not make it easy to reduce them, or parts of their bodies, to sexual objects. A daughter who can internalize her value as a person who is sexual will feel different about herself and likely make different clothing and behavior choices than a daughter who sees herself primarily as a sexual being. The difference is subtle. The first daughter focuses primarily on herself as a person; the second focuses primarily on herself as a sexual being.

How girls relate to others is another way daughters are encouraged to be sexy. Playful teasing or flirting between the sexes is fun, and most of us, if we admit it, remember and recognize the titillating fun of teasing. Unfortunately, flirtatious behavior is easily misunderstood and can escalate into unwanted sexual experiences. Melissa, a college student, was raped by Jeff after following him to his room in the early morning hours. She said they had spent a number of hours talking and had playfully joked about "things of a sexual nature." When he wanted to progress from making out to intercourse, she said no. Melissa says she said no repeatedly. Jeff said, "I didn't think she meant it." He would say her prior behavior had communicated an interest in and desire for sex. This scenario repeats itself over and over on our college campuses. Our daughters need to know how their behaviors could be interpreted. When Melissa was asked why she went to Jeff's room, she had no answer. Hindsight has taught her what she needed the foresight to know.

Furthermore, our daughters need to learn to be assertive and clear with boys with whom they interact. They need to know that a man never has the right to force himself on a woman. The goal is not to make our daughters fearful but to encourage them to be intentional. Girls and women who are aware of their sexuality, intentional about their choices, and who have confidence in their voice, will be at lower risk for unwanted sexual experiences than those who lack confidence and find themselves caught off guard by their sexuality and male responses to it.

"Sex is Recreational; It Doesn't Have to Mean Anything"

While girls growing up in Christian churches may know the above statement is not true, they will have to be able to defend it with something stronger than "my church doesn't believe in premarital sex." We are helped by the presence of an unfortunate array of sexually transmitted diseases, AIDS being the most frightening. But avoiding sex only because it may bring disease is not adequate as a rationale. Why do Christians believe sex belongs only in marriage? Why do we insist that it *does* matter if you have sex with multiple partners? Upon what principles do we base our values? Parents need to help their daughters answer these questions in ways that are meaningful and can be defended.

Learning about Sex and Sexuality in All the Wrong Places

College women talk about finding themselves in a "situation" without a plan. It is tough to be intentional and thoughtful about expressing one's sexuality appropriately when one is trying to make up the rules as one goes along. Likewise, it is tough for a twelve-year-old who has just begun to menstruate to feel good about her sexuality if she has only been given vague cues about the awfulness of it all.

If daughters are not taught about their sexuality from parents, they will learn about it on the playgrounds, in the streets, and from teen magazines and the television and movie industries. The messages communicated from the playground-street-magazine-TV culture reflect two major themes. One theme reflects our postmodern belief that there are no absolute values regarding sexuality in our culture. Since there is no one particular value set that is any better than any other, each girl is to determine her own values. The other theme flows from this one and suggests that the best value regarding sex is the one that says sex is for pleasure—eat, drink, and be merry, for tomorrow we die. In both cases, God's design for human sexuality is substituted with distorted values or a lack of value. In either case, our daughters sense a normlessness and uncertainty about their sexuality arising out of our brokenness as a culture. Researchers Sol Gordon and Judith Gordon conclude that children whose parents are able to talk to them about their sexuality are in a better position to maneuver through adolescence in a sexually responsible way than children whose parents cannot talk to them.[4]

Mark and I have always talked with our girls about our thoughts and values regarding sexuality. There was no specific point when we had "The Talk." When they asked questions, we answered them honestly, though gauged the answer according to their developmental age. Along the way they got a clear picture of our ideas about menstruation, childbearing, and sexual expression inside and outside of marriage.

As I talk with my daughters, we inevitably discuss their relationships with boys. Sometimes the topic settles on physical expression in relationships. While our daughters know Mark's and my values, we have not insisted that they share them. We will have parented them well if they are intentional about choosing values that reflect God's call on their lives and their responsibility as image-bearers of God. We encourage them to be specific about their values and to have someone hold them accountable for the values they set.

Our daughters can be encouraged to develop values and views of their sexuality based on an understanding of God's good gift and intention in creating them as sexual beings. But only if we offer it to them. We cannot count on our churches or schools to do it for us. Although there is general agreement (among both Christians and non-Christians) that sex education should begin in the home, schools and churches have become increasingly involved as parents feel uncomfortable or unable to discuss sexuality with their children. Forty percent of the women surveyed in *The Janus Report on Sexual Behavior* said they learned about sex at home, followed by 33 percent who learned about sex from peers. School ranked third with 25 percent and church fourth with 2 percent.[5] A student and I attempted to build on this finding. One of our survey questions asked teens who attended a large suburban high school to rank the level of influence peers, family, school, and church had on their sexual behavior. We found our ranking of which group *influenced* sexual behaviors the most matched the Janus report's finding on *where* boys learn about sex. High school juniors and seniors said peers influenced their sexual behavior the most, followed by family, then school, and finally church. This may be significant. If the primary source for our daughters' information is also going to be the source which exerts the most influence, then parents who would like to be that influence will do best to talk, and become comfortable talking, with their daughters about sex.

Much of our ability or lack of ability to talk about sex comes from our own family experience. However, old habits can be broken and new habits learned. Our friends Stan and Brenna Jones have written a book titled *How and When to Tell Your Kids About Sex.*[6] They have also developed a related series of books aimed directly at helping parents teach their children about sex at different ages. These books, and others like them, provide a good resource for parents who find it difficult to talk to their children about sex. If parents don't teach their daughters about their sexuality, their daughters will find a world ready and eager to fill in the gaps.

The Wounding of Sexual Violence

"The worst thing about being a woman is we get raped and killed," a ten-year-old said, explaining to her interviewer why she would rather be a man than a woman. "Women can get killed by their prettiness," she said.[7] A culture that teaches that women are valued primarily for their sexuality will lead to women becoming targets of sexual violence. One convicted rapist told an interviewer:

> Rape is a man's right. If a woman doesn't want to give it, the man should take it. Women have no right to say no. Women are made to have sex. It's all they are good for. Some women would rather take a beating, but they always give in; it's what they are for.[8]

This is an extreme and unusual perspective; most men detest sexual violence and the barrier of distrust it creates toward men in general. One male college student told me, "I hate that there is sexual violence against women. I don't like that women fear me just because I am male." Yet a subtle and pervasive belief that men are entitled to sex with women who are made for sex emerges predictably from within our culture and has led to sexual violence. Some of this belief is a by-product of a culture where men are the ones in control—the leaders of and providers for the women who are to submissively follow. Some of this belief is a by-product of a culture with few restraints on the sexual violence depicted in all forms of mass media.

By the time our daughters reach their eighteenth birthday, an estimated 27 percent of them will have been sexually abused.[9] In 63 percent of reported rape cases, the perpetrator will have been someone she knew, 80 percent if she was raped under the age of twelve. Sometimes the perpetrator will be the boy or man next door, a total stranger, or a boyfriend. Sometimes the perpetrator will be a brother, an uncle, or a father. The incidence of sexual abuse is difficult to determine because much of the abuse girls and women experience goes unreported, especially those incidents that occur within the hidden confines of the home.

Two types of families are at risk for incest. One is the chaotic family encumbered with many problems that go back several generations. They tend to have a low socioeconomic status and low education and vocational achievement. Problems with the law and alcohol or drug abuse are common.[10] We hear about these incest victims, and our daughters likely know some.

The second type of family at risk for incest is the normal-appearing family. This family looks great from the outside. It is usually financially stable, in good standing in the community, and often structured with the man as the head of the house. But, inside these homes, parents are emotionally immature and needy, and a drug or alcohol abuse problem is often present.[11] The sexual abuse that occurs within Christianity often occurs in these kinds of homes. Our daughters know these victims, play with them, are them.

When our daughters experience sexual violence, the core of who they are is broken, sullied, and lost. But our God is a God who restores brokenness, washes clean that which is sullied, and redeems that which is lost.

EMBRACING A REDEEMED SEXUALITY

The fight to redeem sexuality for our daughters is embraced by a number of different groups, both Christian and secular. They agree that enabling girls to say no to sex, preventing sexual abuse, aiding their recovery from sexual abuse, and enhancing women's enjoyment of sex are important aspects of redeeming sexuality.

Saying No to Sex

Girls today have sex for all kinds of reasons—to fit in, to feel loved, or because they didn't know how to say no. Seldom do teenage girls have sex because of the sexual pleasure it brings. While motives may differ, Christians who otherwise are uncomfortable with feminists, join them in the battle to teach our daughters to say no to sex. Feminists (both Christian and non-Christian) are concerned that girls have sex for the wrong reasons and are committed to empowering girls with the ability to say no. Both groups want girls to be able to resist and refuse participating in sex even though cultural values have pressured them to say yes. While the Christian feminist values chastity until marriage for both men and women, the non-Christian feminist would assert that a girl should not have sex until she is mature enough to understand the implications of sex. Christians (both feminist and not) value the faithfulness and loyalty of keeping sex reserved for two people who commit to each other for life. Sexual faithfulness demonstrates loyalty, trustworthiness, an ability to be patient, and a desire to experience a communion of intimacy that reflects our ability to be intimately in communion with God.

There does seem to be a turning of the tide in the battle to decrease teenage sexual activity. In the late 1990s, a *Newsweek* article quoted teens around the country about their decision to remain virgins. Author Michele Ingrassia says,

> A lot of kids are putting off sex, and not because they can't get a date. They've decided to wait, and they're proud of their chastity, not embarrassed by it. Suddenly, virgin geek is giving way to virgin chic.[12]

The teens surveyed cited a number of reasons they were choosing to wait. Some were just on hold until they met the right person, although 71 percent said they wanted to wait until they got married to have sex. Eighty-seven percent said they wanted to wait until they were in a committed relationship; 84 percent wanted to wait until they were older. Eighty-five percent worried about sexually transmitted diseases, with 83 percent worrying specifically about AIDS. Another 84 percent worried about pregnancy. Forty percent said they abstained for religious reasons. The tide may be turning.

Christian youth are also renewing their pact with chastity. During the summer of 1994, the campaign called "True Love Waits" drew 22,000 teens and young adults to Washington, D.C. They brought 210,000 pledge cards with them from others who had made a promise to abstain from sex until they got married. At another gathering in February of 1996, 18,000 teens and young adults brought 340,000 pledge cards. The "True Love Waits" campaign is an ongoing attempt to encourage chastity through conferences and conventions both nationally and internationally.[13] The sex part of our daughters' sexuality is being redeemed by pockets within culture that see the need to do so.

But sexuality goes beyond the choice about whether to have sex. Restoring sexuality is also about teaching our daughters how to protect themselves and helping them recover when they become victims of unwanted sexual experiences.

Dealing with Unwanted Sexual Experiences

Parents whose daughters have been molested often feel guilty for not being able to protect them. Thus parents carry two pains— their own sadness, grief, and guilt as well as pain for their daughters, whose ability to feel safe, to trust men, and to embrace their sexual essence have been crippled.

Girls who have been sexually abused learn not to trust the men they are told should protect and care for them. Our culture is broken. Little girls should be able to grow up feeling safe, rather than wishing they were boys so they wouldn't get raped or killed. Parents want to protect their daughters from the ugliness of a broken, sinful world, yet girls need to be prepared for it. We need to teach our daughters what is safe and unsafe, what is good touch and bad touch. To reduce their vulnerability as targets, we need to affirm their ability to be bold and assertive in nonsexual situations so they can be bolder and more assertive in sexual ones. We need to have a listening, trusting relationship with our daughters where they talk to us, knowing they can come for help should they ever be victims of sexual abuse.

The effect of sexual abuse on girls depends on several factors. These factors include the length of time over which the abuse occurred, the girl's relationship to the abuser, whether or not (and how soon) she was able to seek help, support, and counsel, and whether or not she has a strong sense of resiliency. Parents can strive to develop the latter two. As parents work to have relationships with their daughters that encourage open communication, they build a foundation that makes it possible for daughters to disclose abuse. So much shame is associated with abuse that victims often remain silent. Girls believe the abuse is their fault, that they could have avoided it. Parents can build resilience in daughters by reinforcing their picture of themselves as strong women. As they face and overcome lesser challenges that are beyond their control, they learn they are capable and resilient.

Keeping the Value of Virginity in Perspective

When one of my daughters was thirteen years old, she and I were together in the car when the song "Freshman" came on the radio. It's a song about a couple in high school who had sex; the girl got pregnant and committed suicide. The singer is grieving and regretting (I think) the choices they made as freshmen. After the song my daughter said, "I would commit suicide if I ever got pregnant." I asked her why. "Because it would be so bad to have had sex before I got married, and it would be easier to die than to have people find out about that." I was startled and dismayed by her reaction to sex and pregnancy before marriage. I told her I didn't think getting pregnant was the *worst* thing that could happen to her—nor having sex before she got married. While getting pregnant would certainly change the course of her life in dramatic and largely negative directions, as her mother, I thought it would be worse if she became addicted to drugs or alcohol. That response startled her. She had internalized a keen sense of the importance of staying a virgin until she got married. I am *thankful* for that. But, somewhere along the line, she also picked up a belief in the extraordinary awfulness and shame of sexual sin. We need to help our daughters keep their "sins" in perspective. My primary concern is that if a daughter were ever in a situation where she did get pregnant, she wouldn't feel so much shame she could not tell us or get help. A secondary concern is that she know that people with good intentions still make mistakes. Our gracious God is a redemptive God and seeks to reconcile and heal those who sin.

Francis spoke with me in my office after hearing me talk in class about the potential damage overemphasizing virginity can cause girls and women. Once Francis slept with Mike, she believed no one else would ever want to marry her. She had forfeited what she believed to be her most treasured possession, virginity, and as a sullied woman, had dropped significantly in value. Besides, since she had slept with him, she believed they were already married before God. So she kept having sex with him, because the best she figured she could do if she hoped to marry Mike was to keep him happy. But they didn't marry, and she had sex with several other guys along the way too—believing herself unworthy of a good man. Every encounter reinforced her unworthiness. She found a measure of healing in thinking it possible that her virginity was not the most important quality she possessed.

While we need to teach our daughters how to recognize and avoid situations that might explode physically or that might lead to date rape, we need to do so in a way that does not overemphasize their virginity as their most important quality. Our daughters' sexuality is only one part of who they are. While it is an important part, a healthy perspective can be distorted by an overemphasis on it. God graciously seeks to reconcile and heal those who sin.

Celebrating the Gift of Sexual Pleasure

Multiple books (both Christian and not) have been written about exploring and discovering the mysteries and joys of sex. The abundance of these books suggests there is a strong market for them. People know sex is supposed to bring them pleasure, yet many have a difficult time achieving it.

One stereotype we have of the Victorian era is that women did not enjoy sex but performed their conjugal duty by having sex when their husbands wanted it. These wives presumably did not mind that their husbands kept mistresses, because it kept their husbands from bothering them too much for sex. While this stereotype has largely been discounted as a myth, we see women portrayed throughout much of history as the nonstimulated, unexcited but begrudgingly willing partner. The myth suggests that good women are not sexual women. Good women find sex disgusting and do it primarily to procreate and secondarily only to appease the animal nature of their husbands. Some have theorized that these myths abounded in history as a way to control and subdue women's sexuality while legitimizing men's desire for multiple partners. An answer to this repression of women's sexuality emerged in the 1960s, when the sexual revolution legitimized the pursuit of multiple partners for women. However, this did not bring happiness and satisfaction but further alienation from one's sexual essence. God did not intend women to repress their sexual desires. Rather, God designed men and women for sexual experiences that are mutually satisfying and pleasurable and that remind us of our desire for intimacy with God.

Some researchers have studied the hypothesis that the most satisfying sex occurs within the context of loving, committed relationships. It shouldn't come as a surprise that couples in committed relationships find sex satisfying, though our culture often shows us pictures of gratifying sex where the people are physically beautiful, young, and not married—to each other anyway. Good sex requires the trust and willingness to be vulnerable, which emerges out of relationships characterized by deep commitment. One-night stands, however exciting they may be at the moment, lack depth, trust, and the intimacy that enables sex to be truly satisfying. The song "All By Myself" is about a woman who says she never needed anyone and that making love was just for fun. But now she's all by herself and doesn't want to be.

However, just being in a deeply committed relationship doesn't bring about sexual satisfaction. Some women bring inhibitions into their marriages that emerged from broken images and experiences with their sexuality. When the idea that good girls don't like sex is combined with the commitment to say "No, No, No" before marriage, it is hard for some to say "Yes! Yes! Yes!" after marriage. This is compounded for those who have been broken by sexual abuse. My friend Marilyn and I were both nursing our babies when she told me it took several months of marriage before she was comfortable enough with her sexuality to have intercourse with her husband. She was painfully inhibited and unable to release herself to sex, much less to sexual pleasure. The patience and love of her husband and her commitment to working through her inhibitions had brought her to a point of healing and enjoyment in her sexuality. That God gave us bodies that *could* experience such incredible physical pleasure ought to encourage us to embrace sex as wholly good within the context of a deeply committed relationship. A discomfort with sex reflects the brokenness of our sexuality. To seek help if we find ourselves disgusted and unable to enjoy the pleasure of sex is to seek wholeness.

It is healthy for daughters to know their parents *have* sex. It is healthy for daughters to know their parents *like* sex. Not that children should hear parents having sex or know when they are having sex (which are inhibiting factors for the sexual pleasure of many couples). But our daughters should recognize the normalcy of sex as an ongoing part of a healthy marriage. One girl told me she figured her parents had "done it" only twice—once for her and once for her brother. At least she was fairly young at the time. Hopefully she knows otherwise by now. Hopefully it *is* otherwise for her parents.

WHERE TO GO FROM HERE

Helping our daughters embrace a healthy sense of their sexuality is a challenge for any parent. We confront so many obstacles, such as media messages, peer influence, our own broken sexuality and embarrassment. The following suggestions may offer some help in starting a process that leads to other conversations about sexuality, leading to a healthier view of sexuality.

1. Reinforce the Value of Being Human apart from Being Sexual

My thirteen-year-old daughter's thoughts on pregnancy and suicide made sense in a horrible kind of way. Messages she receives from culture tell her she is valued primarily as a sexual being. Boys and men will notice her according to her physical beauty and how sexy she is. Since being noticed by boys is valued in our culture, girls are supposed to be sexy. But girls, especially from religious homes, are also supposed to be virginal—that is, unaware of their supposedly dormant sexuality. These daughters sense their value lies in their virginity: "Boys," they may be told, "may want to play around with loose and seductive girls, but they'll want to marry a virgin."

What these somewhat contradictory messages have in common is the assumption that what matters most is a girl's sexuality. So much focus on one's sexual state can result in a lot of confused thinking and obsessing about one's sexuality. We need to remind our daughters that their value as humans supersedes their value as sexual female creatures. They have been created in the fullness of God's image; that includes the capacity to think creatively, to be in relationship with others, to know God, to enjoy creation, to help guard and keep creation.

2. Recast Menstruation in a Positive Light

Most women remember their first period. Some think they are bleeding to death, others have had the cycle explained to them and know what is happening. Some have embarrassing stories about finding blood on their pants at school. Some feel good about arriving at the dawn of womanhood, others dread it.

Donell was ten or eleven when a family friend gave her a little cosmetic bag that held a washcloth, a plastic bag, a pad, and a new pair of underwear. The friend explained menstruation to Donell and told her she might want to carry the bag with her to school or keep it in her locker. Donell told me that story as she was preparing to give "The Menstruation Talk" to the fourth grade girls at the school our children attended. I thought the cosmetic bag was a brilliant idea and made a mental note to do likewise for my children.

Such preparation helps keep our daughters' first experience with menstruation from being overwhelmingly negative and embarrassing. Parents can influence their daughters' perceptions of menstruation by preparing them for it and by celebrating this physical rite of passage that moves them from childhood toward womanhood. To give the commencement of menstruation honor and blessing is simply to recognize its arrival in your daughter's life, to welcome her into womanhood, and to perhaps share your feelings about menstruation when you were a girl. None of my daughters had a lot *they* wanted to say at the time, but they appreciated my willingness to talk to them and to recognize this event as significant for them. Our daughters need affirmation that the sex they have been ascribed is a good thing—a blessing, and not a curse.

3. Recast the Value of Life Giving

As God brought forth life, so he gifted women with the ability to bring forth life. This is a powerful identification with the Creator that God granted uniquely to women. To think of life-giving capabilities as a curse rather than a blessing is to blemish a profound way that the Creator crafted women in his image. More broadly, we also need to restore the value of being female for our daughters. We need to remind them that God created both males and females in his image and charged them to rule together over creation. One male student in a Gender Roles class captured the wonder of the life-giving capabilities of women this way:

> We talked about female sexuality this week. I was mostly struck with the wonder of the thing. It doesn't really seem like guys have a male equivalent. The ability to bear children is wonderful in the highest sense of the word. I can only imagine. If men had this ability we'd think we were gods. Perhaps this is part of the reason why the subjugation of women has been so important to men. If life is the most valued thing, and women have the ability to produce it, men, if controlled solely by the will to power, seem left with two options in relation to women: worship or control. History shows us which option has been most popular.

Views that limit or devalue women are being challenged—and a primary source of that challenge is women and men who recognize the value of women's contributions *because* they are women. These men and women do not want equality to be achieved by women becoming just like men. They do not value women only for their ability to bear and nurture children, but they recognize them as having more to offer society than reproductive abilities. Growing strong daughters includes growing daughters who can celebrate and embrace motherhood, but who do not believe their value and worth to society is wholly defined by their ability to reproduce and nurture children.

4. Learn to Communicate about Sexuality

The easiest way to communicate with daughters about sexuality is to start when they are toddlers. When they ask questions, answer them. At this point, questions are vague and answers can be simple. To answer these early questions builds confidence for parents and a sense for daughters that her parents are approachable. Parents who have never talked with their daughters about their sexuality will find it difficult (but not impossible) to begin in adolescence. Parents who cannot talk to their daughters forfeit some of their influence to peers. If this is a disconcerting thought, get help learning to begin these important conversations—either through books or friends who you know are able to talk with their daughters.

5. Provide Good Models—Revisited

Parents cannot address all the issues our daughters confront regarding their sexuality. We are a generation removed from the nuances that shape each generation's challenges. Even if we *can* understand the challenges, our daughters are rarely convinced this is true. Thus, the power of models returns yet again, but this time the models are older daughters, usually someone else's daughters. College-age women who have survived the challenges of middle and high school can become models for younger girls. This modeling has mutual benefit. Becoming one who talks with and encourages others reinforces her values for the one who is sharing. And girls who listen to women only a few years older feel connected to the challenges and encouraged by their stories.

Some of these opportunities are formalized in Big Sister and church-based programs. Churches with the benefit of a college-age population are blessed with a pool of potential models. Students can be "adopted" by families (some churches formalize this). Many college women yearn for older women who will take an interest in them and listen to their stories. When you enter such a relationship you bless the parents of these college women by nurturing their daughters when they are away from home. Parents who value the input of college women will seek ways to set up opportunities for these women to interact with their daughters. Meredith, a college student who attended the same church we did, volunteered to get Sarah started learning the guitar; for several months she came over once a week to teach her, and in the meantime, she modeled a confident woman who had made it through adolescence. I value the Merediths who are willing to be role models for younger girls.

CONCLUSION

The creation story brings a sense of wonder and blessing to sexuality. God created two embodiments of his image—male and female. Men and women were created to find each other's bodies attractive, stimulating, and sexually satisfying. When a man and woman become "one flesh" they reflect the unity of a triune God who also has distinct embodiments. Human sexuality reflects the unity of a triune God and our God-given drive toward intimacy.

Yet this beautiful aspect of creation was distorted so easily. Women, who reflect the life-creating aspect of God's image in their ability to grow and bear children, are uncomfortable with their bodies and the reproductive process. Bodies and sex are separated from personhood, and women (and some men) are exploited and sexually abused.

But sexuality can be redeemed. As parents, we can redeem it for ourselves and strive to nurture a healthy view of sexuality for our daughters. Some of us need to start by seeking healing for our own woundedness. Then we will be better able to recognize distorted ideas about sexuality and more effectively nurture and pass on a restored and redeemed perspective to our daughters.

CHAPTER EIGHT

MALES AS FRIENDS, MORE THAN FRIENDS, AND HUSBANDS

"Men and women can never be friends you know," Harry said.
"And why not?" Sally asked.
"Because the sex thing always gets in the way."

—*When Harry Met Sally*

A TWENTY-SOMETHING FRIEND told me about an evening spent with three of her friends, two men and another woman. "Halfway through dinner John leaned over and whispered, 'By the way, I'm paying.' I thought, Oh, no, this is a date."

Can men and women just be friends? A lot of parents worry about the men their daughters will marry, a fair number worry about the boyfriends their daughters will have, fewer concern themselves with the friends their daughters have who happen to be boys. Maybe most of them, like Harry, do not believe males and females can really *be* friends anyway, so they don't think to concern themselves over their daughters' friends who happen to be boys. Yet the foundation our daughters build with boys who are friends will influence what they look for in boys who are "more than friends," as well as the kind of men they will seek for lifetime partners.

FRIENDS WHO HAPPEN TO BE BOYS

College students almost unanimously disagree with Harry. The men, of course, are somewhat perturbed at Harry for sweeping all men together as having such lustful intentions. The women, while somewhat perplexed, flattered, and disturbed (as is Sally) that all males perceive female acquaintances as sexual conquests waiting to happen, are equally perturbed at the suggestion that the men with whom they are friends want to have sex with them.

Our daughters' generation may be doing a better job than previous generations at building cross-sex friendships. Boys and girls are less segregated into the typical male and female activities that used to define the sexes as opposites. Girls play sports now too and learn how to make shelves, clocks, and coatracks at school. Boys learn how to make lasagna and banana nut bread and show up to cheer the girls' basketball team after school. Girls and boys have more in common and thus have more to talk about and more they both like to do than in previous generations. While boys and girls might still fear each other's cooties in grade school, boys and girls in adolescence do not see each other as entirely different creatures. They have some similarities and more interests in common. The main attraction is not *only* an awakening sexual urge that they are told will make them want to have sex eventually so as to fulfill an instinct to perpetuate the species.

At least in my idealized world, relationships between boys and girls are not primarily about sex. Rather, strong daughters and strong sons interact on a whole array of levels about subjects they share in common. In reality, a lot of the messages our daughters and sons receive still encourage them to focus more on their differences (and sex as the main attraction) and less on their shared humanity and purpose as God's stewards.

Regardless of where they fall on the what-they-share-in-common spectrum, women and men have more opportunities for friendship than prior generations. Men and women work together more than they did fifty years ago. Men and women go to college together more than they did fifty years ago. Whether or not they want to, most women and men will need to learn how to be friends without the sex thing getting in the way.

While a significant part of the ability for boys and girls to be friends is dependent on what parents teach sons about girls and women, parents can grow daughters in ways that foster their ability to be friends with males. Much of this emerges as daughters are encouraged to have a strong sense of being created in the image of God. Strong daughters are confident and interdependent, and they interact boldly with the boys growing up in their neighborhoods. Of course, this is much easier if those boys are comfortable with confident, interdependent, bold girls. If girls are confident in their intellectual ability, they will not shy away from conversing with males. If they are confident in their physical abilities, they will more likely join in a coed volleyball, football, or softball game. However well this generation is at building cross-sex friendships, eventually, for most of our daughters, a time will come when relationships move into something more than friendship.

More than Friends

Becca's relationship with Sean sent her into a downward spiral. Becca was one of my students and only told me about Sean after her schoolwork had plummeted, her relationship with God had become distant, and the few friends she had became weary of her depressed emotional state. She wanted to leave him but couldn't. She knew Sean was not good for her, yet she could not leave him, partly because he did a convincing job showing her he loved her and needed her, and partly because he promised he would change. When Sean started dealing and using drugs again, Becca knew she was at a critical decision-making point in the relationship.

The boys and men to whom our daughters attach themselves will have a profound impact on their lives, whether or not they eventually marry them. Historically, Mr. Right was selected by Mom and Dad, the village elders, or a matchmaker—the "more than friends" category didn't exist. For the most part, girls did not attach themselves—either emotionally or physically—to another boy prior to marriage. As countries industrialized, they tended to move away from the traditions of agricultural societies, including arranged marriages. Our independence-valuing culture balks at the lack of personal choice and freedom in arranged marriages. The majority of my students cannot imagine allowing their parents to select their mates, though most of the students I've had from India see parental involvement as having merit.

The style of dating that emerged on the American scene in the early twentieth century introduced new complications and implications for how women and men chose each other. As in the days of courting, men maintained the power to initiate (though this is beginning to change), and women maintained their power to reject a would-be suitor or date. Yet without any official guidance from parents, elders, or a professional matchmaker, our daughters and sons took over the responsibility of making the right choice.

An underlying assumption of dating is that one needs to try out multiple boyfriend/girlfriend arrangements in order to find the right mate. Thus our sons and daughters are exposed to greater risk of rejection and disappointment from losing the love one hoped would lead to marriage. Figuring out whether or not one is *in love* (perceived by many as the most important variable in determining whether or not one should marry) became the task of the young.

Growing strong daughters includes teaching the subtle implications of a dating system where men are typically the risk-taking initiators and women the rejecting or accepting respondents. Rather than being swept along by the current of our confusing system, daughters can maneuver with more certainty and intention regarding how they relate to boys and men.

The Dating Scene

At the colleges where I have taught, students do not date much. By "date," I mean two uncommitted people who agree to go out together at some predetermined time to some predetermined place.

"Dating" means a variety of things. Sometimes it refers to two people who are "seeing each other" on a regular basis and have some sort of exclusive commitment for the time being. I have talked with a number of students who were not sure whether they were in a dating relationship (meaning the relationship had some sort of commitment) or just hanging out together on a semi-regular basis. The confusion was, of course, disconcerting to them.

We talk about dating in several of my classes. Students say the Christian campus environment stifles dating because couples cannot date casually. If you date the same person twice in a row—at least at Christian colleges—other students assume you are talking about getting married. Even if other students do not assume you're talking about marriage, the male (in most cases) worries that the female might think (and hope) that *he* is thinking about marriage. One male student said, "You get this sense that some girls are desperate to find a husband before they graduate, and it makes me nervous about dating at all."

The following quotes about dating reflect some of the attitudes of students in my Marriage and Family classes. These are only a few of the many that spoke negatively about dating.

> Dating is just not fun for me. Hanging out with my male friends is a lot of fun. But going out with one person and kissing him goodnight, getting attached to him and then breaking up is just not my idea of a good time.

> I wonder if anyone really honestly likes dating anyway. It is so awkward. I know I would so much prefer a good friendship over a dating relationship. A friendship, not a dating relationship, is the right place for marriage partners to start. (From a male student)

> How do you get to know someone without dating? Be her friend. You find out a lot more about a person by just hanging out than you do by dating.

Dating seems to be a major disappointment for a number of women and men—at least those who attend Christian colleges. Inherent flaws in the dating system explain at least part of the disappointment. Young people often have unrealistic expectations of dating. Dating is supposed to be a fun way to get to know members of the opposite sex and may lead one to one's mate. But few find it fun anymore, and many find it a disconcerting way to find a spouse.

How Dating Works—the Implications

Dating is supposed to work this way: Chuck has a class with Julie. Chuck finds Julie attractive. Chuck invites Julie out on a date. Julie says yes. They go and have a wonderful time.

More often dating works this way: Chuck has a class with Julie. Chuck finds Julie attractive. She is funny, cute, and seems intelligent. Chuck thinks about inviting Julie out on a date but worries that she might say no. What if she laughs him off? Chuck asks around. Does Julie have a boyfriend? Do you think Julie would go out with me? After a long while Chuck gets up his nerve and asks Julie out on a date. Julie does say yes (but sometimes Julie says no, and this is the rejection that hardly makes asking worth it). Before the date, Chuck and Julie both worry a lot about what to wear, whether or not they will say stupid things, and whether or not they will find anything to talk about.

Chuck and Julie go out. They both try hard to be funny, thoughtful, intelligent. Whether or not Chuck finds himself attracted to Julie, he wants Julie to like him. This is true for Julie too. Chuck, a poor student, is conscious about the money he is spending. However, he doesn't want to appear cheap. He either goes cheap anyway and hopes Julie is gracious enough to understand, or he spends money as though he has it by putting it on his credit card, adding debt to his already heavily charged card. At the end of the evening, Chuck drives up to Julie's dorm to drop her off. Julie wonders if Chuck expects a kiss, or more. Maybe he does, maybe he doesn't. Maybe they kiss at the end, maybe they don't. Regardless, it is an awkward moment. They both say they had a great time, though neither of them have, not really anyway. They both spent so much energy trying to be funny, thoughtful, and intelligent, and trying to second-guess how they were being perceived, that they didn't enjoy the evening as much as they hoped. It seemed like a lot of work.

Whether or not they enjoyed it and whether or not they even like each other, Chuck and Julie will probably spend a fair amount of time thinking about the evening. "It was stupid to tell that story about my sister," Julie will decide. Chuck will reprimand himself and feel the flush of embarrassment again for accidentally calling Julie, "Mary" (his last girlfriend's name). She will wonder: *What does he think of me?* He will wonder: *What does she think of me?*

What fruitful pieces of information did they learn about each other that would help them decide if this was a relationship worth pursuing? Likely not much. At least not much that represents who they really are. If the purpose of dating is to have fun, then maybe, sometimes, dating meets those expectations. If dating is the mating selection process for our culture then it has some major problems. To begin with, couples do not generally get to know each other through dating. Students say they only get to know the dating persona—the funny, thoughtful, intelligent actor they all learn to play on dates. People on dates do not learn much about the person reading the script. (However, those who play the part best end up going out on the most dates and so might be able to use the system to become popular.) Apart from the problem that dating does a mediocre to poor job of meeting either of its two typical goals (to have *fun* or as a mate-selecting process), it introduces other negative, unintended consequences into relationships.

The Unintended Consequences of Dating

One of the nasty by-products of dating has to do with the power differential between boys and girls. Since males are the initiators, they have more control over how the relationship develops. Historically, men have tended to possess selection power over the women they bartered for or courted. Even though women can reject the invitations of initiating males, this is only reactive power—they can refuse to enter a relationship. Women have been discouraged from exerting proactive power—directly initiating a relationship they would like to develop. Thus, males and females both experience several indirect and negative consequences of the power differential between them.

First, boys *have* to initiate. This is not always a blessing. Initiating means males have to assume all the up-front risk of rejection. It also means they are expected to assume all the financial and creative planning responsibilities. When only men had access to money, it made sense that they foot the bill for courting. But men are not the only ones with access to money anymore, and a number of male students say they would appreciate being able to share the rejection risk as well as the financial and creative planning responsibilities with women.

This sharing of responsibilities opens the door to balance the power differential, because it grants girls the right to initiate. Without this right, daughters have only indirect means to capture the attention of Mr. (Potential) Right. Thus a second negative consequence is that girls develop a flirtatious language of seduction, which can help them woo a date from the man of their attentions. One student described the technique as "placing yourself in his path." A female was to find out where the male who held her interest would likely be hanging out, and consistently, for a time, get herself there as well, giving the male ample opportunity to notice her and initiate a relationship. The method had worked for this student, and she was advocating it for her friends. However, if a girl refuses to be scheming, manipulative, or flirtatious, she can only hope Mr. Right will notice and pursue her anyway, instead of someone who is vividly flashing "available and willing" signs. Mr. Right may notice her eventually, but only after he has checked out all the other girls vying for his attention. Waiting patiently to be noticed for one's virtues rather than one's vices is a frustrating and oppressive alternative to directly pursuing a man who has captured her interest.

Ultimately, with the power differential as it is, our daughters have little control over who they marry. While they have the power to say no to an interested male, they do not have the power to be initiators who seek out a man.

The men in my classes say they would appreciate a woman who would be bold enough to ask them out or initiate a friendship. They have less difficulty adjusting to the idea of women being initiators than the women do. Many women are not sure they want to risk rejection or assume financial responsibility for dating. Gaining a balance in the distribution of power is not worth it to them. They prefer the safety of rejection power, and besides, they like being catered to and taken care of. Of course they do. Who doesn't? The dating system reinforces an unequal distribution of power, but the negative consequences are serious enough that parents ought to consider whether or not they favor such an imbalance of power in their daughters' adolescent relationships.

A third negative consequence concerns physical intimacy expectations. Since males largely have to initiate the relationships, assume all the risk of rejection, *and* foot the bill, a potential problem with "payoff" expectations arises. The dating system introduced physical intimacy into casual relationships. During the days of courtship or arranged marriages, physical intimacy between couples who were not committed to each other was discouraged. Fooling around happened some anyway, but it was not sanctioned in the same way it is today. Some amount of physical intimacy is considered normal— even within Christian communities. Youth group leaders (those bold enough to do so) discuss, "How far is too far?"[1] Regardless of a youth group leader's or parent's values, some amount of physical exploration is considered the norm and is expected to occur in adolescence, largely through the process of dating and "more than friends" relationships.

Therefore, if some male thinks a kiss is the least owed him for all he has contributed to making the evening delightful and pleasing, he is only responding to a social norm that he has internalized. Maybe he thinks sex is a more appropriate payoff—at least by the third date. This too is within our fuzzy spectrum of social norms regarding premarital sexual activity. Maybe he doesn't expect any kind of physical reward (males in my classes say they do not). But even if he doesn't, a girl will wonder whether or not some payoff is expected, and it puts her in an awkward, disadvantaged position.

Since girls have primarily learned to communicate indirectly with flirtatious techniques, many are not comfortable communicating directly. They still have the power to say no, but many do not have a voice that can do so. One student expressed it this way:

> Society tells me that it is good to kiss—that I should kiss. So I go on a date with a guy that I don't know very well at all, and at the end of the date he wants to kiss me, because that is what is accepted and expected. But I don't want to because for some reason I think that kissing is more

special than that. But he moves in for the kiss, not giving me a chance to gently reject, so now it's either forcefully reject, hurting his feelings, or compromise my wants and just do it—knowing that I am doing a special act that is not special at this time. And so far, every time I've taken the latter option. I tell myself that it shouldn't be a big deal, that everybody kisses, and I almost convince myself of that. But it is a big deal and I let my voice be lost anyway. To combat this now I just don't go on dates. It's easier to say no when I'm asked out than it is later.

Date rape is rooted both in payoff expectations and the world-view that says women are to be passive while men are dominant. In *Against Our Will: Men, Women and Rape*, Susan Brownmiller says, "All rape is an exercise in power, but some rapists have an edge that is more than physical."[2] As stated in the previous chapter, since men are granted the leader and provider roles in society, they are given a powerful edge over women, who are to be recipients and followers. Some men will feel justified taking sex as payoff for their leadership and provision. Some will be convinced by the myths that suggest girls really want it anyway. Some will be influenced by media presentations that show women as sexually available and power-less. One goal for parents who want to raise strong daughters will be to mitigate the power differential between our daughters and the boys and men they date.

Although some men seem ready for women to initiate and be equal partners in moving relationships forward, one female student said she thinks the men only *say* they would go out with a woman who initiated. She thinks the stereotype of "that kind of woman" is ultimately too threatening and negative and that most men are turned off by it.

There is a negative stereotype attached to women who are confident and willing to initiate relationships with men. The value underneath this stereotype reflects the belief that men ought to be the leaders and women the followers. One perspective in Christianity continues to affirm a hierarchical social structure for men and women. A second perspective in Christianity keeps reemerging—one that affirms the mutuality of men and women. What our daughters determine about the structuring of men's and women's relationships will influence the kind of partner they will be look-ing for and the kind of partner who will find them attractive.

Encouraging the Impossible: Fighting Dating Traditions

Daughters who are encouraged to relate to males as mutual and equal partners rather than subordinate and dependent partners will be less likely to be caught in situations where they are fighting off unwanted sexual advances.[3] However, those who value a hierar-chical model can teach their daughters the same skills that help balance and diffuse the power differential. If your daughter is going to date, the easiest way to balance the power differential is to have her pay her own way. If she pays her share, there is less of a sense that she owes her date any favors. A second way to balance the power differential is to encourage her to offer input in planning the date. The more involved she is in planning the activity, the more control and responsibility she has for it.

Another, but often the most difficult way to balance the power differential, is to encourage daughters to initiate activities with males. These do not have to be "dates." Girls can initiate a group outing to Taco Bell or invite several people over to watch a movie. They can creatively plan ways to interact with and get to know the people they are interested in getting to know. Inasmuch as dating is following a scripted play, it is not all that useful in getting to know what someone is like beneath the surface. "Hanging out" (a term which can include anything from a Taco Bell outing to studying for an exam or attending a sporting event—as long as it is infor-mal, spontaneous, and usually includes more than two people) seems to better accomplish goals aimed at having fun and getting to know members of the other sex.

MARRYING WELL

That children "marry well" has always been of concern to par-ents. Sometimes marrying well has meant marrying into a wealthy family. Other times it has meant marrying into the right social group—be it religious, political, or occupational. Marrying well often represents parents' hope that their daughters will marry men who will be stable (emotionally, mentally, and financially) and faithful. Since only a few countries, such as India, still involve parents in partner selection for children,[4] parents' input in most industrialized countries is subtle and less certain.

Part of that input will reflect what parents believe God says about the structuring of relationships between men and women, how they model that structure, and how successfully they otherwise impress their values upon their daughters. Scripture has been used to discern God's design, yet two camps have come to different conclusions.

Many of our daughters view women as the second sex who should be followers of men, the first sex. Eve was created after Adam, from Adam's rib, to be Adam's helpmate. She was the one deceived by Satan, and she is the one about whom God said, "And though your desire will be for your husband, he will be your master" (Gen. 3:16b).

Theologians have worked hard to understand the relationship between men and women as God intended it. Even John Calvin and Martin Luther came to different conclusions.[5] Some explain the tendency in society for men to be dominant leaders and women to be submissive followers as fulfilling God's design. Others explain this tendency as representing distortions in female and male relationships that took place because of the fall. The former explanations are better known to most of our daughters, and much has been written about them in Christian literature. The lesser known explanations are asserted by theologians who suggest women should be in mutual relationships with men, where both men and women are direct and intentional about pursuing relationships.

How one interprets the creation account justifies how one defines the roles between women and men. The Council on Biblical Manhood and Womanhood, a group dedicated to preserving the headship model for men, interprets the creation account as a God-ordained hierarchical system whereby men are to lead in love and women are to follow with respect. Christians for Biblical Equality is a group dedicated to bringing back the pre-fall interdependent equality between men and women, and interpret the creation account as a story of God's intent for men and women gone awry.

Gilbert Bilezikian, Phyllis Trible, and Stanley Grenz are three of the many theologians that come from a Christians for Biblical Equality perspective. Following is a summary of their responses to the perspective that encourages our daughters to see themselves as secondary image-bearers of God.

1. Eve was created after Adam and from Adam's rib, to be his help-mate. Trible[6] suggests the possibility that Adam, as a *male*, was *not* created first. Rather, the nuances of working with a Hebrew text leave room for the possibility that the first earth creature *(hā'ād-ām)* was not sexually differentiated. Hebrew, like Spanish and unlike English, has masculine and feminine words. Although *'adam* is a masculine word, as *sombrero* (hat) or *rojo* (red) are in Spanish, the use of it does not equal sexual identification. Not until after *ādām* is put to sleep, and God makes from its rib a corresponding mate does sexual differentiation show up in the Hebrew text. Thus, in some significant way, Eve may have been present in Adam before they were sexually differentiated into two people. This splitting of *ādām* into male and female is the culmination of creation, bringing human companionship and sexuality. Trible's interpretation offers one example of how different emphases and interpretations can be derived from the ancient Hebrew language and text.

Regardless of how one takes Trible's interpretation, one still needs to address God's apparent desire to make a helper fit for Adam. Our culture has defined *helpmate* as a supportive person, usually a wife, who assists her husband in effectively using his gifts. However, once again we find a surprise in the Hebrew word. The word for "helper" in Genesis 2 is used primarily in the Old Testament to refer to God as helper and deliverer.[7] An interpretation that suggests women are to be assistants to support men is not consistent with other uses of the Hebrew word in the Old Testament. Neither should the word be used to suggest a superiority in women. Rather, this word underscores how the image of God in men and women is to reflect the interdependent nature of triune God in humanity. Women, who bear God's image in every way that men do, bring creation to completion. As corresponding males and females we reflect God's image. If we subdue, steward, and rule over creation together (as we are charged by God to do), we will be better able to do so with balance, made possible because we were created as corresponding males and females.

2. Eve was the one deceived by Satan and illustrates the need for women to be under the leadership/guidance of men. Even if God's intent with creation was for joint-ruling, some believe that Eve's deception by Satan resulted in her being placed in a subordinate position under Adam, or that Eve's deception illustrates women's need to be under the authority and protection of men, who are less easily deceived. While those who hold to a headship position tend to believe God ordained a hierarchy from the start, some believe God made the hierarchical arrangement a consequence of Eve's sin. The end result is the same—joint-ruling was no longer God's plan. This belief has been dominant, and as women subscribe to it, their ability to accept the charge to rule creation jointly with men is greatly diminished.

It is undeniable that Eve was the one deceived by Satan. However, a careful look at the text regarding her exchange with the serpent challenges our perceptions of Eve and thus of women in general. Eve's dialogue with Satan does not sound like that of an irrational, emotional woman but rather reflects a thoughtfulness that spoke to her ability to reason, to function as a moral agent, and to make disobedient decisions independently (however damning their consequences).

Moreover, the plural form of the Hebrew word the serpent uses to address Eve implies that Adam is present with her at this exchange.[8] Genesis 3:6 makes this explicit, "She also gave some to her husband, who was with her." Eve is actively engaged in dialogue with Satan. She can articulate what God has commanded and what the consequences will be for disobedience. She hears Satan's challenge and listens to his attempt to correct her understanding of God. She desires that which Satan offers and makes a decision to eat the forbidden fruit. Her choice to disobey is deliberate and reasoned. Adam has remained passive and silent during this exchange. He did not interrupt her, and we are given no indication that he tried to stop her. Adam did not act as though his role was to lead and guide Eve. We might argue that if this *had* been Adam's role, could it be that *he* committed the first sin since he did not attempt to stop Eve from disobeying God? Did he sin by refusing to even try to fulfill his role as her leader?

Devastating consequences followed the fall. Humans' perfect union with Creator God was broken. Our ability to function as image-bearers of God was grossly perverted. God's declaration of the consequences of sin included two curses and two proclamations. Because of the serpent's actions, serpents are cursed above all the other animals. Because of sin's introduction into the world, the earth is cursed, and only through sweat and toil will it produce. God proclaims the consequences that will follow humans throughout time— consequences that reflect a state of brokenness from the original plan. Adam and Eve are told that what could have been produced effortlessly (childbearing for Eve, food for Adam) will now be produced with pain, sweat, and toil. In addition, Eve is told that while she will continue to desire her husband, he will now rule over her. She will yearn for her husband (perhaps for the pre-fall intimacy and mutuality they shared), but instead he will be her master.

The effects of this master-dominance become apparent immediately following the creation account and are seen in various stories of broken image-bearers throughout the Old Testament. Lot offered his daughters to the men who wanted to gang rape the male visitor he had received into his home. A Levite man visiting in a town of Benjamin was also accosted by the men of town who wanted to rape him. He offered his concubine to appease them, and she was abused and raped all night and left for dead in the morning. The Benjamite man with whom the Levite was staying also offered his virgin daughter, but only the concubine got pushed outside. King Ahasuerus followed a legitimate tradition in his era when he claimed as many young and beautiful women for his harem as he desired, regardless of whether or not they would choose it. The tragic list of stories illustrating broken relationships between men and women continues well into and through the twentieth century.

Those who desire to raise strong daughters or be strong mothers do not have to agree with a particular critique of the creation story to do either. Nevertheless, what our daughters understand about their proper place in marriage is affected by their interpretation of the creation story. If they believe God ordains a hierarchy in relationships, they will limit their functions as image-bearers to those consistent with subordinate roles. This can be done with integrity as men strive to love their wives and wives seek to respect their husbands. These women will define their abilities by the roles they believe God has given them and by being enthusiastic helpmates to their husbands. They can still be strong women who speak boldly for what is right, have confidence in their roles, minister to younger women in the church, and serve powerfully as Jesus did. They can build strong communities of faith and reach out to neighbors. They can reflect God's image in the useful and good things they create. Being a strong woman is more about how we perceive ourselves as women created in the image of God than the way we define or structure our roles.

Those who believe that God was describing a consequence of the fall rather than ordaining a hierarchy when God said Adam will be Eve's master understand the purpose of our sanctification as believers differently. These women become concerned with renewing God's image in women by restoring the mutuality and interdependence between men and women that existed prior to the fall. Those who take this perspective believe part of Jesus' ministry was directed at this restoration and carried on in the early church. As the church became more and more institutionalized over time, old patterns of patriarchy again dominated male and female relationships. These theologians believe we have allowed our assumption that God ordained a hierarchy to shape our interpretation of Scripture. Scholars who challenge the assumption of a hierarchy have gone back and reexamined Old and New Testament passages from the perspective of God ordaining a mutuality and interdependence between men and women. They see the wholeness of the relationship God intended for men and women as constantly at risk of getting lost in the brokenness of sin.[9]

Because Mark and I believe God designed us for an interdependent relationship that would bring balance to the ruling of creation, we desire to parent our daughters in ways that encourage them to be strong image-bearers of God in the latter tradition. This means Mark and I model an interdependent and mutual relationship for our daughters. We pray for husbands who will nurture them to use their gifts broadly. Our daughters will not likely want husbands who desire to be the primary leader in their relationships but rather men who want women with whom they can partner as equals. We, along with our daughters, will be looking for men who believe women and men are capable of jointly ruling over creation together, including participation in public arenas. Mark and I would encourage our daughters to initiate a relationship with this kind of man. And if they marry one, we will believe they have met one criterion for marrying well. What parents believe about God's plan will shape the nature of the relationships they encourage daughters to seek out.

WHERE TO GO FROM HERE

Mark's and my goal has been to help our daughters learn to recognize healthy relationships with boys that will lead to healthy relationships with men. We define healthy in the following four ways. First, that our daughters are honest and direct in their communication rather than coy and indirect. Second, that they are confident in their ability to be equal partners in the friendship. Third, that they are able to appreciate gender differences that make relationships with the other sex interesting and fulfilling. And fourth, that they will be interdependent—that is, neither too dependent nor too independent in their relationships. Following are several suggestions for how parents can encourage these characteristics in their daughters' relationships.

1. Affirm the Value of Males as Friends

Too often battle lines get drawn between males and females, and they forget how much they need each other. Some women decide they would just as soon steer clear of men altogether. I didn't have Andrea in any of my classes, but she had heard about me and wanted to talk to me about men. Rumor had it I was a feminist of some sort, so she figured I hated men as much as she did. She was surprised to find out I didn't. Not only did I not hate them, but I was *married* to one and even spoke *highly* of him. I also named a few other male colleagues she should speak with so she could see that not all men are bad guys. Her idea that progressive women do not want to have anything to do with oppressive, arrogant, and chauvinistic men—which, of course, accounted for all of them in her estimation—emerged from some painful experiences with men in her life.

Fear undermines relationships between males and females. Sometimes this fear arises from a previous abusive experience with a male. Sometimes it arises from parents' fear that men will take advantage of or harm their daughters. If the fear inhibits girls from developing friendships with boys, then the ability to value men as partners is crippled.

Avoidance of men, either through disdain or fear, is counterproductive to the goal of working interdependently with men to bring about the caretaking of God's creation. Getting a daughter counseling for past experiences, or working through our own fear-related issues, will move broken people toward wholeness and a broken reflection of God's image closer to a renewed one.

While friendships with men change after our daughters marry, they should not have to disappear. If our daughters work, they will most likely have male coworkers. They need to know how to be friends with men. Much wholesome pleasure and growth is found in continuing to interact significantly with people of both sexes after one has committed oneself in marriage.

Men and women were created to work together to bring hope, justice, mercy, and love to the world and its creatures. Our daughters cannot fulfill this responsibility alone; neither can men. Friendships with males strengthen our contribution as stewards. Women and men who remain single need the other sex in their lives as friends. Ruth, a single woman in her seventies and one of the six in our monthly pinochle group, says she appreciates how Mark and Michael, the other male in our group of six, are like younger brothers to her. I think she appreciates that she can be playful with them and talk with them about politics, theology, and social issues, as well as the ordinary stories that make up the stuff of life. If we let it, the perspectives of the other sex can sharpen, challenge, and clarify for us what we cannot see from our own perspective. We need each other. God created us to need each other. And we need to affirm the goodness of males and females being friends for our daughters, rather than fear those relationships or cast them off as insignificant.

2. Get to Know the Boys Your Daughters Have as Friends

My mother always went into her parents' room when she returned home from a date to let her mother know she was home. She would end up sitting on the edge of the bed, quietly telling Grandma all about her date. I imagine that Grandma, who made herself available in the late night or early morning hours, gained a pretty good sense of the boys Mom was dating.

Mark and I had our own idealized view of how we were going to get to know the boys our daughters wanted to date. Our plan went like this: Before one of our daughters could go out on a date with a boy, we had to spend some time with him. That meant he could join our family for a picnic, a movie, dinner, games, whatever. However, we did not account for changes in how teenagers do such things in the intervening twenty-five years since we were teens. Since teens tend to hang out in groups more than date exclusively, our plan would have taken the occasional casual date and given it a significance that implied we thought they were moving toward serious commitment. To act as though commitment was imminent might, in fact, create a premature idea in their minds that they *should* be more than casual friends.

Besides, according to my daughters and college students, the current trend is not casual dating but for boys and girls to hang out in mixed groups. Thus, it became a challenge to get to know the guys our daughters found interesting. When they came over to our house, it was usually in the context of a group. More often, I got to know them kind of like my grandmother got to know Mom's dates. But instead of after-date conversations, we'd have evening walks or talks over a latte when I'd ask them what they like about their friends and why. Having to articulate who they like and why helps our daughters formulate a picture of the kind of person they are looking for to be a good friend, maybe more than a friend, maybe a lifetime partner. I remember when Danielle described a particular friend. She said, "He's the kind of guy, who, when I am around him, makes me want to be a better person." Once she articulated this as a value, she began to internalize it and look for it in her friends.

As our daughters moved into more serious relationships, we welcomed and worked more directly at getting those young men into our home. A couple of them were particularly comfortable hanging out with our family. One of Danielle's friends who came home with her for a weekend visit from college stayed behind while Danielle and Sarah went shopping. He chatted with me on the porch and then mowed the lawn while I did some weeding. We have valued the opportunities for boys our daughters are interested in to interact with us in our home, whether visiting for the weekend, having dinner with us, or attending a Cubs game together. We've even taught one of them to play bridge and enjoy occasional evenings around the card table.

3. Walk the Line with the "Bad Boyfriend"

Try to pull apart a deck of cards held together by a rubber band. The more you pull, the greater the resistance. You may succeed in getting the cards separated by a few inches, but once you release them they will snap back together—or else splatter all over the floor. I knew my parents were uncomfortable with a man I was dating my first year in college. In their wisdom they did not forbid me from seeing him or try to get me to break up with him. However, they strongly discouraged me from accepting his invitation to fly out and visit his family over the summer. I didn't go, and looking back, soon decided their counsel was wise.

Walking the parental interference line is a difficult one. We are preparing to send our daughters off, which includes letting them make many decisions on their own. To send them off with confidence we will teach the value of supportive relationships that include the ability to seek out the counsel of others (maybe even ours!). We also need to be willing to let go, trusting them into the care of God.

Family specialists give different answers to the question of dealing with the "bad boyfriend." Some suggest a tough love approach: "Break up or move out!" This may be appropriate, especially if the relationship is endangering or negatively influencing siblings. Others suggest a tolerant and loving acceptance. Sometimes this may be appropriate—especially with older daughters who are no longer living at home.

Becca, the student whose life was on a downward spiral, needed encouragement and support in her attempts to disengage from Sean. She did not need ultimatums from her friends or family. Becca came to the point of knowing she needed to break up, but it was not going to be easy. For Becca to be successful she needed to move elsewhere, somewhere far enough away that Sean could not contact her. This required a lot of encouragement and support on the part of her parents.

The following three general guidelines may be useful for assessing options in handling a relationship you think is dangerous or potentially damaging to your daughter. First, determine whether your action of choice is in your daughter's best interest or yours; you may need some help from trusted and honest friends to determine this. Second, consider and weigh the possible unintended consequences of implementing your action of choice. Try to anticipate and be prepared ahead of time for the potential fallout; you may need some help with this too. Third, rest in the knowledge that your daughter belongs primarily to God, not you. God loves her more than you do, has her best interests in mind, and is an expert at picking up pieces and building beautiful vessels.

4. Encourage Small and Large Group Activities

Mark and I were quite content that our daughters were more interested in being with boys in the context of groups rather than on dates. Group interaction puts less pressure on boys and girls to act within a certain script; it is more honest, and it eliminates some of the second-guessing about motives and desires. Group activities also diffuse the opportunity for physical involvement and help keep the power between boys and girls more balanced. And a lot of teens, as well as college students, think hanging out with a group is simply more fun.

Early on we tried to encourage group activities by buying Danielle a teen version of a Murder Mystery game. She never used it (though Megan did several years later), but she got the idea we were supportive of mixed group activities. All three girls come up with ideas for how to have fun with boys and girls in the context of their youth groups and different friendship groups. However, group activities are not always wholesome. Parents still need to be aware of who the kids in a group are and what the activity entails. We still veto certain activities and are more comfortable allowing greater independence with some groups than we are with others. Knowing our daughters' friends and plans is an important part of being able to guide them. Encouraging groups rather than individual dating is a good way for them to get to know males in a more natural, less artificial setting.

5. Challenge Models of Unhealthy Relationships

If our daughters can recognize unhealthy relationships in others, they will be better able to discern the health of their own relationships. I asked Sarah what people thought of Mandy after observing her at a party Sarah hosted. Mandy, whom I didn't think had a boyfriend, was sitting on a boy's lap, communicating very clearly a message of interest and availability. Sarah said, "Oh, Mandy is just like that. It makes me mad sometimes—it makes all of us mad sometimes. She knows she does it. She can't seem to help it." Sarah was several steps ahead of me. She had already figured Mandy out and determined that Mandy's way of relating to boys had developed into an unhealthy pattern. Our daughters can be taught to recognize overly dependent relationships ("she won't go anywhere without him"), overly independent relationships ("they don't even seem like they're married"), possessive relationships ("he gets mad if she even talks to another guy"), and manipulative relationships ("she can get him to do anything for her"). The more they come to recognize the ways relationships can be broken, the greater the likelihood they can recognize their own vulnerabilities.

6. Use Tangible Symbols as Reminders of Commitments Made

A number of people have promoted promise rings or chastity rings as a symbol for girls, and sometimes boys, of their commitment to remain virgins until they get married. We offered our daughters promise rings as a rite of passage when they turned thirteen. But we broadened the commitment and wanted to be sure they knew they were making a promise to themselves and to God, not to us. Offering our girls a ring reflected our decision to grant them more independence to the degree they demonstrated the ability to make wise choices. Accepting a ring symbolized a commitment on their part to strive to make good choices about their friendships and activities. Tangible symbols can be strong reminders of decisions and commitments our daughters make.

CONCLUSION

While the friendships our daughters establish with boys will influence their later marital relationships, how our sons and daughters relate to each other as friends is also influenced by what they believe about marriage. There is no ambiguity about how God intended people (friends, more-than-friends, or spouses) to treat each other. That we are to love, be honest in our communication, act with faithfulness and integrity, and serve each other is clear. These make up the essence of relationships. Less clear are the roles men and women have been given to play. One conclusion that can be pulled out of the ambiguity concerning roles is that how we *structure* our relationships is less important than the essence of them. That we support relationships where our daughters are encouraged to bear God's image with confidence is more important than supporting relationships where the roles are assigned a particular way. God left much room for humans to construct various social structures. Communities, churches, families, and marriages have all been constructed differently across times and cultures. However, any structure that claims to be godly ought to attend to the essence of how God would have us treat each other.

Meanwhile, the perceptions our daughters develop about men in general will flow from their friendships and more-than-friend relationships with boys and men. While parents cannot choose their daughters' mate, they can still influence perceptions they hold about men as friends, as well as what their daughters might be looking for in a husband.

CHAPTER NINE

FATHERS AND DAUGHTERS
with Mark R. McMinn

My father has often shared with the family those things which have been on his mind and heart. There have been times when my dad has become emotional when talking about something of great importance. When these instances came about he did not leave the room but allowed us to see the way something deeply moved him. These instances showed us that it is okay to show your emotions and that it is okay for men to cry.

—female college student

A BOOK ABOUT GROWING STRONG DAUGHTERS would be incomplete without a chapter addressing fathers and daughters. Instead of attempting to write this myself, I recruited my husband to write a chapter that covered some of the issues he thought important in raising strong daughters. This chapter represents his reflections and ideas as shaped by his experiences with fatherhood and influenced by his academic discipline—psychology.

One of our friends spent a week with his fourteen-year-old daughter at an adventure camp in northern California. He came back with great stories about performing height-defying acts of courage such as rock climbing, rappelling, and riding a zip-rope together down a peak into a cool mountain lake. The two of them shared risks, created memories, and strengthened the bond between them.

Unfortunately, most of us don't have the opportunity or the resources to zip down Mount Shasta with our daughters. And even those who have the chance for a week away in the mountains have to come down from the mountaintop to the daily challenges of parenting—working out curfew times and driving privileges, lying awake wondering and worrying about the temptations our daughters face each day, and trying to maintain some form of authority while remaining flexible and compassionate to our daughters' needs.

So how do we handle the daily demands of fathering in ways that inspire strength in our daughters? What do we say to the fourteen-year-old who disagrees with a request for her to be home by 10:30 P.M.? She protests with the passion of a martyr and the grace of a freight train: "You're still treating me like an eight-year-old! All of my friends can stay out as late as they want. I just won't go if I have to be home by 10:30."

So, Dad, what are you going to say? What are you going to do? And what response might hold the greatest promise for building inner strength in our daughters? In many ways the demand for independence is the same sort of demand we face with two-year-olds and six-year-olds and sixteen-year-olds but adorned in the details of a fourteen-year-old's life. If you have experience raising children, or if you have experience being a child, you realize how stupidly obvious it is to say there are no easy answers to this dilemma. It seems the only option is tension and conflict. Tension, conflict, and praying for age twenty-five. But rather than fighting the tensions of fathering daughters, perhaps there are lessons to be learned in the midst of the tensions. This chapter is organized around three basic tensions that all fathers know or will know. These tensions cannot be escaped, but they can be understood and used to invest wisely in the lives of our daughters.

TENSION ONE: MAINTAINING ATTACHMENT WHILE SUPPORTING AUTONOMY

As a farm boy in Oregon, I remember how we used to plant a stake near young walnut trees and tie the sapling to the stake for firm support. But as the tree grew, we always removed the cord and the stake to let the tree face the gusts of life on its own. Breaking free from the stake was the only way for firm roots to grow and provide the necessary support for a growing tree. Fathers need to be strong supports, yet they must also know when to let go and allow their daughters to learn strength on their own. This is a difficult task that calls us to great wisdom and courage.

John Bowlby, a British psychiatrist, developed a theory of attachment that suggests infants are born with a biological drive to connect with their caregivers. Daughters love their fathers, not because their fathers are such great guys, but because they are biologically programmed to love their fathers. Of course their fathers may be great guys too, but the point is that every infant is born with an instinct to attach to caregivers. Bowlby's psychological observations also make sense from a theological perspective. Being created in God's image means that all humans—including fathers and daughters—are born with a desire to be in relationship with one another.

Given half a chance, young daughters are willing to follow their fathers almost anywhere—to the hardware store, underneath the car to change the oil, to the store to pick up a gallon of milk. They care less about learning how to change oil than about being with the man they love. As they grow, they become interested in other activities and other males, but they never completely outgrow their attachment needs for Dad. As a psychotherapist, I have heard dozens of stories from grown women about their unfulfilled longings for their fathers' attention and love. The emotionally absent father is a great curse—often leaving a daughter feeling unloved and unlovable. A daughter longs to be emotionally attached to her father.

And yet, you may be thinking, my adolescent daughter does not show any longing to be close to me. She is wrestling away from my grip, trying to stay out as late as possible. She is looking for independence, not attachment. This is a tension we need to get used to, because it affects every daughter-father relationship throughout childhood.

A daughter will struggle for independence while longing for attachment. We see it when the eight-month-old daughter is tired of Dad's way of feeding her Gerber green beans, so she grabs the spoon and does it her own way. We see it when the grade-schooler decides Dad just doesn't understand and spends the evening silently avoiding him. We see it in high school, when a daughter can't wait to get out of the home and go to college. But, all the time, there remains this inner desire for connection and closeness. So how does a father maintain attachment with his daughter while also supporting her autonomy?

Of course there are ways we should *not* handle this tension. We should not suppress our daughter's autonomy and insist on continual closeness. Think, for example, of the father who insists that his adolescent daughter kiss him good night each evening. At some point in adolescence, this may become uncomfortable for the daughter, and if our goal is to raise strong daughters, then we want her to have some control over her own lips. Forcing a good-night kiss won't produce strength—it will produce passivity and compliance along with a dose of hidden resentment and anger.

At the other extreme, we should not encourage so much autonomy that we never see our adolescent daughters. Even if they don't know it, our daughters need the warmth of appropriate touch—a pat on the shoulder that says, "I'm glad to see you," a hug in a moment of sorrow or joy, a high five as congratulations. Strong daughters need to spend time with their fathers, even when they don't know it. Fathers can find a balance between healthy closeness and appropriate independence. Following are four suggestions.

Fight the Stereotypes

One of the biggest struggles we face in being attached to our daughters is the stereotypic view of being male. We are told that a real man is one who provides for the family and leaves the emotional stuff for the women in the house. I recently found an amusing "Real Man" quiz reverberating in the e-mail humor circuit. One of the questions went something like this:

> You're awakened by your wife early in the morning. She tells you that she is sick and that you will have to get the children ready for school today. Your response is:
>   a. Do they need to eat or anything?
>   b. They're in school already?
>   c. There are three of them?

Each of the multiple-choice options is progressively more "manly." This is funny because it resembles a stereotype that is relatively common: Men don't fool much with parenting stuff.

So the first challenge for fathers wanting to establish a healthy attachment with daughters is to fight the stereotypes. We need to learn the language of feelings that may not come naturally to us. We need to dispel the myth that quality of time with our daughters is more important than quantity of time—both are essential. Sometimes we need to turn off the football game and talk with our daughters. Sometimes we need to keep the football game on and invite our daughters to watch it with us. We need to take them out for breakfast or dessert, shoot hoops with them in the backyard, build Lego™ structures with them in the living room, read books to them, have pretend tea parties, ask about their friends and virtual pets. We can share the tenderhearted privilege of parenting with our wives if we break through the unfortunate stereotypes of being male.

Seize the Day!

Fathers need to be ready to spend time with daughters when they are ready. We can't always force them to conform to our schedule; sometimes we need to conform to theirs. Recently I chatted with nineteen-year-old Danielle for what I thought would be a one-minute conversation about household chores. But she sat down at the table as we were talking. I knew what that meant. She was willing to talk for more than one minute and about topics more meaningful than vacuuming carpets. So I sat down too. We had a delightful conversation that lasted almost an hour. She was ready to talk, so I grabbed the opportunity.

Be Part of Their World

One of the most consistent ways I have found to spend time with my daughters is by encouraging them in the activities they have chosen. They receive the benefits of autonomy, because we are talking and thinking about their lives. Yet they also receive the benefits of attachment, because they are spending time with the gray-haired monster when he doesn't seem like a monster. For example, I try to learn about my daughters' athletic events whenever I can. Everything I know about cross-country and volleyball and track and field, I have learned from my daughters. They have welcomed me into their world and are happy to teach me the nuances of a good bump or the mental game of staying in front of another runner. Or sometimes they feel closest to me when I can help them figure out a tough algebra problem that is due tomorrow. When they invite me into their world, and I come with a cheerful attitude, they experience both attachment and autonomy at the same time.

Show Confidence in Their Abilities

Criticism is the enemy of both attachment and autonomy. When fathers criticize their daughters, they feel less attached ("What does he know—he's just a gray-haired monster") and less autonomous ("I guess I'm not as capable as I thought"). The converse is also true: Placing confidence in our daughters builds both attachment and autonomy. Confidence like this can be expressed through simple statements of affirmation, such as:

You're doing great in school this year.
You have such a nice smile.
It's really nice to be with you.

These simple statements and millions of affirmations like them can increase our daughters' sense of confidence and autonomy, while also communicating the closeness and emotional warmth for which they long.

Tension Two: Modeling Strength While Affirming Voice

One way fathers grow strong daughters is by displaying strength in the family. In many families, fathers are seen as a voice of firm authority. This provides an important role model that daughters and sons observe during their formative years. Parents are confident and assertive and can make decisions—even tough decisions. Daughters can learn strength from watching strength. Modeling is a powerful way to learn.

But not all strength is good strength. Sometimes a father's leadership comes in ugly packages. Some of the strongest fathers are the ones with intolerant, dogmatic, authoritarian views of leadership—remnants of the Archie Bunker school of parenting. Daughters of these fathers may learn how to be strong in some situations, but usually their confidence and voice is squashed under the burden of their harsh father.

A harsh father may tell his fourteen-year-old, "There is to be no talking back in this household. I will not tolerate this kind of attitude from you. You have lost your chance for tonight and for the rest of this week. If you would like to do something with your friends next weekend, I suggest you control your words better next time." Off she goes to her room. She has seen strength, but has lost her voice. So a father's strength is not enough. It must be balanced with a desire to encourage his daughters to gain their own voice and their own strength.

Those who study parenting styles would probably agree with the time-honored adage, "There are two ditches on every road." Veer too far one way and we become wishy-washy, laissez-faire fathers who model passivity rather than strength. This is what developmental psychologists call *permissive parenting*,[1] and the result is children who lack self-confidence, are aimless, and do not achieve much with their lives. Veer too far the other way, and we become controlling autocrats who foster passivity in our daughters. This is the so-called *authoritarian parenting* style. Children from authoritarian homes are often hostile, discontented, and uncooperative later in life. But what does it look like in the middle of this road?

The ideal balance is what developmental psychologists call the *authoritative parenting* style. Authoritative fathers are able to take firm leadership positions when necessary, but they are also able to be flexible and negotiate with their children. Authoritative fathers can both teach and learn from their strong daughters. Daughters from these homes grow to be high achievers who are friendly, cooperative, assertive, and self-confident.

Assuming we have convinced you that authoritative fathering is the right choice, answer the following three questions to see how you are doing with your parenting.

1. Do you maintain rules in your home, and expect your daughter to obey them without question? Okay, it's a trick question. Ideally, you should have answered "yes" to the first part of the question, and "not necessarily" to the second part. A home without rules and expectations can give our daughters too much freedom of choice, leaving them to wander aimlessly through the developmental challenges of childhood. But if the rules are enforced as nonnegotiable dictums, then we smother our child's voice. So the ideal balance is to have clear rules and expectations, including firm consequences when those rules are not followed, but also a willingness to learn from our children about the fairness of the rules we set. Let's face it, things are different than they were when we parents were children. How can we learn the unique challenges facing our children and set appropriate guidelines unless we listen to and learn from them?

Returning to our example of the fourteen-year-old who believes a 10:30 P.M. curfew is way too early, perhaps it would be good to hold fast to the expectation, but invite future dialogue at the same time: "You have had a very busy week, and I want you home by 10:30 tonight. If 10:30 seems unfair, I am willing to sit down with you tomorrow and listen to what you have to say. But tonight you need to be home by 10:30." Here parents give clear expectations while maintaining a listening ear.

2. Does your daughter understand the reasons for the household rules? If you answered "yes," you are heading in the right direction. Except when parenting very young children, who may not be capable of understanding the reasons for some rules, it is important to let our reasons be known.

As toddlers begin to experience the curious world around them they start asking, "Why?" "Why do chickens lay eggs?" "Why is the sky blue?" "Why do people die?" I remember being in the middle of answering one of my daughter's why questions when she interrupted me and asked, "Dad, why are you talking?" Kids are curious. They want to know why, just as we adults are curious and want to know about our world.

Of course, we don't want to answer why questions forever. We can tolerate the incessant questioning during the toddler years, but it gets obnoxious if our teenagers are still asking, "Why?" every time we make a request or statement. One way to prevent this is to slip into an authoritarian posture and reply, "Because I said so!" After enough of these messages, our daughters stop asking why, but not for the right reasons. They stop asking because their voices are squashed by our harsh words.

There is a better option. Authoritative fathers are willing to give reasons for the rules and expectations of the home. Daughters who learn to expect wise and well-reasoned answers to their why questions eventually feel less need to keep asking why. They come to expect that the rules and expectations of the home are reasonable. Often, they can figure out the reasons themselves, and when they cannot they have learned to expect a calm answer from their parents. And sometimes they even see their parents changing rules that have been unreasonable.

3. Are your daughters able to say no to you? Yes, it's another trick question. On the one hand, if you answer yes to this you may feel like a wishy-washy, permissive parent. On the other hand, we *want* our daughters to learn how to say no to males, even males in authority positions over them. With epidemic rates of date rape and sexual harassment in the workplace, we need to find ways to teach our daughters to say no to males. The challenge is teaching daughters to say no while instilling the ability to respect appropriate authority. If Jocelyn decides to come home at midnight after she was clearly told to be home by 10:30, should we just view it as a way for her to develop a voice independent of her father? Probably not. Here we must make a distinction between directives and choices.

Directives are clear, specific expectations that reflect a parent's position of authority. Parents issue directives to children throughout their formative years. "Susan, pick up your toys and put them in the toy box" is a directive. Although permissive parents might tolerate a "no" to such a command, authoritative parents will insist on compliance. When children do not comply with directives, there should be unpleasant consequences so they will be more compliant next time. So Susan heads to the time-out chair for three minutes, and then she is given another chance to pick up her toys. This models parental strength. As children grow, there is less and less need for directives. The instruction to be home at 10:30 may be the only directive our hypothetical fourteen-year-old has received from her parents in the past several days. But, hopefully, she has learned enough about directives by age fourteen that she doesn't fool with the consequences anymore.

When we give our daughters two or more options without forcing their decision, we are giving them choices. Choices should start early in life but will be the predominant mode of parenting by the time our daughters reach adolescence. An authoritative parent will work to give choices or to combine choices with directives, whereas an authoritarian parent is content with directives alone. For example, another effective way to respond to the fourteen-year-old might be, "You have had such a busy week that I want you home at 10:30 tonight. I am open to considering the possibility of you staying out until 11:30 next Friday, but if you want to do that you will need to slow your schedule down this coming week and get more sleep than you were able to get this week."

Here a directive, home by 10:30 tonight, is combined with a future choice, next weekend. Choices give voice where directives model strength. We need to balance directives and choices while keeping in mind the importance of increasing choices and decreasing directives with age.

There are two critical features of good choices that ultimately promote voice in our daughters. First, choices should be honest choices. Consider the following conversation at the McDonald's counter:

Dad: What would you like today?
Daughter: The Big Mac looks good. Can I get one of those?
Dad: Well, that's too big for you. You wouldn't be able to finish it.
Daughter: Okay. Can I have a chicken sandwich?
Dad: That's pretty big too, and I was hoping not to spend that much.
Daughter: Well, I could just have a hamburger.
Dad: Okay. That sounds good.

The father had the right idea in giving his daughter a choice about her meal, but it wasn't such an honest choice. It was one of those you-can-choose-if-you-choose-what-I-want-you-to-choose kinds of choices. It would have been more honest to limit the choices with the initial question: "Would you like a hamburger, a cheeseburger, or the Chicken McNuggets today?" The second principle of effective choices can only work if this first principle of honest choices is firmly established.

The second principle is that choices should ultimately replace directives, even when parents have strong preferences for their daughters. By the time of adolescence, our daughters need the freedom to make choices that we would not choose for them. Let's imagine your seventeen-year-old daughter wants to date a boy that you would not choose for her. What are your options? One option is to give an authoritarian directive: "You may not date him." This gives your daughter the choice of rebelling against your directive or complying. If she rebels, your strength gets undermined while affirming her voice; if she complies, your strength is affirmed while undermining her voice. A second option is the permissive parenting option: "You're old enough to decide who you date—it's none of my business." This option affirms your daughter's voice but communicates a kind of anemic response on your part. A third option, more authoritative in nature, is to give your opinion plus an honest choice: "I would prefer you not date him [and explain your concerns], but you are old enough to make your own decision." This option communicates your strength (you have an opinion and are concerned for your daughter) while also giving voice to your daughter (you are not required to agree with me or do what I suggest). Choices such as this should not replace directives too early in life, but eventually we have to let go, just as we had to let go of her bicycle after taking off the training wheels.

Authoritative fathers promote confidence in their daughters while also modeling strength. They are able to set clear rules and expectations, yet they are also willing to listen to their daughters' opinions, remain somewhat flexible, and negotiate the rules as needed. They encourage voice by listening well to their daughters, yet they take seriously their position of authority and are willing to make unpopular decisions at times. They model strength while affirming voice.

TENSION THREE: CRAFTING COMMUNITY WHILE TOLERATING TENSION

There is one other tension illustrated in the brief discussion about fourteen-year-olds and curfew times. How much should fathers tolerate tension and anger from their daughters? In our efforts to affirm our daughter's voice, how do we handle the ugly, shrill voice that sometimes expresses itself with rage and accusation? As with the other tensions discussed in this chapter, this calls for wisdom and balance.

When Tension Is Not Tolerated

None of us cares much for conflict and tension, but the essence of true community always brings the possibility of conflict. To whatever extent our families represent interdependence and a healthy sense of community, we can expect tension from time to time. Sometimes we fool ourselves into thinking that the best families are those with no apparent conflict, but there is often long-term damage from families that suppress conflict at any cost.

Psychologists who study eating disorders in adolescent girls, as well as psychologists studying more severe personality disorders, have identified the *perfect family* as a breeding ground for these problems. In the perfect family, conflict and tension are suppressed in order to maintain the reputation of the family. Family members look perfect when they go to church; they imply to others that their family is perfect; they seem perfectly happy in their interactions with other family members. But all this perfection comes at a cost. When things *aren't* perfect in a perfect family (inevitably they are not), no one can talk about it. The myth of family perfection is so strong that no one dare crush the myth with a complaint or reveal a family secret to someone outside the family. When the myth of perfection is marred by occasional conflict or misconduct, every family member knows that this conflict should never be discussed with others outside the home. "Don't tell" is a theme of the perfect family.

Almost every perfect family has an authoritarian leader—most commonly the father. Whether intentionally or not, the father somehow gets the message across that the image and reputation of the family are more important than individual expression and growth.

A six-year-old daughter in a perfect family may feel angry at the dinner table, because every time she talks, her twelve-year-old brother makes fun of what she says. How might she respond? If she expresses her anger, she will be told that this is not the time or the place to be causing trouble. If she asks when the right time and place would be, she will be told not to talk back. So she learns to keep the anger inside, where it often ferments into self-doubt or even self-hatred. By the time she is sixteen, she is longing for ways to express her individuality, to resist the control of her father. In essence, she is looking for the perfect way of exerting some control in her own life without risking the condemnation of the man who has so much control in this family. Eating disorders are the natural solution. No one can *force* someone else to eat. They *may* be able to make her chew and swallow, but they have no control over what she does in the locked bathroom after dinner. This quiet rebellion occurs often in a perfect family. It is a daughter's way of distinguishing herself from her controlling parents.

Of course there are many other causes of eating disorders, some of which have little to do with parenting style or family structure. My point here is not to describe the cause of eating disorders as much as it is to suggest that fathers need to tolerate tension and conflict and disagreement in the home. Conflict is a natural part of being in relationship with one another, and if we suppress tension in our homes, we may find our daughters expressing their strength and independence in unhealthy ways.

When Community Is Not Crafted

Ironically, there is another extreme that also seems prevalent in the home lives of adolescent girls with eating disorders and other, more severe, forms of personality disorders. The so-called *chaotic family* is a place where anger and tension and frustration are often expressed, but where the family community is never intentionally crafted. Family members come and go as they wish, rarely thinking of the needs of one another, viciously snapping at those who interfere with their own desires and needs. There are no clear expectations to provide emotional boundaries for children in chaotic homes. Children wander aimlessly through those critical adolescent years, learning values by trial-and-error.

We want our homes to be sanctuaries—safe places where family members meet at the end of their busy days to spend evening hours reading, chatting, eating together, or recreating. Imagine the chaos if home were not a sanctuary. What if home were only a place of more conflict and more turmoil? What if the stresses of a busy workday or school day were more comforting and relaxing than home? This is the picture of a chaotic home—more like an unkempt zoo than a sanctuary.

How do fathers play a part in crafting a home community where relationships are valued and tension is tolerated? How can both occur without veering into the ditches seen in the perfect family and the chaotic family?

Fathering and the Bowl Metaphor

One of the most useful images I have of my job as a father is serving as a container for my daughters' emotions. Admittedly, it is an unusual metaphor to see ourselves as bowls, but let me explain. First, bowls are places to put things. Now that I have three adolescent daughters, I realize that much of their emotional lives remain private. They have no interest in talking about every feeling they have throughout the day. But sometimes they want to talk about their feelings. Maybe they are worried about a friend, saddened by losing an important relationship, upset by family rules or expectations, or anxious about the demands of a busy schedule. My job is to be a container where they can deposit these feelings temporarily, look at them carefully as they speak with me, and then retrieve them and carry on. This means I have to listen well.

Second, bowls don't swallow things. A bowl just sits still and contains; it never swallows and consumes. It is not my job to fix my daughters' lives so they don't have pain. Every human through all history has known pain. My daughters will not be exempt from pain. Sometimes I am tempted to try to fix things by giving unsolicited advice or trying to solve their problems for them. Sometimes I even feel angry that they have pain, because I cling to the neurotic belief that good fathers keep their daughters from pain. But just as good bowls don't swallow or consume their contents, I have to remind myself that my daughters don't want or need me to fix every problem in their lives. They need me to listen and care, just to contain their burdens long enough for them to gain the strength they need to face their personal challenges.

Third, bowls have boundaries. A bowl has sides; otherwise it could not be used for storage. If I am to be an effective father, I must have certain expectations of myself and my daughters. For example, we need time together. How can we build community unless we see one another? This means saying no to traveling sometimes. It means setting limits to how many evenings our daughters spend with friends, school activities, or church activities. I employ boundaries when I distinguish between the content of what one says and the way it is expressed. There are some ways of expressing emotions that simply do not fit within my boundaries as a father. I want my daughters to feel comfortable expressing any emotion or experience, but I do not necessarily accept all possible methods of expression. I need to be willing to tolerate tension, while also remembering the importance of crafting a sense of community within the family. When one family member attacks another with cruel and accusing words, we are not crafting community. In true community we are able to speak our differences, even with intense emotions at times, but we do so with a respect for one another.

So how might this bowl metaphor relate to a conversation about curfews? The daughter is upset because she is expected home by 10:30. She accuses her parents of treating her like an eight-year-old, reminding them that all her friends can stay out as late as they want. And then she zings them with guilt by saying she just won't go if she has to be home by 10:30. First, bowls are places to put things. It is important to allow her to express her frustration and anger. However crudely, she is learning to have a voice—to express her preferences and wishes even to a powerful male in her life. To suppress this right and tell her that she has no right to feel the way she does is to slip into the ruts common in authoritarian parenting and perfect families. So our first conclusion is that we ought to let her talk. Second, bowls don't swallow things. These are her feelings and her decisions. There is no need to evaluate her emotions or try to talk her out of them. They are hers. If she chooses not to go out with her friends in order to induce a bit of guilt, then that is also her decision. Third, bowls have boundaries. Parents are not required to change the curfew time just because the daughter got upset. Also, though she expressed her feelings, she may not have done so in the best way. The daughter and her dad may want to have a conversation the following day about more effective ways to express frustration and disappointment.

Conclusion

Whether rappelling rocks on Mt. Shasta or negotiating the Friday night curfew, there are adventures to be faced in effective fathering—many more adventures than can be summarized in one chapter. Raising strong daughters is not for the fainthearted. To whatever extent we succeed, we can expect some degree of tension in the home. But these tensions are not signs of failure, they are signs of success. Properly handled, we can use these tensions to craft the character of daughters as they grow strong. Three tensions have been considered in this chapter. As we model strength while affirming voice, we move toward authoritative parenting—a style that promotes confidence, assertiveness, and security in our daughters. As we maintain attachment while supporting autonomy, we experience closeness with our daughters while learning to respect their independence. Eventually, they invite us into their world more as friends than as authority figures. As we craft community while tolerating tension, we accept our daughters as individuals, created in God's image, with the capacity to feel and think on their own while contributing to the welfare of the family unit.

Our daughters are created in God's image. What an enormous privilege and tremendous responsibility it is to be stewards of that image during their formative years.

CHAPTER TEN

MOTHERS AND DAUGHTERS

Mummy herself has told us that she looked upon us more as her friends
than her daughters. Now that is all very fine, but still, a friend can't take
a mother's place.

—Anne Frank, *Diary of a Young Girl*

THE CAMERA ZOOMS IN on a pregnant woman standing by
the window, the curtains and her hair gently moving with the wind.
Her hand is on an empty cradle. She awaits motherhood with wise
and gentle anticipation.

A nursing mother rocks her infant. Her hair falls loosely across
her face and within the grasp of the nursing child's fingers. She
smiles, the baby smiles.

A mother kneels down by her preschool child, buttoning up the
yellow slicker before sending the child out to play in the rain. Mothers
pack lunches, do laundry, braid hair, cook meals, drive carpools,
bake cookies for Christmas parties—all for the beloved children
who appreciate her efforts to make their lives safe, fulfilling, healthy,
and pleasant.

214

Suddenly adolescence hits and media images of mothers change. Mothers become those exasperated middle-aged women who don't understand anything about teenagers, who have unrealistic expectations that their children be polite to those over twenty, dress "appropriately," and keep the floor of their rooms visible. Mothers are portrayed as worried, helpless, and hopelessly incompetent. And if daughters become promiscuous or rebellious, mothers are blamed for not loving enough, not being strong models, or not being authoritative enough in their discipline. In short, mothers ruin their daughters' hopes for happiness and their chances to be well-adjusted adults. From adolescence on, depictions of mothers continue downhill. Mothers are hard to get along with in adulthood and impossible to please. Mothers-in-law are interfering and overly critical.

Teenage daughters feel enough tension and confusion in adolescence without having relationships with their mothers undermined by a culture that expects those relationships to be awkward and difficult. A daughter, according to contemporary culture (and developmental theory), is supposed to separate from her mother—to "differentiate" and become her own person. The easiest way to do this is to strive to be everything Mom is not. Mom is neat; daughter becomes messy. Mom cares about the environment; daughter uses *lots* of paper and leaves the lights on. Mom is punctual; daughter is perpetually tardy. Mom runs late; daughter becomes punctual and is driven crazy by Mom's tardiness. Mom doesn't wear much makeup, so daughter wears a ton. Mom likes makeup and dressing stylishly, so daughter wears no makeup and dresses in alternative resale shop clothes.

Yet in spite of trying to be what Mom is not, most daughters still desire approval and affirmation from her. They want their moms to like their friends, appreciate how they dress, and approve of what they do with their free time. During Sarah's retro-style era, she asked if I liked her shiny polyester green and orange outfit. I said, "If I liked it that would mean it wasn't outrageous enough. Am I *supposed* to like it?" She smiled a little. Sarah wasn't really asking if I liked her outfit. She wanted affirmation of her choice to be the kind of girl who wore retro. In a counterintuitive sense, she wanted approval for something she's doing which is *supposed* to make adults in general, and perhaps mothers in particular, shake their heads in befuddlement.

What is motherhood about? On its most surface level motherhood is about reproducing, nurturing, socializing, and sending off the next generation. We do the necessary work of changing diapers, getting our children immunized, teaching them manners, paying school registration fees, packing lunches, signing field trip permission slips, paying more school registration fees, purchasing clothes and school supplies, being Girl Scout, Pioneer Girl, or Awana leaders, teaching driving skills, and on and on.

On a deeper level, motherhood is about tasting God's capacity to love us. As we experience loving our children, even though we love them imperfectly, we come closer to an understanding of how God loves us—with a perfect, unconditional love that seeks our best interests. We grow in our knowledge of God as we love, accept, and serve our children.

Thus, mothering is not only about preparing and sending off the next generation. It is also about experiencing and coming to know God. As we grow our children through infancy, toddlerhood, early and later childhood, and adolescence, we recognize our own spiritual journey with God. We struggle with God as our daughters struggle with us. We look to God for comfort as our daughters look to us. The value in motherhood goes beyond what we can do for our daughters; it is also about bringing us closer to God.

Since we learn more about God's love as we strive to love our children, we can look at how God parents us for principles regarding how we should mother our daughters and sons. The first part of this chapter will consider two of these principles: availability and flexibility. The second part will deal more specifically with some of the relationship challenges mothers confront as they try to raise strong daughters.

THE PARENTING OF GOD

Images of both mothers and fathers are used to depict God's relationship with humans in the Old and New Testaments. Sometimes God is like a tender and compassionate father (Ps. 103:13). God is called the father of orphans and defender of widows (Ps. 68:5). Sometimes God is like a mother eagle teaching her babies to fly or a protective hen gathering her chicks under her wings. As a parent, God nurses, carries, protects, disciplines, and teaches; and he is ever present, available, and approachable.

Availability

During the agricultural era of history, families lived and worked in close proximity to each other. With the advent of the industrial revolution, fathers began to leave the family every day to go to work. They entered the cities and worked in factories or budding businesses. The effect of absent fathers on children has been documented in numerous studies and books.[1]

For a time, only unmarried women worked. They mostly taught school or worked as nurses. But not too many decades after fathers left home for work, mothers also left home to work elsewhere. They too entered the cities and worked in factories or businesses. For most of them, work became an economic necessity. Families were not living on farms anymore, where they could provide much of their own food and livelihood. The industrial revolution did bring progress, and an increased standard of living, but not without cost. The increased standard of living itself became costly and burdensome. Some of the consumerism associated with an increasing standard of living could be rejected; other aspects of it became entrenched in the American way of life.

For instance, phones are fairly standard now. Some of our daughters will try to convince us that multiple lines and call waiting are also standard. I recently received an ad in the mail promoting the necessity of a second *car* phone, which, of course, the company would gladly give me for free if I would sign a two-year contract for service. Most people feel they need at least one phone to function in the United States. Thus, the standard of living goes up a notch, and phone bills have to be paid. Most people live too far from work to get by without a car. In 1970, 28 percent of households had two cars. In the 1990s, 54 percent of American households had two cars.[2] The standard of living is raised another notch. Most of our food now comes from a grocery store (or local fast-food restaurants), and more people heat with gas or electricity than with wood. At least some of the increased expenses in living are unavoidable.

Families committed to subsisting on one income often live well below the standard of living. In 1999, one full-time, minimum-wage job paid about $11,000 per year. Only the middle and upper classes can live off one income.

Some mothers leave home to work, not only out of economic necessity, but because they desire to use other gifts and abilities beyond mothering. As men find satisfaction in work, so women desire to contribute and find meaning in work.

The availability argument should not be reduced to "working mothers do not care for their children and at-home mothers do." Rather, we can take the reality of what is—some mothers work and some do not—and identify the strengths and challenges within each choice. Rather than pointing fingers or feeling guilty, the goal becomes overcoming challenges and enhancing potential strengths so parents can be available to their children.

At-home Mothers: a Strength

Mothers who stay home full-time can provide a greater sense of presence and availability than are found in dual-career families. Since parents are not omnipresent, like God, they cannot be in two places at once. As it is, most children already miss out on the presence and availability of dads—when Mom goes to work the availability of parents is further reduced. Once social scientists identified the decreasing availability of parental time with children, the quality versus quantity argument arose to justify men and women working full-time. The argument suggests that the quality of time together is more important than the quantity of time together. A mother who stays home with her kids and watches TV all day provides less nurturing for her children than a mother who works full-time but is actively involved with her kids when she is home. True, theoretically anyway, but the children do not necessarily see it that way. Quality and quantity are both important, and children will tell adults so. While teaching a Marriage and Family class at a large public university, I learned that many women students were hoping to stay home with their young children. Their mothers had not been home for them, and the students wished they had been. Children want and need the availability and presence of parents. One college male wrote this about his mother.

> My mom is a full-time homemaker. She doesn't work outside the home, but works extremely hard inside of it. It has always been this way for me. For all of my nineteen years my mom has stayed home with us. I do not know what it would be like to have my mom working. I can say, however, that I think all three of us children benefited greatly from having a homemaker mom. There were countless times that I needed help with something, or needed to talk about something, or just wanted some company, and she was there for me. Others might say she is old fashioned, but I respect her for what she is doing. I am thankful that she has chosen homemaking for her lifestyle.

Having a full-time homemaker can make home life a haven for everyone else, though it doesn't always. Women who stay home and see their calling as being home (an important qualifier) tend to cook more, do more of the family chores (e.g. laundry, cleaning, errands), and thus create a comfortable space for children and husband. Their lives become a sacrifice of service to their families. So much is the absence of their role noted, that many career mothers say they need a wife to help them keep track of birthdays, bake for school parties, and take their turn driving the carpool. Mothers who stay home are available and present for their children and husbands.

At-home Mothers: a Challenge

While children and husbands are served well by mothers and wives who stay home, that role can be so taken for granted that neither children nor husbands learn to become servant-like. Boys with at-home moms often grow up expecting a wife who will do their laundry and cook their food. The idea of serving in this capacity themselves will often seem demeaning to them as males. Household work is women's work, they think. Unfortunately, this refusal to share the household duties undermines the value husbands of at-home wives claim to give it. If the work at-home mothers do is supposed to be held in high esteem, then sons and husbands affirm its esteem by their willingness to serve by participating in it.

In *Women's Ways of Knowing,* the authors describe a number of mother-daughter relationships. The most admired mothers were perceived as being able to speak from their intellect as well as their gut. They may have stayed home, but pursued lives beyond serving the needs of children and husbands.[3] They were perceived as confident, capable, and interdependent. Some of my students whose mothers never worked express feeling that their mothers did not live up to their potential and were doormats for the family, especially their husbands. One of my students said she had found some poetry her mother had written in her early twenties. The poetry was beautiful, poignant, and intelligent. My student felt as if the woman who had written that poetry had disappeared somewhere during the next thirty years, and her daughter grieved that loss, both for her mother's sake and for her own. To overcome this potential challenge, mothers who stay home after their children are older can develop outside interests that build confidence, independence, and the ability to contribute meaningfully outside the home. For a daughter to respect her mother's choice to stay home, she needs to see her mother as intelligent and capable of choosing something else.

Working Mothers: a Strength

The male student quoted earlier, with the stay-at-home mom, had a father who made over $100,000 a year. If his dad made only $20,000, I imagine he would have a different story. Consider this female student's home:

> My parents struggled financially as I was growing up. They believed in doing whatever they could to keep us in a Christian school. Because of this, my father worked two jobs and was rarely ever seen. My mother was also very involved in her work, which mainly involved counseling and teaching women. This created an environment that was hard on us children. When there was a problem or a question, it was hard to find someone in the family who could help. Often I found friends, or a youth spon-

sor at church, or someone else to fulfill my needs. Mainly, I just became very independent.

This story illustrates both the strengths and challenges of dual career families. The combined yearly income of this family was $27,000. Sending only Dad off to work was not a feasible option. And it came at a price. These children did not feel as if their parents were either present or available. However, they did see a mother partner with their father to carry their financial burden. They saw her as a willing, strong, and capable woman able to contribute meaningfully in a ministry of counseling and teaching other women. In addition, they learned how to seek help outside their own family. Given that only God can parent us perfectly, that only God is always available and present, we need to teach our daughters to build relationships outside our families to help meet their needs. Neither a spouse, parent, or sibling will always be present and available. Another strength the female student gained was an ability to function independently. Children whose parents both work, learn to cook, do laundry, and clean. They learn how to be responsible for themselves.

Working Mothers: a Challenge

In an ideal world, men and women will both find their work satisfying and fulfilling, whether that work is accomplished inside the home or out of it. As God is available both as mother and father, so parents would both be available and actively involved in the parenting of children. Somewhere along the way we assumed it was the mother's responsibility to be available to children. It made sense if Dad had to be off earning the income. But this too came at a price. Dads became distant. They did not know their children, and their children did not always find them approachable. With dual career families, mothers can also become distant; they can lose touch with their children. Mothers (and fathers) can mitigate this weakness when both parents see it as a joint responsibility to be available and approachable. Whether or not both parents work, when both share this responsibility, children receive balanced parenting by two people whose different parenting styles reflect the different ways they bear God's image. In an ideal world, parents' work schedules and finances would be such that they work, yet have time and energy for each other and their children. Since this isn't an ideal world, and careers are often most demanding during the years children are most needy, then parents need to work this joint responsibility out between them.

For Mark and me it was relatively easy. I wanted to stay home with our girls when they were young. We worked creatively to make that feasible financially. Early on it meant we lived in subsidized housing. We planted a garden, canned and froze food, and seldom went out to eat. Our entertainment consisted of walks, playing games, and being with friends. Intermittently I went back to work one or two shifts a week to keep my RN license current. Later Mark started a part-time practice in addition to his teaching. We look back on our early years fondly. Our lives felt rich, though we lived on a very small income. When our youngest went to school, I pursued my own career calling. That meant Mark had to back off his career-building enough to become a more involved father and househusband—picking up the girls after school and sharing the cooking and cleaning responsibilities.

Because parents are not omnipresent, we have to give more attention to how we sequence our lives so someone is available and present for our children. A myth parents have to confront is that children don't need them once they are old enough to read, make a lunch, or ride a bicycle. Our daughters will still want us to be around, even if they do not always show it. As Mark and I were heading out one evening, we asked fifteen-year-old Sarah (a private adolescent who spent a fair amount of time alone in her room) whether or not she wanted us to wait to go until the ride for her baby-sitting job came. She thought a minute and then said, "Actually, I want you to stay, but I probably won't talk to you." Danielle, home for the summer after her first year of college, told Mark and me that she still wanted us to act like parents to her—to listen to her and give her counsel.

Our daughters need us as they stretch through adolescence toward adulthood, just as they needed us when they were babies and schoolchildren. Because of the many expectations that girls face to be sexual, or rebellious, or boldly experimental—and, above all, to separate from parents—they need mothers (and fathers) who are available. Because daughters will hear messages (sometimes from the voice of their own uncertainty) that they are incapable and likely to fail, they need affirmation that they *are* capable and *can* succeed.

Daughters need mothers (and fathers) who can sit down together for a latte and conversation, or run to the library to pick up some needed resource for a paper, or cheer them on as they run, kick a soccer ball, or dribble a basketball. Daughters need the affirmation that their mothers are available and care about the woes and wonders of their lives. Some careers allow this flexibility. Some do not. Most of us have at least a measure of control over choices that affect how flexible we can be.

Flexibility

When my daughters hit adolescence, I had to get used to the idea that they usually would rather go to the mall or out for coffee with friends than with me. I also had to get used to the idea that they would share more of their personal lives with their sisters, friends, and youth leaders than they would with me. I secretly hoped they would love to spend all that time with *me,* and would tell *me* all about their lives like they did when they were in elementary school.

A couple of summers ago my mother, two sisters, sister-in-law (who is very much like a sister), and I extended a family reunion to spend two and a half days on the Wilson River in Oregon. We left our children and husbands (except for one nursing baby) and gathered together to reminisce and reflect on our lives. We brought photo albums to help stimulate memories as we shared various stories from our childhoods. Mom heard a lot of these stories for the first time. I asked her later how that felt. She said it was a bittersweet experience. On the one hand, she enjoyed hearing the stories and learning more about her daughters' adolescence than she had known before. On the other hand, the stories brought a painful awareness of how much she had been on the outside of our lives.

We mothers need to expect to be on the outside sometimes. We need a flexibility that allows our daughters to change and go through stages, sometimes growing away, sometimes drawing near. As God graciously flows with our idiosyncrasies, allowing us distance, patiently waiting for us to draw near, being the ever steady Rock of security amidst the changing seasons of our own journey, so we ought to flow graciously with the seasons of our daughters' lives. And as God welcomes the various ways we will relate—song or silence, raised arms or reserved postures, liturgical recitation or the speaking of tongues—so we would be wise to welcome the various ways our daughters may choose to relate to us. Some relate by sitting quietly in the same room while working on separate projects. Some relate by playing games, going on walks, writing notes, joking, touching. The way our daughters relate to us will not necessarily be the way we would prefer. As God is flexible in dealing with us, so we should be flexible in dealing with our daughters.

MOTHER/DAUGHTER RELATIONSHIPS

I look at pictures of my infant daughters and cannot imagine they are the same people who now fill my house with their voices, thoughts, and *persons,* impressing themselves upon me as uniquely different than me—yet still of me. We nurture our infant girls, teach them to become somewhat self-sufficient, and then feel a wrenching as they move away from us to become women. Walter Wangerin speaks of this process as a mystery to him, a man.[4] That women would do this birth and letting-go thing amazes him. He describes how mothers sacrifice twofold for their children—and twice. First, she labors to make room for the child to grow within her (sacrificing all sorts of personal comforts), and then labors to empty her womb so her child can *be.* Second, she makes room for the child in her life, sacrificing again all sorts of personal comforts, and then again labors to let the child she has nurtured leave home and go out of her life.

Somewhere around adolescence, many mothers decide they are ready for the second send-off and that it's a lot easier to empty her house than it was to empty her womb! Given the tensions surrounding many daughter/mother relationships in adolescence it would be easy for mothers to decide to check out of their daughters' lives for a while, and figure they will reconnect after they go away to college. Indeed, many of my college students have confirmed that they appreciate their mothers a lot more since leaving home. However, our daughters need us during adolescence, and if we want them to become strong women through the challenges of adolescence, we need to proactively mother them. We are supposed to be the more mature of the pair and to keep on giving even when our efforts are not appreciated. Our relationship can be an anchoring point for our daughters in the midst of their own uncertainty and the uncertainty around them. To be this anchor and encourage our daughters to grow strong, we need to find ways to invest in their lives and stay connected, yet be willing to let go. We need to find ways to speak the language of love, and if we need an image of hope, to develop and hold on to one.

Investing

A winter day some years ago . . .

The aroma of chocolate chip cookies meanders through the house, drifting up to the loft and back to the bedrooms. Sarah, in her green apron appliquéd across the front with a brown teddy bear, is my number one assistant. She stands on a chair by the counter plopping spoonfuls of cookie dough on the pan in drunken rows. Megan, in her green teddy bear apron, is my number two assistant. She sits on the counter, mostly sneaking licks from the bowl when she thinks I'm not looking.

Me, I'm the chief chef, in my green teddy bear apron. Today I'm relishing this moment, this breath of time when my children are young, at home, all mine. Already one is in school. Already I sense a pulling away as she seeks to stretch out and grow.

Sometimes I hear mothers say they cannot wait until their child is old enough to go to school so they can get on with their lives. I said it myself sometimes. Often I lost the beauty of those early childhood days in my aspirations for some tomorrow. In our impatience for tomorrow, some of us feed our daughters "Miracle-Gro"

225

in hopes of bringing tomorrow sooner. But we lose something precious in this speeding up of growth. The chocolate chip cookies are for moms too. Tomorrow can wait. Today has fulfillment of its own. Tomorrow will come, perhaps after all, too soon.

Many years ago a friend asked if mothering daughters was what I had anticipated. I mused over my spiced tea and said, "Mostly. We don't bake as many cookies, stroll through the park, and pass time in the rocking chair as much as I thought we would, and we have more messes, noise, and frustrations. But mostly mothering is what I thought it would be."

"Do you like it as much as you thought you would?" she asked.

"Sometimes I don't like it much at all," I replied, "but mostly I like it more than I thought possible."

I still agree.

Our attitudes about mothering will affect what we do with the first few years of our daughters' lives. Some of us have no choice but to work, some of us are blessed with the choice. Some of us will choose to follow a career call and seek to balance parenting with our partners. In any case, mothers can feel overwhelmed with the added responsibility of a career or resentful of putting our goals in storage for a few years. If we see the early years of our daughters' lives as an interruption of or intrusion in our lives, we may not realize the value of investing in them. We may toss those early years off as insignificant, only later to discover how significant they were, both for our daughters and ourselves. We build later relationships based on earlier experiences. It will be easier to connect with our daughters in adolescence if we connected with them in preschool. As women, we are affected by motherhood. Who we and our daughters become reflects the mother/daughter relationship we have had. The time when our children are young is as the dawn—fleeting, yet full of possibility for the day to come.

> The cookies are done now. We pull out the baked ones and slide in some more.
>
> "Are they cool enough to eat yet, Mama?" asks Sarah.
>
> "Cookie!" says Megan.

Staying Connected

Staying connected requires flexibility and knowing how your daughter connects. Each of mine connects differently. A couple of summers ago, Danielle and I shared a wonderful connection point when I invited her to help me figure out trendy clothes combinations I could teach in. Sarah and I connected on walks and through written notes. Megan and I connected over lunch or coffee, or while playing cards, or in conversations we had in the hammock.

A friend of mine used to take her elementary age children out of school and out for lunch—an idea that had never crossed my mind (would the school *let* me do that?). The teacher thought it was *great* that a parent would want to come take a child out to lunch. So I took my friend's inspiration and we established a lunch date pattern. I picked up one of my daughters for lunch one day a week, so I had lunch with each one once every three weeks. Sarah liked KFC, Megan liked McDonald's, and Danielle liked going different places. We enjoyed the intersection of our lives at an unusual point in the day.

Another connecting point that worked best with Sarah was letter writing. She expresses herself more easily in writing than in speaking. For a while we had loose letters I was trying to track and keep. Finally, I bought blank journal books and started exchanging letters in the journals with each of them. Now we have an easy way to keep them. Danielle and Megan haven't exchanged letters with me as often as Sarah, nor at as deep a level. Daughters will have different points of connection.

Learning Ways of Loving

We also need to learn to express love to our daughters in ways they most feel it. In *The Five Love Languages*,[5] Gary Chapman discusses five basic ways people express love and like to receive love. While he is mostly writing to couples, an application to our daughters is appropriate. Some daughters like receiving and giving gifts as a way to express love. Others feel loved mostly through words of encouragement. Some love and feel loved through acts of service. Some love and feel loved by spending time together; for others it is through touch. Our daughters likely use and respond to several of these expressions of love. Our job as mothers is to become conversant in all of them, to identify which speak most clearly to our daughters, and then use those to communicate our love to them.

Believing Our Images of Hope

At an extended family reunion one summer, my sister-in-law, JoLynn, was asking people for nuggets of wisdom about how they were parenting their children through adolescence. Teri, one of my cousins, said something like this:

> I picture them in adulthood—having survived adolescence and emerging with all the strong and good characteristics that have always been part of who they are. Then I hold onto that image as hope.

That is an insightful piece of wisdom. It also reflects a twist to the Thomas theorem we talk about in sociology. W. I. Thomas said: Situations that are defined as real become real in their consequences. When one believes something about oneself and then acts on the belief, often the belief creates and becomes reality. If a girl moves to a new school and believes she is incapable of making friends, she will not go out of her way to try. Since she does not try, her inability to make friends becomes reinforced; thus the belief "I cannot make friends" becomes a reality. In a similar way, what a mother believes about her daughter can come to be internalized by her daughter as true. As our daughters learn that we believe them to be developing into strong, confident, capable women, so they will begin to see themselves as such. Mothers carry a significant voice for their daughters. We can tell them we believe in them when they are unable to believe in themselves. We can identify and affirm strong characteristics forming within them. Because daughters identify with Mom (whether or not they want to), what Mom believes about who they are and what they are capable of can help anchor them in the midst of uncertainty.

Letting Go

Mothers can hang on to their daughters in one of two ways. One is to literally want them to stay close, especially if their daughter is single. Maria was a student of mine and is an only child. Her mother is a single mom. The truth is, Maria's mother has done a remarkable job of raising a strong daughter who is confident and independent. Maria's mother loves that Maria has been able to carve out a life that is meaningful and productive. Another truth is that Maria's mother yearns to live closer to her daughter and wishes Maria would come back home to live. Yet she doesn't call and nag or pester her to do so. Maria's mother has done a remarkable job of letting go, giving Maria the chance to forge ahead in the making of her future.

While mothers may desire to be as intimately connected as they were when their daughters were growing up, mothers need to develop their own network of friends and not rely on daughters to fulfill their needs for intimacy and friendship. When we see God at work in our daughters' lives we need to affirm their choices, even if they separate us. We need to let our daughters grow up . . . and away.

Another way mothers need to let go is to accept our daughters' choices when they are not the choices we would make for them. Our daughters are wired to want our approval. In Amy Tan's novel *The Joy Luck Club,* one frustrated daughter tells her mother how burdened she has felt her whole life with the need to always try to please her. Her mother begins to cry and says, "You have made me very happy." Needless to say, this did not improve her daughter's relationship with her.

For our daughters to have peace about pursuing God's leading, mothers must be willing to let go of their own expectations. Mothers are the vessels God uses to bring forth children. But the children belong to God. We must learn to release them back to God. Daughters will find it easier to stay close to mothers who allow them space to go down a different path than their mothers did. God may call our daughters to fulfill their stewardship role by preparing them for different challenges that match the needs of a changing world. We need to let go of our daughters so they can freely follow the call of God on their lives.

CONCLUSION

Mothers get mixed messages about the role they are supposed to have in their daughters' lives. We are supposed to be close, yet our daughters are supposed to create distance from us at some point. This distance, or even rejection of us, is the only way society says they will ever become their own persons. In *Mother Daughter Revolution,* the authors astutely observe that "We live in a world where blaming mothers is the yellow brick road to 'health' and a 'positive adjustment' to society."[6]

Yet mothers can invest in relationships with their daughters when they are young and strive to stay connected to them through adolescence. Some daughters will still reject Mom for a while; others will be able to stay connected and use their mothers as an anchoring point for the challenges and changes they confront.

Our daughters will be reflections of us as their mothers and the choices we made as we parented them. We will see bits of ourselves in our daughters, as we have seen pieces of our mothers in who we became. But our daughters are unique creations of God that reflect the shaping and calling of God in their lives, more than the shaping and calling of us as their mothers. If we can ultimately relinquish our expectation that they be daughters in ways we define it, then they will be free to become our friends.

And hopefully, through our mothering, we will come closer to understanding God's love of us. As we sacrificially love and serve our children, so we feel how God sacrificially loves and serves us. God yearns to be in relationship with us as we yearn to be in relationship with our daughters. And, in a very tangible way, when we love and sacrificially serve our children, we bring honor to God by reflecting his image as a Parent who cares, nurtures, and loves.

EPILOGUE

WHEN JANA, my backpacking partner and colleague, and I envisioned and ultimately birthed "Glorious Endurance," we wanted to offer a backpacking experience for women that would stretch them physically and invite them to worship in God's pristine creation. With each trip, we intentionally acknowledge and construct a community of journeying women who will talk, laugh, cry, and pray—often together, sometimes alone.

How I long to prepare my daughters for the glorious endurance of life! They will need to be strong so they can endure the challenges of a culture that is not ready to let them be strong and has particular ideas about how females are supposed to be. To be gracious, empowered women they will need strong shoulders to carry the load God prepares for them and well-seasoned spirits that know they are capable of much.

Preparing our daughters for the glorious endurance of life means giving them a sense of the glorious—of the privilege to be called by God, created in the image of God, and gifted with femaleness, which enables them to balance maleness as stewards over creation. God has given us abundant life—meant to be glorious. Yet God knows life will bring challenge and pain. God also knows that challenge and pain make us strong and enable us to better experience the glorious.

Parents have a unique task in growing daughters. We need to be intentional about building confidence, independence, and voice in our daughters, especially because they live in a culture that easily erodes confidence, independence, and voice. We need to be intentional about restoring a healthy sense of their physical and sexual selves so they can see their bodies as worthy and wonderful vessels that house the image of God. We need to encourage our daughters' relationships with men to reflect interdependency and a sense of partnering together over creation.

Examining how our daughters have been created in the image of God has implications for how we encourage them to listen to the calling of God in their lives. Now that our culture is broadening our daughters' opportunities, they may be called to places that we have traditionally been more comfortable sending our sons. We do not need to fear the opportunities but help our daughters evaluate them in light of an understanding of how God has created them—as capable of discerning, reasoning, creating, and ruling.

In *Streams of Living Water*, Richard Foster talks about our sense of calling. He defines calling using many of the characteristics discussed in this book that relate to the image of God essence within us. Foster says, in part:

> We have a sense of creativity that enables us to place the autograph of our souls on the work of our hands. . . . We have a sense of meaning and purpose for we know that we are working in cooperation with God to bring the world one step closer to completion.[1]

May a restored image of God enable our daughters to approach life with confidence and with a certainty that God has given them what they need to walk through and experience the glorious endurance of life. And may we grow our daughters to be strong so they can fully use their God-likeness in cooperation with God to bring healing to a broken world.

NOTES

Introduction

1. This is discussed at length in Amitai Etzioni's, *The Spirit of Community: the Reinvention of American Society* (New York: Simon & Schuster, 1993), 23–24.

2. Church historians and theologians suggest some of our modern understanding of Christianity is a result of distortions beginning with the fall, which Jesus began to set straight with his radical approach to women. These writers also suggest that distortion began to occur again shortly after Jesus' time on earth, as the church became institutionalized and women's contributions in the early church and society became marginalized and forgotten. These trends continue to damage our daughters at the dawn of the twenty-first century. See for instance, Gilbert Bilezikian, *Beyond Sex Roles* (Grand Rapids: Baker, 1985), Phyllis Trible, *God and the Rhetoric of Sexuality* (Philadelphia: Fortress Press, 1978), Stanley Grenz, *Women in the Bible* (Downers Grove, Ill.: InterVarsity, 1995), Mary Stewart Van Leeuwen, ed., *After Eden* (Grand Rapids: Eerdmans, 1993), and Catherine and Richard Clark-Kroeger, *I Suffer Not a Woman: Rethinking 1 Tim. 2:11–15 in Light of Ancient Evidence* (Grand Rapids: Baker, 1992).

Chapter 1: *The Strength of an Image*

1. Rosemary Agonito, *History of Ideas on Woman, a Source Book* (New York: Perigee Book, 1977), 41–54.

2. See Augustine, *On the Trinity*, 7.7.10, translated S. McKenna, vol. 45 of *Fathers of the Church*, ed. H. Dressler (Washington, D.C.: Catholic University of America Press, 1963), 351–52 and Agonito, *History of Ideas on Woman*, 73–90.

3. See Anthony A. Hoekema, *Created in God's Image* (Grand Rapids: Eerdmans, 1986), 67. Hoekema uses the generic man throughout his writings, though notes the intent that women are to be included. Hoekema states one feature of the image of God is its universal nature that is bestowed equally on women as well as men. Also see Millard Erickson's discussion of image of God in *Christian Theology* (Grand Rapids: Baker, 1985), 514–15.

4. Hoekema, *Created in God's Image,* 68–69.
5. This list is derived from Berkhof's discussion of the structural elements in Hoekema, ibid., 59.
6. Claire M. Renzetti and Daniel J. Curran, *Women, Men and Society,* 3d ed. (Boston: Allyn and Bacon, 1995), 108.
7. "The New Theologians," *Christianity Today* 43, no. 2 (February 8, 1999): 46.
8. Stanley Grenz, *Women in the Church: A Biblical Theology of Women in Ministry* (Downers Grove, Ill.: InterVarsity, 1995), 170–71.
9. Robert Coles, *The Call of Service* (Boston: Houghton Mifflin, 1993), 1.
10. Ibid., 5.
11. Hoekema, *Created in God's Image,* 83.
12. Ibid., 26.
13. Millard J. Erickson, *Christian Theology* (Grand Rapids: Baker, 1985), 514–15; Hoekema, *Created in God's Image,* 74.
14. Augustine, *Confessions* (Brewster, Mass.: Paraclete Press, 1986): I1.
15. Those who do not believe women have been created in the image of God to the same extent as men would also argue that women are only rulers/stewards to the extent they do so under the authority of male leadership. Stanley Grenz is one theologian among many who offers an excellent response to this point.
16. Hoekema, *Created in God's Image,* 85.

Chapter 2: *Masculinity and Femininity: Origins and Implications*

1. This has been done in numerous good books, such as Mary Stewart Van Leeuwen, *Gender and Grace* (Downers Grove, Ill.: InterVarsity, 1990); or Renzetti and Curran, *Women, Men and Society.*
2. Most notably the work of Margaret Mead.
3. John Bristow argues this point in *What Paul Really Said About Women* (New York: HarperSanFrancisco, 1988).
4. Plato, *Timaeus,* trans. H.D.P. Lee (Baltimore: Penguin, 1965), 42A-C, 90C, 91A.
5. Bristow, *What Paul Really Said About Women.* Also Agonito, *History of Ideas on Woman.*
6. Bristow, *What Paul Really Said About Women,* 28–29.
7. Gustave LeBon as quoted in Stephen J. Gould, *The Mismeasure of Man* (New York: W.W. Norton, 1981), 10–45.
8. Edgar Berman, M.D., "Letter to the Editor," *New York Times,* 26 July 1970. In Stewart Van Leeuwen, *Gender and Grace,* 89.
9. Elizabeth Debold, Marie Wilson, and Idelisse Malave, *Mother Daughter Revolution* (New York: Bantam Books, 1993), 10.
10. *Boys and Girls: The Difference* ABC Special. (John Stosell reporter, May 29, 1992).
11. Renzetti and Curran, *Women, Men and Society,* 362–63.
12. Ibid., 396–97.
13. Ellen Goodman as quoted in Stewart Van Leeuwen, *Gender and Grace,* 90.
14. Carol Cohn, "Wars, Wimps, and Women" in *Men's Lives,* Michael S. Kimmel and Michael A. Messner, eds. (Boston: Allyn and Bacon, 1995), 131.
15. John Arnold, Letters to the Editor, *Newsweek,* May 5, 1997, 20.
16. Manny Kiesser, Letters to the Editor, *Newsweek,* May 5, 1997, 20.

Chapter 3: *Daughters and Confidence*

1. Mary Field Belenky, Blythe McVicker Clincy, Nancy Rule Goldberger, and Jill Mattuck Tarule, *Women's Ways of Knowing* (New York: Basic Books, 1986).

2. Ibid., 170.

3. Mary Pipher, *Reviving Ophelia* (New York: Ballantine Books, 1994), 19.

4. Naomi Wolf, *The Beauty Myth* (New York: Anchor Books, 1991), 215.

5. Mary Pipher mentions these three factors in her discussion of why girls spiral downhill. *Reviving Ophelia*, 22–23.

6. Jerome Kagan, *The Nature of the Child* (New York: Basic Books, 1984), 29.

7. Margaret Jablonski, "The leadership challenge for women college presidents," *Initiatives* 58, no. 4 (1996): 1–6.

8. Renzetti and Curran, *Women, Men and Society*, 119. Also Pipher, *Reviving Ophelia*.

9. Renzetti and Curran, *Women, Men and Society*, 113.

10. Catherine Krupnick in "Who Needs Boys?" *20/20* segment, ABC (John Stosell, reporter, May 29, 1992).

11. Debold, Wilson, and Malave, *Mother Daughter Revolution*, 11.

12. The original study was conducted by K. Deaux, *The Behavior of Women and Men* (Monterey, Calif.: Brooks Cole, 1976), as reported in Renzetti and Curran, *Women, Men and Society*, 123. More recently this has been explored by Janet Swim and Lawrence Sanna in "He's Skilled, She's Lucky: A Meta-analysis of Observers' Attributions for Women's and Men's Successes and Failure," *Personality and Social Psychology Bulletin* vol. 22, no. 5 (May 1996): 507–19.

13. Traci Watson, "Study: Girls get higher grades," *USA Today*, 12 August 1998, sec. A, 5.

14. Mary Pipher, *Reviving Ophelia*, 24.

15. Susan J. Douglas writes a very entertaining and persuasive case for this in *Where the Girls Are: Growing Up Female with the Mass Media* (New York: Random House, 1994).

16. This information was passed on to me by my wise psychologist husband, Mark McMinn.

17. Christina Boyle, "The Ultimate Prom Survival Guide," *YM Prom* (April 1997): 94.

18. B. R. Sandler and R. M. Hall, "The Campus Climate Revisited: Chilly for Women Faculty Administrators and Graduate Students," Washington, D.C.: Project on the Status and Education of Women. As reported in Renzetti and Curran, *Women, Men and Society*, 133.

Chapter 4: *Daughters and Independence*

1. See Hoekema, *Created in God's Image* and Erickson, *Christian Theology* for a more complete discussion.

2. Stewart Van Leeuwen, *Gender and Grace*, 44–46.

3. "I Am a Rock," from Simon and Garfunkel's Greatest Hits album (CBS Inc., 1972).

4. Fritz Pappenheim, *The Alienation of Modern Man* (New York: Monthly Review Press, 1959), 31.

5. Certainly men have historically acted in independent ways that have also brought about long-term negative consequences for humanity. One need not look very far in Scripture, or history, for examples of these as well.

6. Susan J. Douglas, *Where the Girls Are*, 7.

7. N. Darnton, K. Springen, L. Wright, and S. Keene-Osborn, "The Pain of the Last Taboo," *Newsweek,* October 7, 1991, 70–72.

8. See Trible, *God and the Rhetoric of Sexuality,* Bilezikian, *Beyond Sex Roles,* and Grenz, *Women in the Church* for a more complete discussion of this and related issues.

9. D. Stanley Eitzen and Maxine Baca Zinn, in *Conflict and Order: Understanding Society,* 5th ed. (Boston: Allyn and Bacon, 1991), 319.

10. Linda L. Lindsey, *Gender Roles: A Sociological Perspective,* 3d ed. (Englewood Cliffs, N. J.: Prentice Hall, 1997), 106.

11. Tracy Lai, "Asian American Women: Not for Sale," in Estelle Disch, *Reconstructing Gender: A Multicultural Anthology* (Mountain View, Calif.: Mayfield, 1997), 53.

12. Lindsey, *Gender Roles,* 133–53.

13. Renzetti and Curran, *Women, Men and Society,* 360.

14. Robert Lauer and Jeannette Lauer, *The Quest for Intimacy* (Madison, Wis.: Brown & Benchmark, 1994), 211.

15. Ibid.

16. Lindsey, *Gender Roles,* 259.

17. Katie Hafner, "Girls Soak Up Technology in Schools of Their Own," *The New York Times,* 23 September 1999, sec. D, 7.

18. 20/20 segment, "Who Needs Boys?" ABC (May 29, 1992).

19. Lisa McMinn, "Women and education," senior research project at George Fox University (1991).

20. U.S. Bureau of the Census (1995), in Lindsey, *Gender Roles,* 257.

21. U.S. Bureau of Labor Statistics, *Employment and Earnings* (January, 1992): 185–90, reported in Macionis, *Society: The Basics* (Englewood Cliffs, N. J.: Prentice Hall, 1994).

22. Hoekema, *Created in God's Image,* 59–73.

Chapter 5: *Daughters and Voice*

1. Debold, Wilson, and Malave, *Mother Daughter Revolution,* 112.

2. Deborah Tannen, *You Just Don't Understand: Women and Men in Conversation* (New York: William Morrow & Company, Inc., 1990), 75–78.

3. Edith M. Schulze, "Gender Dynamics in the Classroom at an Evangelical Christian Liberal Arts College," (dissertation at Loyola University of Chicago, 2000), faculty presentation; 5.

4. Tannen, *You Just Don't Understand,* 75–78.

5. Phyllis Trible, "The Pilgrim Bible on a Feminist Journey," *Perspectives* 6, no. 9. This article is taken from a 1988 address delivered at a program, "What Women Theologians Are Saying," sponsored by Auburn and Union Seminaries.

6. William Lane Craig, *Reasonable Faith: Christian Truth and Apologetics* (Wheaton, Ill.: Crossway, 1994), 276.

7. For instance, Grenz, *Women in the Church,* 39–40. Also discussed by Maria L. Boccia, Catherine Clark Kroeger, and Gilbert Bilezikian.

8. Debold, Wilson, and Malave, *Mother Daughter Revolution,* 16.

9. Cynthia J. Neal and Michael W. Mangis, "Unwanted Sexual Experiences Among Christian College Women: Saying No on the Inside," *Journal of Psychology and Theology* 23, no. 3 (1995): 171–79.

10. Renzetti and Curran, *Women, Men and Society,* 120.

11. Wolf, *The Beauty Myth,* 17.

Chapter 6: *Physical Essence*

1. As quoted by Karen Schneider, "Too Fat? Too Thin? How Media Images of Celebrities Teach Kids to Hate their Bodies," *People Magazine,* June 3, 1996, 65.

2. Eric Levin, editor, *Unforgettable Women of the Century* (New York: People Weekly Books, 1998), 15.

3. Elayne A. Saltzberg and Joan C. Chrisler, "Beauty Is the Beast: Psychological Effects of the Pursuit of the Perfect Female Body," in Estelle Disch, ed., *Reconstructing Gender: A Multicultural Anthology* (Toronto: Mayfield, 1997), 137.

4. Schneider, "Too Fat? Too Thin?" 71.

5. Ibid., 73.

6. "The 50 Most Beautiful People," *People Magazine* (May 1997).

7. M. Boskind-White, "Bulimarexia: A Sociocultural Perspective," in *Theory and Treatment of Anorexia Nervosa and Bulimia,* ed. S. Emmet (New York: Brunner/Mazel, 1985), 113–26. As cited in Renzetti and Curran, *Women, Men and Society,* 478.

8. Wolf, *The Beauty Myth,* 182.

9. Ibid., 185.

10. Jean Antonello, *Breaking Out of Food Jail* (New York: Simon and Schuster, 1996), 228–35.

11. Renzetti and Curran, *Women, Men and Society,* 476.

12. Joan Jacobs Brumberg, *The Body Project* (New York: Vintage Books, 1997), 122.

13. Saltzberg and Chrisler, "Beauty Is the Beast," 134–35.

14. Ibid., 136.

15. Ibid., 136–37.

16. Lucette Lagnado, "Women Find Breast Surgery Attractive Again," *Wall Street Journal* (14 July 1998), sec. B, 1.

17. Wolf, *The Beauty Myth,* 247.

18. David Garner, "Special Report: The *Psychology Today* 1997 Body Image Survey Results," *Psychology Today,* January/February 1997, 42.

19. Lagnado, "Women Find Breast Surgery Attractive Again."

20. Claudia Kalb, "Our Quest to Be Perfect," *Newsweek,* August 9, 1999, 57.

21. Dorinda Elliot, "Hong Kong's Canary," *Newsweek,* June 16, 1997, 41.

22. Renzetti and Curran, *Women, Men and Society,* 460.

23. Ibid., 461.

24. Women's Sports Foundation, Eisenhower Park, East Meadow, NY 11554, as cited in Mariah Burton Nelson, *The Stronger Women Get, the More Men Love Football* (New York: Harcourt Brace, 1994), 34.

25. As reported in PBS special, *Baseball: American Game, Japanese Rules,* 1988.

26. Renzetti and Curran, *Women, Men and Society,* 462.

27. Mary Ulmer, "Half Empty or Half Full? Commentary in SportsTalk," *Chicago Tribune,* 4 July 1999, sec. 3, 16.

28. *20/20* segment, "Wrestling and Girls," ABC (February 28, 1999).

29. Frank DeFord, "The Women of Atlanta," *Newsweek*, June 10, 1996, 71.

30. Mary Pipher as quoted in Karen Schneider, "Too Fat? Too Thin? How Media Images of Celebrities Teach Kids to Hate Their Bodies," 74.

31. As quoted in Sarah Ban Breathnach, *Simple Abundance: A Daybook of Comfort and Joy* (New York: Warner Books, 1995), September 8.

Chapter 7: *Sexual Essence*

1. Wendy Griffin, "The Embodied Goddess: Feminist Witchcraft and Female Divinity," *Sociology of Religion* 56, no. 1 (1995): 35–48.

2. Some translations have substituted other words that fit a picture of a male God better—such as "created you," or "brought you forth."

3. Jean Kilbourne, *Still Killing Us Softly* (Cambridge documentary 1990).

4. S. Gordon and C. Snyder, *Personal Issues in Human Sexuality: A Guidebook for Better Sexual Health* (Boston: Allyn and Bacon, 1989) as cited in Olson and DeFrain, *Marriage and the Family*, 203.

5. S. S. Janus and C. L. Janus, *The Janus Report on Sexual Behavior* (New York: Wiley, 1993).

6. Stan and Brenna Jones, *How and When to Tell Your Kids About Sex* (Colorado Springs: NavPress, 1993).

7. As quoted in Renzetti and Curran, *Women, Men and Society*, 338.

8. D. Scully and J. Marolla, "Riding the Bull at Gilley's: Convicted Rapists Describe the Rewards of Rape," *Social Problems* 32, no. 3 (February 1985): 251–63.

9. N. Darnton, K. Springen, L. Wright, and S. Keene-Osborn, "The Pain of the Last Taboo," *Newsweek*, October 7, 1991, 70–72.

10. David H. Olson and John DeFrain, *Marriage and the Family, Diversity and Strengths* (Mountain View, Calif.: Mayfield, 1994), 493.

11. Ibid.

12. Michele Ingrassia, "Virgin Cool," *Newsweek*, October 17, 1994, 59–69.

13. True Love Waits now has a website (truelovewaits.com) listing their mission, history, and upcoming activities.

Chapter 8: *Males as Friends, More than Friends, and Husbands*

1. Personally, I think a better question might be, "What is the *purpose* of a physical relationship outside of marriage?" A couple of follow-up questions could be, "How will I appropriately express affection to a male friend after I get married? Why—and *is*—some greater expression of affection to males appropriate before I get married?"

2. Susan Brownmiller, *Against Our Will: Men, Women and Rape* (New York: Fawcett Columbine, 1975), 256.

3. Cynthia Neal and Michael Mangis, "Unwanted Sexual Experiences Among Christian College Women: Saying No on the Inside," *Journal of Psychology and Theology* 23, no. 3 (1995): 171–79.

4. Shanthy Nambiar, "Love with a Proper Stranger," *Washington Post*, 17 November 1993, Sec. STYLE, CO1.

5. Grenz, *Women in the Church*, 156.

6. Trible, *God and the Rhetoric of Sexuality*, 72–143.

7. Ibid.; Bilezikian, *Beyond Sex Roles*, 28; Grenz, *Women in the Church*, 165.

8. Trible, *God and the Rhetoric of Sexuality*; Grenz, *Women in the Church*.

9. See Bilezikian, *Beyond Sex Roles*, and Richard Clark Kroeger and Catherine Clark Kroeger, *I Suffer Not a Woman: Rethinking 1 Timothy 2:11–15 in Light of Ancient Evidence* (Grand Rapids: Baker, 1992), and Stanley Grenz, *Women in the Church*, for a thorough treatment of this issue.

Chapter 9: *Fathers and Daughters*

1. Helen Bee, *The Developing Child, 2d edition* (New York: Harper and Row, 1978), 325.

Chapter 10: *Mothers and Daughters*

1. For instance, David Blankenhorn, *Fatherless America* (New York: HarperSanFrancisco, 1995), and Sylvia Ann Hewlett, *When the Bough Breaks* (New York: HarperSanFrancisco, 1991).

2. George J. Church, "America Then and Now," *Time Magazine*, January 29, 1996, 38.

3. Belenky, Clinchy, Goldberger, and Tarule, *Women's Ways of Knowing*.

4. Walter Wangerin Jr., *Ragman and Other Cries of Faith* (New York: HarperSanFrancisco, 1984), 99–100.

5. Gary Chapman, *The Five Love Languages* (Chicago: Northfield Publishing, 1992).

6. DeBold, Wilson, and Malave, *Mother Daughter Revolution*, 25.

Epilogue

1. Richard Foster, *Streams of Living Water* (New York: HarperSanFranciso, 1998), 270.

Lisa Graham McMinn is an assistant professor of sociology at Wheaton College, where much of her class work and informal student contact intersects with the issues she raises in this book. Lisa and her husband, Mark, are the parents of three daughters. They live in Wheaton, Illinois.